Per Wästberg was chief editor of *Dagens Nhyeter* (Sweden's major morning paper) from 1976 to 1982. Since 1979 he has been President of International PEN. He was the co-founder of both Swedish Amnesty International and the Swedish Defence and Aid Fund for southern Africa. He has also collaborated with the Swedish International Development Agency's commission for humanitarian aid since 1964, and was made a member of the European Academy of Arts and Sciences in 1980.

He is the author of twelve works of fiction and eighteen documentary works, mainly on Africa and Stockholm. Among these are *Forbidden Territory*, travels and political analysis of Rhodesia (1960), and *On The Black List*, a similar book about South Africa (1960), which were both translated into nine languages. A trilogy of novels published between 1968 and 1972 sold one million copies in Scandinavia. The second volume *The Air Cage* (1969), was not only filmed and translated into many languages, but also won the Swedish Booksellers' Prize for that year. Per Wästberg's latest publication is a collection of poems, *A Distant Affinity* (1984).

Assignments in Africa

Reflections, descriptions, guesses

Per Wästberg

Translated by Joan Tate

Farrar, Straus & Giroux
New York

Translation copyright © 1986 by Joan Tate
Originally published under the title Afrika—ett uppdrag,
copyright © 1976 by Per Wästberg
All rights reserved
Library of Congress catalog card number: 86-80952
Published simultaneously in Canada by Collins Publishers, Toronto
Printed in the United States of America
First American edition, 1986

Contents

Preface vi
Back to Africa 1
Mondlane's house 15
Enos – guest-worker in his own country 55
Pula – give us water 70
Snails in Tanga 82
Resting place in Zambia 90
The example of Mozambique 109
The Assignment 169

Preface

In a poem by the South African writer, Oswald Mtshali, the boy swings higher and higher. The world swirls by, points of the compass meeting as he shouts out the questions he has never dared ask: 'Mother! Where did I come from? When can I have long trousers? Why is Father in prison?'

Questions are accumulating all over Africa.

Hardly a day has gone by over the last eighteen years without my thinking about Africa and occasionally acting on my thoughts. I have come to live with Africa, involving myself with foundations, societies and committees and making contacts with friends, politicians and refugees. I have travelled in several countries south of the Sahara, but it is the white racist countries which are still my great interest.

When I first went to Africa in 1959, I knew far too little. Today, I sometimes think I know far too much – to be able to see clearly. I have eaten of the tree of knowledge and am less easily surprised. My innocence has gone, if not also my naivety, and therein lies the difference from the person I was when as a student I found myself on a white farm outside Salisbury in Rhodesia.

I was no longer travelling into the unknown, but into familiar country, a familiar country of contradictions, in which solemnity and laughter are irreverent neighbours.

Africa is a continent of multiplicities, in unexpected and uneasy turmoil. This book has become splintered in much the same way as my own experience of Africa has become. It is about a great deal, and yet not about much. I think I have shone a torch along a personal pathway through the forest, hoping that somewhere there is a connection with the public highway system.

The subtitle comes from the heading of the sixteenth chapter of Charles John Andersson's *The River Okavango*, published in 1861. I think that we – or at least I – have come no further on our African journey. We still make our way with descriptions, reflections and guesswork.

1976

Ten Years After

This book deals with events in the late Sixties and early Seventies. It is a very personal account written some ten years ago, slightly different from the more factual approach I attempted in the reports and editorials for my newspaper. My book was read in Sweden against the background of two earlier volumes, *Forbidden Territory* and *On The Black List* which deal with Rhodesia and South Africa. Because of my writings I was thrown out of both countries and could not return to Zimbabwe until the Independence celebrations in 1980. I maintained many contacts with South Africa by visits to neighbouring countries.

Through these visits I have become convinced that, regardless of foreign aid, internal development in most of Africa has declined. Neither socialist nor capitalist theories seem to provide a solution. Industrialisation as a short-cut to welfare and prestige has turned out to be a failure. Large parts of the continent are on their way back to a household economy, and the overall importance of agriculture remains crucial. Of the countries I mention, Uganda is a perennial tragedy with no end in sight, Kenya may be on the verge of a breakdown or a harsher one-party tyranny, Tanzania is impoverished, while Zimbabwe, although something of an economic miracle, is threatened by South African intruders and Matabele dissenters, and is reacting savagely against both.

At the time of writing South Africa is the focus. About 900 people have been killed within a year. Now and then I meet

Oliver Tambo, President of the African National Congress, who recently told me: 'We have asked whites to join us in the struggle to get rid of the tensions that come with apartheid. We hoped that together we could build the non-racial South Africa. There would be no violence at all if we did not have the violence of apartheid. To be a victim of apartheid means to be many, many things apart from losing a job, which you are losing all the time anyway. And the way we look at it is: the more effective sanctions are, the less the scope and scale of conflict.'

Listening to Tambo, I wish President Botha would dare a bold step forward, releasing Nelson Mandela and other political prisoners, rescinding apartheid legislation and initiating discussions on how to devise a non-discriminatory system. At the same time the ANC should be asked to suspend its campaign of violence and the international community to cease hostile acts against South Africa.

Basically, it is all about caring for *people*. When five thousand people in Dreifontein were dumped in the wilderness, without schools, arable land or much water, Saul Mkhize wrote a letter to the Head of State in South Africa: 'In the name of God, Your Excellency, is this mercy?'

The reply was a bullet in the chest and torture for his son.

Stockholm   P.W.
November 1985

Back to Africa

1.

Back to Africa.
I am flying over Lake Rudolf, where the very first human beings were found, three and a half million years old. The survey map shows mountains, rift valley, sea and coast. No geographical boundaries can be seen from up here, no political realities. Down there is the Third World, worse for wear, yet not lost, plundered, yet not exploited, the world which was once man's first. It still has a wealth of resources in its soil and the poorest people on its surface. It is melancholy to look down on this dry earth, often regarded by Africans as a womb, the beginning and end of the universe, where they buried their dead, curled up like foetuses.

How quickly it has gone. The white tribe arrived, the first to be incapable of forming a natural union with what it found and saw, and after only a century, a single breath drawn in Africa's life, the wildlife and rich savannas are disappearing together with much of African culture. In a stroke, man has cut his ties to the environment which for millions of years he developed in mutual understanding with all other living things.

Since my first visit to Africa, the Third World has risen like an Atlantis out of a sea of oblivion and ignorance. Now it is on the map, in most people's minds and also in our budgets and finance bills. In 1959, the words "undeveloped country" were not in use, SIDA* not even thought of. De-colonisation was just beginning when I arrived in Rhodesia, 'the land of unlimited

* The Swedish International Development Agency

opportunities', as it was called in the handbook for North-European immigrants.

The 1950s are distant to many people, a decade of apparent calm, when problems were swept under the carpet. Stalin ruled, children reported their parents to security forces, Senator McCarthy was hunting communists, and tension between East and West remained. Mount Everest was as unconquered as the planets, no one was looking for coal in the Antarctic or searching for oil along the continental shelf of Africa. Plankton had not been polluted, lakes were clean and cancer-forming preservative additives had not been discovered. Scarcely any massacres, floods or earthquakes were reported – assuming they occurred in poor countries.

The threat of the atom bomb and the cold war was considered the greatest danger of the 1950s. There were not a great many other things to worry about. The population explosion was rarely mentioned, and the thought that it was possible to misuse the resources of the world had not yet reached the newspaper leaders and cultural pages. Marshall Aid concerned Western Europe and was a field in which the underdeveloped countries had no part. When the United States expanded its aid to the underdeveloped countries, it was mostly in the form of providing armaments to obedient regimes. The same applied to the limited contributions of the Communist states. They did not want to pay off the colonial debt.

The Second World War had been a white war, sometimes fought in what were then called backward areas. Colonial power structure was taken for granted. A colony might possibly change owners, but economic oppression was never questioned. It was not easy for the facts about enforced poverty to penetrate the wall of official indifference. Today it is hard to understand this relatively recent silence surrounding colonialism. There were exceptions, in Sweden perhaps Gunnar Alvar and Jan Myrdal first and foremost.

The lot of the colonies was to produce raw materials. Their poverty was inevitable and was considered to have picturesque elements. Then in 1957, Ghana gained independence. England and France (but not Portugal and Spain) admitted that every country had a right to independence, though the reasoning behind this was not entirely idealistic. The mother-countries considered political independence would advantageously conceal the fact they could no longer afford to maintain power. During the first four years of the 1960s, twenty-one colonies formally gained independence.

A time of expectations . . . in the middle of the twentieth century the Africans were considered to be so steeped in European outlooks and technical methods that they were ripe for the political institutions which grew out of the Industrial Revolution in Europe. Africa was regarded as a miniature of liberal Europe: capitalist economy, education for all, parliament and laws and central bureaucracy. The model was to be constructed by the African middle-class, with sensible European advisers in the background.

The 1950s were for Africa a period of liberal joy and faith in the future. Freedom for the colonies – healthy economic links would be thus strengthened. Education for all – but in British and French culture. Parties for all – but on the European pattern of right, centre and left. Greater freedom of choice, i.e. the possibility of choosing between a hoe and a briefcase, between a drill and a judge's wig.

The air resounded with elevated intentions. Old African parishes and kingdoms provided names for the new nations: Ghana, Mali, Malawi, Zambia. Kenya was already there, the white man's mispronunciation of the Kikuyu word *Kere Nyaga*, the streaky white mountain today called Mount Kenya. New flags were made, preferably with fields of yellow, green and black, and to mark a farewell to the past, national anthems were composed, though a fragment from a Beethoven symphony or a mission hymn remained behind as a reminder.

It is easy to be wise after the event and say that the nationalist leaders who fought colonialism saw it in far too narrow political terms. They saw the transfer to independence as a holy war against an implacable enemy, while what actually happened in most quarters was a conscious retreat. Force played little part for the French, the British and the Belgians. The debate was about timing: now, or in two years, or in five.

The big commercial companies in Europe noted very early on in which direction development was heading. More clear-sighted than other groups, they started out from the acceptance that the time of white imperialism was over. They made contact with the black middle-classes, they appointed Africans and aimed at manufacturing consumer goods for the local market. The copper companies of the Congo and Northern Rhodesia (later Zaire and Zambia) were so powerful, that over the heads of governments they were able to deliberate with black resistance men and the emerging trade unions. A company such as Unilever – with an annual turnover greater than the gross national product of Nigeria with her sixty million inhabitants – was able to carry out its own policies in an apparently radical, mutual understanding with the new African élite. In this way, it avoided becoming the scapegoat of retreating colonialism. In countries such as Kenya and the Ivory Coast, the number of whites also increased after independence.

Not until after the dissolution of imperialism did the multi-nationals get their real chance, and the boundaries of their preserves, though invisible, had greater impact than those of the Berlin Congress. A representative example of their policies is how the Volta Dam in Ghana was built by companies based in Europe and America. The socialist Nkrumah was enthusiastic. The country would be transformed and cease to be slave to cocoa exports. But to maximise profits, they built the dam with capital-intensive methods. So few new jobs were created, while the level of wages for those who got jobs was so high that a socially dangerous labour force arose. Instead of using local bauxite, raw materials were imported, and instead of becoming the basis of a major industrial complex to the advantage of the whole of West Africa, the Volta Dam became a foreign investment, depending for its capital, materials, and experts on foreign decisions. Investors had no intention of risking nationalisation.

While political decisions were left in the hands of indigenous rulers – to the delight of progressive Europeans – commerce was still under foreign control. World prices of copper, coffee and cocoa and crucial investments were decided on in London, Paris, Brussels and New York. An African government could decide about hospitals, schools and roads, but if there were to be money or not depended on forces beyond their reach. Raw materials poured out of the continent. Every nation did indeed acquire factories for its own soft drinks and cosmetics, but not one a steel-works. Will Africa be forced to accept the multinational companies now being squeezed out of Hong Kong and Taiwan and looking for cheap labour, low taxation and freedom from environmental regulations?

This persistent colonial dependence has many manifestations. The French colonies gaining independence in 1959-1960 were tied to a new French commonwealth – except Guinea, which stood outside and so was deprived of all aid. French arms and officers came to determine military coups. French aid balanced the budget. Thousands of young Frenchmen preferred to be teachers in the ex-colonies rather than do military service. France had almost a monopoly of investments and was able to reckon on the support of their protégés in the UN in exchange – or at least on discreet silence on the sale of planes and nuclear reactors to South Africa.

African independence was a good thing in itself. It exposed what colonialism had neglected or delayed, problems rising to the surface and becoming visible. But there were no cures except what had been inherited from the mother power, the hitherto applied idea of universal suffrage and the laws on preventative detention. Radical and well-meaning people in Europe wanted the Africans to take on a form of government which for a century at most had existed only in England, the USA and Scandinavia. This at a time when a great many people in Europe had come to realise that the parlimentary system was by no means perfect. Just as Africa was trying to reap some dividends from cultural and political loans, various Europeans themselves were beginning to question bureaucracy, centralisation, commercialism, consumerism, the blessings of industry, the usefulness of competition and an alienated labour force.

Yet Africa's political freedom, however badly administered it may be in some countries, cannot be compared with colonialism which in its very nature entails alien oppression, a denial of man's responsibility for his country and his own destiny. The liberation of the colonies meant a revolution in ideas and ways of thinking, probably the greatest in the history of humanity. Freedom for coloured people was an inconceivable thought only a few generations ago – as preposterous as the idea that porpoises could speak and people could walk on the moon.

The fault of colonialism lay in its faith in its own rightness.

It arrived with the torch of civilisation. It brought with it enlightenment, i.e. trade technology, to those who abided in the darkness. With the help of Christianity, these worldly pieces were glued together into a totality that looked good at a distance, in Europe. White imperialism encouraged or enforced the cultivation of crops which could be sold abroad – cotton, cocoa, coffee, sisal. It broke up small self-contained units and tempted or ordered Africans to apparently increased prosperity through work in mines, on farms and in factories.

The result was that African culture – far too resistant to be completely destroyed – was hollowed out and regarded as inferior. Many Africans ask themselves: why did we allow ourselves to be deceived? Why weren't we able to unite? The answer lies in some colonial teaching: you knew nothing and were ignorant. You were not mature enough to take responsibility. They were taught to sit open-mouthed and obey instead of questioning and thinking, then told they were backward. The greatest damage, Julius Nyerere says, one can do to a people is to make it ashamed of its origins. Internal oppression dissolves far later than external.

During the early years of independence, black people probably generally believed that as long as the whites were replaced by African legislators and administrators, they would be able to cultivate their own soil themselves without having to serve lords and masters, and a new life would be based on old values, but without the previous misery of disease, superstition and ignorance. African leaders were expected to reform ways of life without threatening the security of tradition. Those are two almost incompatible aims. Perhaps Nyerere has found one possibility in the *ujamaa* villages based on the community of clans and at the same time open to greater national solidarity.

During the 1960s, a great deal occurred to make expectations fade into cynicism. A dozen or so régimes were overthrown unconstitutionally. The use of force replaced political processes. The pan-African utopians led to OAU, but not to any unions. In some countries, massacres between tribes, and public executions as punishment and a warning to others followed colonial injustices. Bribery and corruption became common. Political rights were constantly on tenterhooks. Writing freely in newspapers or holding public meetings were often regarded as obstacles to the collective assault on poverty, that is, a threat to the state.

The new leaders – with the forceful exception of Nyerere in Tanzania – promised prosperity within a few years, but poverty remained and the reasons for that were many: centuries of isolation, tropical climate and erosion of the soil, slavery and the lack of interest by the imperialists in the education of their subjects, lack of organisation, capital investment and professional knowledge.

Yet the paradoxes of Africa show sufficient signs of hope that it may be possible to overcome poverty. Africa is three times as large as the United States, six times the size of Europe. Africa's 340 million people have over three times as much cultivated land per capita at their disposal as have the inhabitants of Western Europe.

The average income is higher than that of India, lower than that of Latin America. If one looks at the number of schoolchildren and doctors and energy consumption, fifteen of the twenty least developed countries in the world are in Africa. Nevertheless, a third of the world's potential water-power is in Africa and of the eighteen most important minerals, Africa has the not inconsiderable number of ten – between 20 and 95% of world production.

It is difficult to know how everyday life has changed for Africans since I travelled all over the continent before the departure of colonialism in 1960. It is also difficult to interpret statistics that show a growth of four per cent a year, an increase in population of about two per cent and increased debts to the rich countries, so that an increasingly smaller share of the national income goes to the good of the people. These figures are for Africa as a whole, but oil supplies and mineral exports concentrate growth in certain countries, while others stagnate. South Africa, Egypt and Nigeria account for half of Africa's income, Zambia, Zaire and Libya for most of the rest.

The majority of black people have scarcely noticed any major changes. When they supported the fight against colonialism, they expected cures for bilharzia, more schools and clinics, higher prices for their maize and cotton, groundnuts and coffee. They were presumably less interested in new airports and hotels, or that the President inspects military parades in distant countries, for such vicarious raising of standards usually appears inadequate. So military coups are often greeted with sceptical goodwill, with a hope of reforms that will be shared by the many.

For Africa's political independence did not achieve that social equality which was the aim during the struggle for freedom. With few exceptions, it led to power being concentrated in a privileged élite. Some members of this élite had already taken up their positions before the new nations were even declared free. This group was of no class. It owned no land or other assets, and it was not monolithic. It consisted partly of the chieftains the colonialists had used, partly of an ancient merchant community along the west coast of Africa, partly of the new men with professional qualifications, most of all in government service: these groups were joined by a growing number of people who were often educated or trained in Europe, army officers, politicians and union officials.

This élite did not inherit its position. Most of them came from ordinary homes and had been given their chance through the family allowing a favourite son to go on to further education. Education, good fortune in business and political chance-taking opened the door to a high position in society, regardless of origin. The politicians gathered at the top of the élite. They took over the command-posts their colonial rulers had left behind them. The state was the largest employer and patron, and that gave the politician economic power as well. He was besieged by relatives and other ethnic brothers who all wished for a taste of his success and to receive some acknowledgement of the support they had given him. Then tribal influence came into the picture. If a man belonged to one party, the whole village joined, but one single tribe rarely came to dominate. Many leaders became skilful at tribal arithmetic and regarded the different tribal groups as so many interested organisations to be weighed against each other.

In most quarters, a chasm opened between this privileged minority who adopted the life-style of their predecessors, and the majority out in the countryside and in the city slums. In Gabon in 1970, people in the countryside earned approximately £38 a year, while government officials earned an average of £1300. This chasm will no doubt stamp African politics in the future. Tax riots, conflicts with bailiffs and chieftains, resistance to allocations of land all added to colonial defeat in Algeria, Kenya and Nigeria. Much of this will probably be repeated, this time against a black élite who would be tempted to call for help from the rich industrial countries on the pretext that they must protect their supplies of raw materials.

Up here in the plane, concealed loudspeakers are playing *Schlittschuhlaufen*, the menu is as large as a marine chart and you have to look hard to catch a glimpse of the huts on the ground. We are travelling from the north, perhaps flying with the *harmattan*, bringing with it drought and blowing the life out of children. We are waiting for the monsoon to come from the sea and set the human body alight again.

Now in the 1970s, we have acquired new facts about this earth and this part of the world, and we have formed a new picture. Magnetic poles were placed differently before, as shown by the position of metal particles in the sediment on the ocean beds. Political fields of power have also changed and have sometimes become clearer in recent years. Thus the picture of Africa changes according to insight and point of view.

So it was not until 1960 that the underdeveloped world appeared in all its shamelessness. The 'welfare' which was the pride of North Europe seemed to many people to be based on non-free foundations. If equality was a global question, then we were no longer social-democrats or liberals, workers or officials, but feudal lords. We made our way ahead on borrowed time, using borrowed money. Others paid the bill, and they could not afford it.

It is easy to become impatient and demand swift solutions to all the terrifying problems. Involvement that does not show immediate results is often abandoned. But seen from an historical perspective, decolonisation itself went quickly and relatively painlessly. Not least in order to counteract indifference and meanness in the rich countries, we must also keep in mind individual positive contributions to the development of the underdeveloped countries, increased average expectation of life and a 25% rise in incomes per decade. Although distribution of incomes is very unequal, this means large groups of people have had their standard of living raised – compared, not with us, but with their own past.

As economic miracles do not occur from one decade to another, a body of opinion that is constant through the years is necessary. This can find support in the Arusha declaration in Tanzania. Neo-colonialism and dependency have seldom been analysed more clearly, nor the wish for self-reliance and economic freedom through one's own labours and sacrifices. Most foreign aid works by oiling the wheels of exploitation. Swedish aid – as is aid from the rest of Scandinavia and Holland – however, is considered fairly free of the selfish and short-sighted motives of power politics. It is proportionately higher than in most countries. Nevertheless, only two per cent of Swedish investment goes to the Third World, the remainder to the industrial countries. Marx's theory on the necessity to invest in poor countries to have access to their raw materials does not work. They have access to them regardless.

The best we can do for the Third World is perhaps to invest in research at home – on family planning, for instance, nutrition, improvement of grain strains, forestry and erosion, research which is of use to the underdeveloped countries, and then offer them the results to exploit at no cost.

Flying over Africa . . . in humanity's latest means of communication over its most ancient dwelling places. The untouched heights above the African landscape favour generalisations. But the confused historical events being staged below on earth cannot be described in these abstract terms of perspective from the air without the truth becoming porous, suspended, ambivalent.

Space is where we have best been able to observe the thinness of the crust of the earth, but it is from the level of grass and stones one sees the breaking of human bonds. Villages and tribal collectives, in which everything has functioned thanks to the fine-meshed protective net of centuries, have been shattered by war, erosion, missions, company demands and government decrees.

These uplands, where the dwarf acacia stretches up to find moisture from the air, and where the Grant's gazelle and the eland trample a path between grazing and water-hole, was once a green wilderness, its lakes still crystal clear, its mountain slopes still not scraped bare of soil. People lived here with the hippopotamus and crocodile, with flints as tools, and eyes that saw the animals of the earth in distant constellations.

From high up in the air – as from deep down in the sediment – it is possible to think that the traces, long ago swept away, will appear again, just as the wash on a calm sea remains visible long after the vessel has passed.

2.

The wing-tips wobble in the turbulence and the clouds gather. Descent to Kampala, disguised as an idyll with lush hills, Indian confectionery temples, white villas with orange tiled roofs. From Zinjanthropus, East African man, who two million years ago left his traces among the scattered rocks of Olduvais, to the anti-man of today, Field Marshal Idi Amin.

We make an intermediate landing in Entebbe long enough for me to have time to telephone a friend at Makerere University and hear that he – he in particular by sheer chance – has survived a dictator insane with fear, arrogance and syphilis. I look out over green Uganda, which I have visited many times before. Africa's most beautiful countryside is ruled by a man whose emotional life is that of a boar. Perhaps he has to kill every day to make sure he is alive. So far.

It is rare that men who have seized power by force and executed every conceivable possible opponent are approved by the UN, OAU and other assemblies, as if they had been appointed by free choice. For Amin is not alone. There are his friends Bokassa in the Central African Republic and Macias Nguema in Equatorial Guinea – and then John Vorster in South Africa, where white police shoot black children in the slums and where a hundred or so maltreated Africans are always waiting to be taken to the gallows in Pretoria at six o'clock each Monday morning.

The homes in Kampala . . . I remember an evening with an Indian family. The next day, the eldest girl, nineteen, was going to London to school, by train to Mombasa – the railway her ancestors built – and then by sea. The talk round the dinner table, the uneasy laughter . . . they wanted to conceal the departure, the melancholy and incredible fact that the family was to be splintered. The girl's eyes were red as if she had been crying sand instead of tears.

The mother rinsed the plates between courses, making large wet patches on her sari. She cleaned the stove and the draining board with long sweeping movements. There was a smell of curry, ginger and soya. Unleavened bread was taken out of the oven, coffee put on, the eggs turned in the pan, and from the red biscuit tin the stately grey-bearded figure of Prince Albert stared straight into the eyes of the children. I was there at the next day's departure, which was making the smallest of everyday preoccupations loom. The younger brothers and sisters were very quiet. I saw them rinsing their hands and faces in rainwater without exchanging a word.

The family were traders, like most Indians, buying and selling goods, working on them, sewing, tailoring, making curtains and lampshades. Maybe their prices were too high, maybe they had saved a little. But I don't think they were wealthy. The house was small, several sleeping in each room, and sending a girl to London was probably a financial sacrifice apart from an unusually emancipated action. The family was a workshop, a co-operative working almost all round the clock. Not until now, after four generations in Uganda, could they afford one son and one daughter some further education.

The sickly angels on the wall, the print of some faintly saintly maiden, the green plastic-covered chairs from Kampala furniture dealers, the refrigerator in the middle of the living-room – it was uglier than any African hut. But what stays in the memory is the circle of life and talk round a table one hot night, a few people subduing their grief over a daughter's departure for what they know might be her happiness. What they don't know is what lies ahead of them.

The memory of them appears because I met them in a country in which the life of individuals no longer counts for anything, in which laws are ignored and a soldiery is seized with murderous hatred for anyone for whom books have some significance.

Entebbe, Kampala, cities of terror . . . in the transit hall of Entebbe's new airport building, the walls are sullied by the be-medalled Field-Marshal, a reincarnation of Göring. I seem to sense the smells from Ocean Road and see that girl before me, uncertain, but her suitcases already packed, an iron filing on the outskirts of the magnetic field of her family. How could I betray you – whether you are now in England or have been killed – by talking about you in such lifeless terms as the predecessors of the petty bourgeoisie, representatives of the unpatriotic, unassimilated middle class, or – to quote a slogan – 'the parasites on the healthy stock of the proletariat'?

For that, among other things, is why I must return to Africa – to wash away this veil of dead words and phrases, to shed the dried snakeskins of sociology and psychology, to stop picking though half-baked terminology and listening to mindless computer jargon.

I fly on over Serengeti and Ngorongoro's crater to Arusha in northern Tanzania.

It is the mid-1970s, years which, like 1960, redrew the political and economic map of Africa. Portugal's colonies are free and the balance of power in southern Africa has shifted. The feudal empire of Ethiopia has ceased to exist, but it is too early to say what will replace it. Economically, they have been unhappy years. World inflation and drought, falling prices of raw materials, quadrupled costs of oil and all kinds of imported goods. These catastrophes have forced the African nations to unite more successfully than before round demands for a new international economic order. For the distance is increasing between what the Third World wants and expects and what the rich world thinks it should be content with.

From Arusha, some of us share a Land Rover to Tanga on the coast. The drought is worse than we had even imagined. Is this how universal thirst starts and a cycle is broken – in an unexpected leap from reasonable prosperity to a life-threatening dearth? The delicate membrane of growth is threatened everywhere. A deer dead by the roadside, its skin like paper, its legs as light and dry as pumice. Panting impala chewing on acacia fruit-pods and in their dung transporting the seeds to more fertile soil.

For long stretches, the road is as bumpy and stony as a river bed. It looks as if water had been here, then ebbed away and now everyone was waiting in vain for the tide to turn. A few zebra, immobile in the pale waves of elephant grass, stare at us like Sunday visitors to the zoo. A giraffe thoughtfully leans over its tall meal of tree-top foliage, sparing the weaver bird's nests hanging like hairy fruit from every branch. A dikdik antelope shakes its head, as if it had water in its ears.

The surfaces of the lakes shrink from year to year, filling up with eroded soil and volcanic soda-bicarbonate which makes them glow as pink as the flamingo they tempt to them. I see herdsmen with tufts of grass stuck in their loin-cloths. They, like the plants, have roots in the soil they entreat the heavens to water. But the outlook is dismal, and the newly installed water hydrants counteract their purpose. Cattle flock to them, graze away all the grass for a mile round them and trample the soil to dust with their sharp hooves. Before more cattle can reach them, a desert has appeared. The animals die just as they catch the glimmer of the water-hole.

No one dares forecast the length of the drought any longer. I hope I am still here if the rains come to Africa, before my stay is over.

Mondlane's House

1. To the Sea

Hardly anyone knows I am here.

The house stands by the Indian Ocean, fifteen miles or so north of Dar es Salaam. Its address is a box number in the central post office. The telephone is on a party line. Three rings means the neighbour. I have seven and I've seldom had to count that far.

I have rented a Land Rover which can cope with the sandy roads. I drive to an Indian store and buy food, most of it imported, except vegetables and bad wine from Dodoma, which tastes of raisins. I buy a newspaper there, the *Tanzania Standard*. It says little about what's happening in the world and much more about speeches by leaders, friendly visits in various directions, and the need to boil and filter your water. But when I buy fresh fish in the market, the market woman wraps my perch in a two month old issue of the *Gothenburg Post*. This surprises me. Who has smuggled it in? Its paper comes from the same forest as that of the *Tanzania Standard*. The *Gothenburg Post* also writes about the shortage of water and water pollution.

The house belongs to a foreign woman, a friend of Nyerere's, who worked a great deal for Frelimo. Eduardo Mondlane, the founder of Frelimo, retreated to this house to write his speeches and plan the strategy of the freedom movement. In 1969, to this stillness, surrounded by sea and sand, to this small house apparently located in an apolitical eternity, a postal packet was sent. It contained a philosophical dictionary in several parts, with death inserted and the knowledge extracted.

Now it is several years later and there is no trace of the explosion. It is strange how easy it is to paint out and repair. The walls are whitewashed. I try out the mosquito nets on their rickety wooden frames. They have stuck in the damp. There are no windows, only openings and frail grilles. On the low bookshelves are dozens of Georgette Heyer's books, the most easily-read author in the tropics. She died a year or two ago. She lived in Tanganyika for a few years. Perhaps she has been here.

An attempt at a garden is slowly silting up with sand. The birds are tearing at the leaves of the thorn bushes. Turtles come up out of the water and slowly crawl across the sand the low tide has revealed. The ant-lion is arranging its traps. As the river rises, the spiders seek refuge on the edge of the shore. They start by kicking up sand, then run up with their little burdens from the bottom of the hole. Sand spurts from holes inches deep. At high tide, they weave a silky waterproof web-tent across the top of the hole. They are safe in there and have enough air until low tide, and then the heat of the sun bursts the roof of the tent.

The ocean is always audible. The wind shakes the wild tomato bushes and their small yellow balloons. Sunrise is shortly after six, the sun coming quickly out of the horizon like a hayrick fire. I go swimming in shallow water, warned about the dangerous currents farther out. A pair of grey herons stand guard on the water's edge, continously thrusting out their beaks as if doing cross-stitch together on a cloth of air.

Among other things, I have to put together a report on the liberation movements, their need for aid and first and foremost their information problems. Contact with the movements is followed by meetings with many individual people wanting help and advice and promises. This is natural, but I can't cope with it. My assignment is not that of a magician. On some days, I feel like a funnel into which requests and demands are being poured.

Why can't I arrange for a scholarship, a house, a publisher, a film company, a journey? I become all white men, rich and well-meaning people in one single fragile figure. Sooner or later a moment will come when I have to do something just for him or her. Addresses accumulate in my notebook. Once again, I must find out about supplementary courses back home, about German and history and sociology, about nuclear physics and pharmacy.

I am pleased to be inaccessible for a couple of weeks. I am tired of the summaries, inferences and smooth conclusions everyone appears to long for: gift-wrapped truths. I am choosing fragments, details, with no expectation that the many splintered pieces will merge into a whole. The cracks must show – glue is the alien element. A great many faces loom out of the mist, none complete, none wholly visible.

'When I open up a dead person,' said the surgeon in Bukoba the other week, 'it's the cells, the tissue I want to get hold of. Not the human being. When I take a piano to pieces, I don't expect to find the note.'

'And by travelling round Africa,' I said, 'I don't expect to find what we call Africa, but just a few ingredients floating through it. People on their way, ideas drifting.'

Dare what I don't see? No. But see what I don't dare.

The storms rumble on, inside nations, outside on the plain alongside the ocean, inside myself. Harmless sounds, intrusive sounds of the heart, grumbles of loneliness, the buzz of five-year plans constantly in progress . . . I shall prepare something: a white paper, a particular statement of the state of Africa. I can't. I'm incapable of it.

Colourless nocturnal insects are attracted to the desk lamp, blinded and incinerated. Black dust on the window-sill, flakes of blackout paper.

Pessimism of mind and optimism of will – Antonio Gramsci speaks of that in a volume Mondlane left behind him in his library – that's what Africa does to me. A dualism of hope and doubt, for such great difficulties correspond with such limited resources.

Africa has demanded endurance, obstinacy and self-control of me. Africa has sucked me dry and given in return rains followed by drought. I would prefer to undertake something in which it would be possible to find joy. That is the egoism of one who lacks a vocation, but it can be used in different ways. I don't share the disposition of Sartre's hero, Roquentin, who reacts with distaste and loathing to the physical world. For him, it is slimy, soft and stinking. He wants the cold and the night. They are clean. Sartre's voice can be heard behind Roquentin's. He is the puritan from the north.

The confused metaphysics in me and my own realistic daylight eyes tell me that happiness ought not to be possible in a world of starvation, oppression and inequalities. I do try, like so many others, striving for it to be a little better somewhere, somehow. Nevertheless, I am happy, the countryside exists, the scents and shapes of plants, people's faces and their multifold expressions, emotions and movements.

It is perhaps a matter of disposition and fortune in life, perhaps linked with a tendency to want to differentiate between light and dark, if for nothing else but to have more variety. Maintaining that the Swedish mixed economy and American capitalism are the same thing is to me like looking at the earth from the viewpoint of an astronaut. Neither can I bring myself – after Johannesburg, Nairobi and Buenos Aires – to regard Stockholm as a stinking slum of maimed and outcast people.

A good day, like a good book, is one in which a sense of life is elevated and condensed – one is alive. Why? Hard to know. The book, the conversation, the action, the meeting with another human being and his or her life . . . or the sense of leisure one evening when you can walk round a big city and listen and look without having to intervene . . .

That happiness is real, only its durability deceptive. Few have been able to describe it. Jean Giono in *The Hussar on the Roof*, Sven Barthel in a few pieces on the Stockholm islands. Vladimir Nabokov in *The Gift*, and in the drawing of Martin Eidelweiss' maturity in *Glory*. Nabokov creates happiness through a certain prose rhythm, a building up of individual pieces into pleasing and sensual glider landings. In *Speak Memory*, there are many such passages: one describes the father, who is seen from the dining-room window to be slowly rising and falling, horizontally, the peasants out in the yard tossing him in a blanket.

But I so often meet people imprisoned in an almost joyful denial. For them, a Swedish summer meadow doesn't exist, except only as an urgent problem of cultivation. They neither understand Harry Martinson's *Midsummer Valley* nor Björn Berglund's *The Raspberry Man*; start describing an African meadow and you are accused of being a fascist fleeing from the suffering of the Third World in its own garden and thus responsible for genocide.

I have never had an ultimate aim in life, and there are undeniably many exciting things to involve oneself in. I do want to continue with Africa, for Africa stands for so much else. Some people ask: what's the point? The misery won't improve from you stirring in it, will it? No – how do I know? Though I think the famous last line in Camus' essay is a possible answer: 'We must imagine Sisyphus happy.'

Go into Africa as if into a dark cave of injustices, affronts, sufferings in such quantity and of such strength that unremitting actions are your only protection against going mad. Renewal and joy are not to be expected, only the meeting with your own death in that of others.

Go out into Africa, out on to the plateaux with their clear air and new outlooks. Free yourself from habitual patterns. Don't be blinded by catastrophes and multifold splinterings, but gaze with critical eyes and sort out the contradictions and connections. Africa as a form of experience, a touchstone, a way to liberate yourself from pretentiousness, provincialism and prudery. I am sitting at the desk Eduardo Mondlane had sat at. I am considerably younger than he was when he opened his parcel of books and a second later . . . it was some time before they found him, because he had asked to be left in peace. He was a unique person and thus irreplaceable for his family and friends. But not for the movement he founded: the murderer could not stop the liberation of Mozambique.

Perhaps it is the memory of Eduardo – his expressions and gestures, his trust in the future when he spoke of free Mozambique, his connections back into western tradition: Tocqueville, Lincoln, Shaw – which so often makes me think in this house about the brevity of life, about death which is not that far away, about how my feelings and interests will disappear like a puff of smoke. Or is it because I have small children whom I regard with an astonished admiration, which would be less had the stork brought them? Or because I now and again meet people who say: we haven't met for twenty-five years. Then I think: I can't have lived that long. Then I think: the expectation of life in Angola, for instance, is thirty-three, not even half that of Sweden.

After that, self-pity. I have not been able to acquire a philosophy of life. I haven't read Goethe, Tolstoy and Shakespeare with any seriousness. What do I know about philosophy and science? The children grow up, I travel, look at old houses, publish some books, drink rougher and rougher red wine, enjoy the seasons, experience a great deal on a superficial level and some things on an inner level.

And yet . . . the wind blowing through the jacaranda trees, drying out the eyes of the turtles. Thoughts on death, Auden says, are like distant thunder at a picnic.

As swiftly as when you loosen a tightly tied bowline, a double-knot, the rope of life glides out of your hands.

It is sixteen years since my first year in Africa. Several people I got to know then are now dead, their voices no longer heard. I cannot go and see them. I hear them talked about, but sometimes no one even seems to remember them. The air full of what is unspoken. I was deported from Southern Africa's countries as well as from some others. But *they* were deported out of existence.

Some were famous and survive as monuments: Mondlane and Cabral, Lutuli, Chitepo . . . but Walter, Mary, Karen, Zimbusu, Joaquim were not among the famous. Their words have not spread, their days not noted down. They lived in the shadow of greater people and events. I don't know where they are buried, if anyone does.

People die, but objects remain, a few plates in a cupboard, a fern-print on the wall, a school book with underlinings in it, a jar of vitamin tablets. But in *their* case, there is virtually nothing left. They died in a road accident, of blood-poisoning, in the mass murder in Burundi, in a Portuguese prison. Guyat, an Indian business man, took his own life when Amin's soldiers seized his store and all his possessions in Kampala and tore up his passport. He wanted to punish them with his death, but they just laughed.

I hurriedly close a window-frame when I go to bed, and something cold and yellow splashes me. I have crushed a beautiful green lizard. I think about our coldness towards cold-blooded creatures – so much easier to kill a fish than a beaver – but the lizard was a mistake, "an unfortunate incident", as American war communiqués used to describe the obliteration of a village. I look for the lizard's family in the darkness, but there is no one to whom the murderer can offer his condolences.

The heat is oppressive. The stars move their counters across the sky. The night is vast, but it seems impossible to flee except to another darkness covering another verdancy.

So I remain enclosed in the cloak of night. I feel obliterated, invisible. Molecules and atoms are not being used. They disappear to find new combinations.

On these nights, when vision ceases and sounds never fade, there is someone with a long pole stirring in the pan of creation.

2. Temptation

One morning, a kite drops the backbone of a rat out of the sky. It lands on my breakfast tray. A little time passes before I identify this gift from above, by which time there is marmalade on it.

A MIG-19, made in China for the Tanzania People's Defence Forces, is practising above the house by the sea. My kingfisher flutters up from its hiding-place – as if someone had flung an amethyst into the air.

President Nyerere, *Mwalimu*, the Teacher, is speaking on the radio. Anyone who does not do a good day's work for good wages is exploiting others who do, he says. Socialism has nothing to do with poverty or wealth. Work decides that. Before independence, we promised each other Freedom and Work. Now we should say Freedom *is* Work.

He is patient, but always sounds as if he were in a good mood. *Ujamaa* is his favourite subject – the extended family's solidarity, 'the opposite of capitalism, which is based on the exploitation of human beings by each other, but equally the opposite of doctrinaire socialism, which is based on class struggle between human beings.'

Most of the youth of the country have to be prepared to work in *ujamaa* villages so the country can become self-sufficient. Many of the older officials think they have to show the poor how they are to live in the villages, while they themselves do not share the life of the poor. Therein lies a generation conflict. The young TANU leaders teach scientific agriculture and co-operative economy, take part in literacy campaigns and well-digging. They live in the villages and try, often in vain, to solve the problems. Why should two people who do not work equally hard receive the same income?

The gap between generations constantly appears in educational programmes on the radio. A girl is studying Swahili grammar, but her mother tears the pages out of her book as wrapping paper for fish. A father sends his son to fetch beer and takes his lamp. But the boy lights a candle, holding one hand round it as he goes on studying. Children, don't give up, retrain your parents – it is the final heretical point.

Frelimo has asked if I will be their publisher, although it is not clear if the publishing is to happen from Dar es Salaam or Lourenço Marques. The strange thing is that they have not made the suggestion through SIDA, but directly to me, via an intermediate contact in UNESCO in Paris. I was to be in charge and encourage the production of educational material – from ABC books and multiplication tables to appropriate revolutionary publications – and, it was implied, ensure that some of Swedish aid was in the form of paper for books and newspapers.

Is this a chance to become Africa's Allen Lane or Per Gedin? Would the family want to come out here? For how long? There is a relationship between words like 'Africa' and 'always'. I happened to read a poem by Peter Porter, the Australian poet. He catches a nostalgia also found in the whites in Africa, a feeling of having missed the European bus:

to have a weatherboard house and a white
paling fence and poinsettias and palm nuts
instead of Newstead Abbey and owls and graves
and not even a club foot;

above all to miss the European gloom
in the endless eleven o'clock heat among
the lightweight suits and warped verandahs,
an apprenticeship, not a pilgrimage –

I do not want to give up Europe. The micro-memory of Sweden overwhelms me, daisies and white clover emerging at the foot of brick-red gasometers in Värtan. A boat-house in April. Washing the winter frost out of boat paint-brushes, hearing the flies waken, seeing them sluggishly making their way up the milky windowpane and meeting ice, the glitter of water.

Why am I here? What am I doing?

In Sweden at this time, I usually put a short-stemmed bunch of celandines and hepatica, yellow and blue and green, into an eggshell-coloured cup on my desk. There's a small etching by Bull on the wall, a barometer, a pair of binoculars, a flute on a rough table and a window open to the sea. Then I have a few prints by Palmstruch, in very narrow wooden frames, portraying various ferns with their seed cases, roots and fruit. I wrote about ferns in a couple of novels, and a woman fern specialist confirmed that she found no ferns in Botswana. An Englishman, a teacher at Swaneng Hill School who had learnt to make furniture with Carl Malmsten, learnt Swedish, and happened to read it. He sent me an envelope with six species of pressed ferns from the savanna round Serowe.

I tell Frelimo that they should try to find someone who knows Portuguese better, and that they would have to have alternative costings for different forms of publications. They realise from this that I have thanked them and turned down the offer.

Sweden: mostly temptation. Africa: temptation and duty. Get a post somewhere, in management, a library, a university, become a peripatetic adult tutor, stay for a few years ... it would be easier if I were a dentist or a highway engineer. For almost two decades, I have travelled back and forth between Europe and Africa, on various assignments and for various purposes, and yet I still cannot see my rôle in Africa. Look at Barbro Johansson, the Swedish missionary who became a Tanzanian citizen, an MP and adviser to Nyerere, giving so much life and humanity and involvement without being in any way obliged to ... and I say to myself: if you can't be like her, you ought to go home.

So I will go home — but not yet.

3. Work

The work goes slowly. I spend time washing-up and cleaning thoroughly, the rituals of solitariness: the house should look as if it were just about to be used. The porcelain is English Copeland and decorated with meadow flowers from northern countries. I sweep the sand from the painted concrete floors, here and there covered with worn rugs with Arab patterns on them. I leaf through books and see Eduardo Mondlane's underlinings. I imagine him here, concentrating on his task, not wasting a moment on daydreams.

Just before he took his own life in London, where he was in exile from his own country, the young South African poet, Arthur Nortje, whom I got to know slightly, wrote:

Some of us must storm the castle
some define the event.

Some act, others define and report. But the boundaries are indistinct.

In the long run, reading is no help. Through necessity you have to experience with your senses, which does not mean that everyone who travels experiences something. It can be the testimony of others which opens your eyes, but it is personal experience which allows them to remain seeing.

In Eugenia Ginzburg's autobiography *English Journey to the Whirlwind* an Italian girl communist flees from Italy to 'the fatherland of all workers'. She is taken straight to Stalin's torture chamber. Eugenia sees her in the prison cellar, the temperature below zero, being showered with cold hosepipes. The girl understands nothing, but keeps on writing: I am a communist, I am a communist.

Africa has taught me a critical guardedness I did not have before I came here. I was an inquisitive and observant person to whom it was a matter of honour to refuse to evaluate. Perhaps that was right, considering my limited knowledge. Perhaps that fitted in with the atmosphere of the 1950s.

Africa has also given me a sense of *déjà-vu* when on other journeys – in Chile, in the Philippines, in Greece – I have seen both the luminosity and oppression of hope which returns and slams the desk-lid on to one's fingers. So much of what I experience reminds me of Africa, resounds against its soil, echoes against its cliffs.

Have you seen it? people ask me. Have you done that, too? Yes, I have seen the drought and the hunger, children dying. I've seen people whose legs have been shot off by the Portuguese, whose nails have been ripped out. I have met people who have survived years in South African prisons and Rhodesian camps.

Seen and not seen. A great many people write about it, well and in depth, and many have photographed expressions of pain and long rows of child graves in Dimbaza, South Africa, bells fixed to the low wooden crosses. And yet it seems as if nothing has been said. I cannot say anything, and people who have been exposed to inhumanity have not spoken.

It is no help to the dying that flowers bloom and birds twitter nearby. But what is unjust in Africa appears to have some kind of idyllic edge. At least it doesn't look like Auschwitz, where the railway lines end near the showers and all humanity ceases among leaves and gravel, in smoke and mist, and nothing appears capable of starting again.

None of the great tasks have an end – that is the starting-point. Making justice conceivable, sharing power, lessening hunger and stopping illiteracy and spiritual impoverishment – all that would be superhuman if one did not see the actual striving as meaningful and the result as only long-term improvements never possible to complete.

Working can never be so in vain as weeping. On winter nights, the sap lies quietly inside the tree. Then it slowly begins to move; nothing is visible and the trees are dry, but suddenly, one warm day after a frosty night, the extremities of the branches begin to moisten.

Maturity includes all movements forward to the moment when we see the fruit.

The sea is unfathomable and brittle, not eternal and terrifying, the trees fragile and sighing, and yet princely, defying rain, thunder and snow. I think of the sea and the trees as our true friends.

'Don't cut down trees,' says Samora Machel, Frelimo's leader, to his people. 'Think how they have protected us for ten years, our troop movements, our schools and hospitals.'

The dragonflies rustle their blue wings across the stones on the shore. After a day of calm, the surface of the water is wrinkled by the wind like a large dark piece of clothing waiting to be hung up to dry. Flocks of gulls as thin as cigarette smoke out to sea.

Ships lie at anchor in Dar es Salaam. The Tan-Zam railway stops here, Zambia's lifeline to the east coast. The vessels unload manufactured goods and take on huge bars of copper. In Dar es Salaam, I catch a glimpse of the country's tallest building, the fifteen-storey block of the semi-state National Insurance Corporation.

They know I am here. I have drunk Coca-Cola with the local TANU leader and now he is coming here to have a beer with me. He wonders if there is anything I'd particularly like to see. Not now, I say. I have seen the training camps for Frelimo guerillas now being used to train thousands of black men from Zimbabwe. I have been to Ubongo Farm Implements Factory, which means a hoe factory. A good hoe is worn down in three years by the hard earth. Six million people use hoes. They need two million a year.

He nods. He is tired. Too many meetings. Soon he will be posted to the countryside. No one is allowed to stay near the town for long. It demoralises them. There had just been a meeting of African foreign ministers in Dar.

'Séances,' says Richard. 'Pan-Africanism is the protoplasm floating round the hall. The interpreters translate between three European languages and Swahili. Pan-Africanism, unity, imperialism, socialism – the words sound alike. The words are talking to each other. We are the ventriloquist's dummies.'

He cuts into a guava, fanning himself with the palm of his hand.

'Most countries in Africa have no particular aim in mind. So they can't fail. Countries which have an aim – for instance, that everyone shall partake in decisions on their country's development – they risk failing.'

'People like you.'

Richard has been on a leader's course at Kivukoni, a kind of adult college for political scientists and administrators, opposite the harbour entrance in Dar. He has never been outside Africa.

Suddenly, a fish-vendor is at the door. I buy a couple of mackerel and suggest to Richard that I fry one each for us. For a moment he is worried I haven't a servant, then adapts swiftly to the situation and chooses to observe my activities with surprise from a chair. That's all right as long as I'm opening beer-cans, but when I open tins and gut the fish, I am adopting a female rôle which troubles him.

He picks up the nearest book and buries himself in it. It is Norman Mailer's *Marilyn Monroe*, which I bought in Dar. I warn him solemnly about this western seduction. It's a piece of platonic necrophilia or – as some of my friends express it – supersensual masturbation.

Mailer sees Monroe as Nana and Madame Bovary rolled into one and has little to say about her drug-strewn road to defeat. Marilyn is 'the Stradivarius of sexuality', Mailer writes, creating a world record in ecstasy over an imagined saint and acting genius – for Marilyn seems to me to lack both saintliness and real talent.

In the end he finds Marilyn and Mailer are names so close that they were perhaps meant for each other – or possibly the same person from the start – that is not made quite clear. Sex for Marilyn is what ice-cream is for others, Mailer thinks, and he interprets Marilyn gazing at some mushrooms as 'probably comparing them with differences she has found between the penises of her husband and her lover.'

I exclaim angrily about this to Richard, with the result that he puts the book down and shares my mackerels, which I serve with fried potatoes, tomatoes and watercress. When I ask him to tell me something about his family, he does so at once with no affectation.

He was born in 1944 and was seventeen when Tanganyika gained independence – he remembers women dancing all night with great palm leaves in their hands and even an old Indian who was the President of the Supreme Court leaping about until about dawn. His grandfather was born in 1890, in what was then a German colony. He was recruited into the German army in 1914, then blown to bits in an ammunition accident. His father, then a few years old, was cared for by poor relations, and at sixteen had to start working on a coffee farm in Arusha.

His father ran away after a few years, was brought back, and when that had happened a few times, he had to choose between the local police station, which meant a thrashing and forced labour on road building from then on, or a thrashing at home. His wailing echoed through the barn all night, as if his very skeleton were creaking its last protest. He survived, and it was my friend's mother who told the story. She was there and heard it, though they hadn't met then, but she had grown up on the same coffee farm.

In the end, both of them ran away from service and took their children to Dar es Salaam, where no one looked for them. The landowner and his son eventually sold the farm for a high price to an African co-operative and moved to Australia.

The boy was sent to school and joined TANU Youth League, then became a member of a township cell and is now a social worker and disciplinary officer in the district north of Dar where I happened to be for a while.

It grows late. I resist the temptation to take the car in to Chez Margot to meet acquaintances, or to the outdoor cinema on the Morogoro road, where ancient American westerns and Kenyan advertising films follow one another in front of thousands of patient socialists. The day's radio programmes end with the national anthem, a variation on the South African liberation movement's *Nkosi Sikel' Africa*. Bless the children of Africa, bless the children of Tanzania.

Out at sea, the spear-fishermen's lights are shining. I am alone with my incompleted tasks. It is twenty-nine degrees Celsius outside.

I see the eyes of a frog low on the edge of the water, scanning its shore preserve. I think of the curved mechanical eyes of human beings twisting and turning back and forth every night across the canopy of the skies from hundreds of observatories.

One day, with a telescopic lens as big as a market square, we will certainly catch sight of something we don't like, a huge phantom squatting out there on the far shore of the sea of space.

4. Books

An empty afternoon, the sand as smooth as an English lawn. I see a cat in semi-profile – what's it doing here? The fishmongers call from the town where the houses are closer along the shore.

A copy of *The Times* comes sailing my way. In it I see that the British Mule Company in Hong Kong has been disbanded and that a passenger plane has been struck by a stone flung thousands of feet up into the air from a volcanic crater. I read that my friend Richard Hughes is assiduously continuing with his European novel cycle – one volume per decade. He is now seventy-five and not well – and he defends the art of the novel: 'We are today sliding back into tyranny, barbarity and violence ... fewer than a fifth of the books printed are novels. That is not just chance.'

No, perhaps it is actually an event. So many new novels are based on documents or pseudo-documents, imitating journalism, creeping closer to a reality that can be coated with facts. They are firmly fastened in a safety-belt of information. The book becomes a footnote to a more absorbing life outside its covers, the reader hastily closing it and hurrying out.

Fiction is to invent lives which serve to condense and complicate the world. Maybe today we should differentiate between cultures needing to understand their lives through literature, and cultures exposed to all the interpretations they can cope with. The old-fashioned novel is still alive in Latin America, India and West Africa, while it suffers from shortage of breath in most parts of Europe.

Does this happen because literature is being edged out by history and sociology? Or is it that our imaginations have no breathing space in the rich world, with its contradictory demands for solutions of vast ecological, industrial and social problems? Proust speaks somewhere of the confidence required to create reality. Perhaps we ought to speak of the confidence required to create literature possible to live with.

Where are Julien Sorel, Anna Karenina and Balzac's young

careerists? In them we found detailed circumstances instead of hypotheses, social environment instead of conspiracy theories. V.S. Naipaul's Mr Biswas is a creation in line with the great nineteenth century characters; that is, a human being we don't forget once we have met him. I see him everywhere. I'll always be thinking about him. No wonder it is the Third World writers who are attempting to identify human beings who have for all centuries lived in the shadow, in literary silence.

With us, like the peoples of the Third World, women have begun to chart their literary past, but on the whole, the patient resistance of reality to our wishes is no longer a main theme in the literature of prosperity. We are more troubled by the plans reality has for us and its troublesome incomprehensibility. It's a question of understanding the conditions under which we live – we are seeking our own Odysseus, a new Orpheus, new myths to still our seesawing lives.

I am generalising all round, retreating into mist, literary scurvy. The ground is not frozen, only the pigs are lazy – or whatever it was Sven Delblanc said about attempts to render literature innocuous. Now and again I find myself about to write about Africa, and then it all falls to pieces. How necessary is it? What driving force have I? It is easy to question yourself – individual self-searching in Mondlane's house by the blue ocean, while liberation movements struggle, or at least discuss strategy.

Describe your books, people in Africa sometimes say – just as one asks someone to talk about his profession. It is difficult to say anything exciting. I do not really see them as dialectical counter-arguments, but more as addenda. They wander like cats round the same hot dish of porridge, the densities of life and the epiphania of experience.

People who don't read ask: Why do you write? Perhaps one writes in order to avoid answering such questions. Or perhaps to get someone to put up a shelf, or stir a saucepan, or mend a torn pocket, or to make people somewhere look up because they remember something they had read, or they hear something said on the radio that stays for ever: Yes, that's true, and I didn't know it.

That's probably roughly what it's all about, and that's quite enough.

Experience persists and accumulates. Here, too, in Mondlane's lonely little house, where I must soon complete a report on innumerable conversations and deliberations with the liberation movement people, one of those countless documents which will not be printed, only copied a few times, but which at best could be the basis for actions and measures taken.

Yard upon yard is added to a thicker and thicker roll of cloth, the colours changing, fading and becoming stronger. If you are an author, you cut a piece of the cloth off occasionally, dye it another colour, wash it, iron it, pull it and fold it – and it becomes a book, an experience cut off and thus transformed.

5. The Impenetrable Forest

Back to Africa, return to Africa – they are common expressions. The white man's grave is presumably also his cradle. Once one has been there, it is a matter of a journey back, inwards, towards the origin.

I read about a recently released Swiss film called *Le Retour d'Afrique*, about a young couple planning to settle in Africa but never getting there. Africa is the magnet, the litmus paper of their everyday life, the lighthouse and buffer, everything between heaven and earth that touches them. But never Africa in itself, never Africa.

However much one wants Africa for the Africans, Africa cannot be freed from the white man's imagination. Africa is a symbol in a way that no other continent is. Jules Verne, Rider Haggard and Graham Greene have all sought Africa in fairytale form, as if Africa were a rock on which were inscriptions and decorations awaiting decoding and interpreting. Africa is still a map on which only rudimentary topographical phenomena have been drawn. The idea that there is an Africa that has to be found, defined and constantly re-described is an old idea. It has a past there is no need to flee from, but which is a necessary sounding-board, so that one doesn't end up in the empty heart, in a clean grave with no memories.

So we are faced with an Africa which serves in a variety of ways as a tool and instrument for white people in novels by

Romain Gary and Joyce Cary, by Laurens van der Post, Doris Lessing and Nadine Gordimer – a search for the truth about ourselves.

When Joseph Conrad was nine years old, he looked at the map of Africa, put his finger on the white area which at the time was the unsolved mystery of the continent, and said that when he was grown-up, he would go just there. When he later achieved his aim, he wrote in *Heart of Darkness*:

'Going up that river was like travelling back to the earliest beginnings of the world, when vegetation rioted on the earth and the big trees were kings. An empty stream, a great silence, an impenetrable forest . . .'

When I was young, I idolised Hemingway's characters. They lived freely floating between drinks, bull-rings, hotels and almost anonymous women. They were so tough, so realistically drawn, and yet they were romantic cocoon creatures who never descended to ground level where most people exist.

Hemingway's image of Africa is of a wildlife park, a reserve, with a few individual black poachers. The lost hero searches in it for his identity, struggling with the elements and drink. The whole world is a cinder-track for his own performance: it is imperialism.

Yet there is something moving about Hemingway's search for an 'untouched' reality, not yet tarnished or written about by his contemporaries:

'I want to go back to Africa, but not earn my living from it. I can do that with two pens and a few hundred sheets of paper. But I want to go back to where it was a joy for me to live – really live. Not just watch life gliding by. Our ancestors went to America because at the time that was the right country to go to. It had been a good country and we'd made a damned mess of it and now I want to go somewhere else, just as we've always had the right to go somewhere else . . .'

I see before me the nineteenth century explorer taking the altitude of the sun, turning a sextant and seeking a direction. For Africa is full of pathways. It is an untrodden country, not untouched. What is so confusing is the endless number of pathways. They criss-cross each other, and which one leads to the swamp and which to the hill, which to the ford and which to a village? The vegetation is too high to allow a clear view.

You take a path at random; they all seem to go the same way, but soon turn off and lead you astray.

So the explorers were in the hands of their guides and the chieftains who provided the guides. Difficulties in coming to some agreement with the chieftains and explaining the reasons for these peculiar journeys through alien territory caused delays described by Livingstone, Baker and Speke as insufferable. Disappointments lay round the nearest baobab tree and behind the huge mountain – drought, no fruit trees, no navigable river, natives who spoke yet another incomprehensible language . . .

Exploring has become an obsolete profession. There are no more white patches on the map, and discoveries of today are made in areas smaller that a square millimetre or larger than the surface of the earth. When man landed on the moon, he saw the earth as a blue and silver bubble somewhere in space. Politically speaking, it is good if we regard the earth as a village in which we all have to live. But for enjoyment's sake, let us go slowly, on foot, by train or canal boat, then it will remain large. The more we see of the world and the less of television, the larger it will seem. But for the person fleeing from a Chile of prisons and torture, seeing himself deported by country after country, the earth is no spacious planet.

Those statues staring out to sea in the ex-colonies: generals, governors and governor-generals. They died of pestilence, fever and hardship, or they returned alive to the coast: both exploits meriting a statue. Many of these are now being stored away in warehouses, irrelevant – the inhabitants themselves knew perfectly well how to live and travel in their own country. There are no statues of Africans in European countries.

No longer does anyone talk about how China and India were discovered. Countries with cultures aren't discovered. Black Africa also had its culture, but it was a long time before anthropologists went there to substantiate it. The Victorians discovered very little in the broad scientific sense. But remarkable people like Mary Kingsley found not only curving rivers and villages to draw on the map, she also frightened her day with a new way of regarding black people: 'The African is no more underdeveloped than a rabbit is an underdeveloped hare.' She was completely at home in the cannibal villages of Gabon. 'If I have a heaven, then this is it', she wrote one morning in the 1890s, as she paddled away in her canoe and went swimming alone before her hosts in the village were awake.

The lives and activities of explorers easily acquire features of nostalgia strengthened by association with childhood stories and imaginative xylography in *Through the Dark Continent*. They lit the darkness and filled maps with mountains and rivers, but most were insensitive to the society and customs of the people. They were heroes, and the unknown Africa was a heroic symbol. It was easier to portray yourself as the conqueror of barbarians in a distant country than as a human being meeting friendliness and curiosity and not knowing how to handle the experience.

The nineteenth century explorers darkened African society rather than discovered it. They added to information on Africa, but knowledge is something else.

Lake Victoria had been used by thousands of people when Speke said he had discovered it. He contributed to the general education of Europeans, no more. But finding the source of the Nile, which no one had seen, and grasping the connection between Lake Victoria and the river, that is charting the unknown and increasing mankind's store of knowledge.

Shaking with ague, attacked by poisonous insects and hostile natives, travellers wrote down their exact observations on damp paper, using thin ink they had made themselves from plant juices. They went home to their royal geographical societies, which enviously refused to believe them, or else they died in the jungle, and posterity first heard of their fates much later. The Swede, Charles John Andersson, leading explorer of South Africa, was awarded an honorary doctorate at Lund University and was expected to go to fetch his laurel wreath. No one knew that he had died by the River Okavango the previous year.

They were rarely grateful for their experiences. In the diaries of Stanley and Lugard, the reader comes across contempt and hatred of Africans, and Richard Burton believed in an inborn depravity in black people. They go no deeper than the descriptions usually found in the margins of old maps. Here, for instance, is one from Boulton's Map of Africa, printed in London in 1795:

'The Hottentots delight in wine, brandy and liqueurs . . . They are considered the laziest peoples under the sun. They prefer to starve or eat dried skins or the soles of shoes rather than hunt for food. They pray to the moon and worship a fly as large as a wasp.'

Livingstone, on the other hand, never dismissed the Africans. He demanded much of them, because he judged them as equals. They did not inhabit another world. Alongside Mary Kingsley a few decades later, Livingstone was the only one of the great explorers to see that initiation rites and other ceremonies were not bestial and heathen, but had an aim and purpose. He showed insight into the developments to come which reminds the reader of Darwin and Marx, his contemporaries.

The new Africa would be dominated by European trade and the exploitation of raw materials, and this would destroy a society based on co-operation, and collective and mutual fulfilment of duty. When the traders brought in cash and the cotton-gin, the teachings of Jesus would trickle into the cracks in society and encourage moral confusion.

Livingstone considered this unavoidable. He knew he himself had been involved in instigating it. At the same time, to the very end of his life, he loved Africa for its natural history, as a continent and as a state of affairs he feared would soon disappear:

'How often have I not regarded scenes that have condensed beauty itself . . . green meadows, cattle grazing, goats roaming, kids leaping round, groups of herd-boys comparing miniature bows, arrows and spears. The women steer their steps towards the river with water-jars unconstrainedly balanced on their heads. The men sleeping in the shade of the fig-tree, old grey-haired elders sitting on the ground, stave in hand, listening to the morning gossip.'

That is how Africans remember their country.

What is moving about Livingstone's diaries are the signs of a weariness he condenses into small hard words, an overwhelming fatigue, perhaps largely due to the fact that he feels ensnared – he has to co-operate with the slave-traders he loathes. He does not go as a Christian preacher, but as the precursor of a force of traders and soldiers with whom he has no wish to identify. He has other ideals, but is probably often regarded as a forerunner of Stanley, with his Maxim-gun, his hippo-whip and simpler formulae: chieftains clapped in irons, a trading station formed, an ingratiating dispatch to the Queen of England, and western civilisation has taken one booted step forward into the kingdom of darkness.

When about a hundred years ago Henry Morton Stanley set out to search for the lost Dr Livingstone, he made tremendous preparations. He starts from Bagamoyo, a sleepy little town by the sea, north of Dar es Salaam, where Frelimo founded its first secondary school with Swedish aid. The caravan, or safari, largely follows the order recommended by the German Reichard:

'At the head of the column, in a long line, one man behind another, are ten or twelve armed men. After them, the standard-bearer, and the flag itself plays an important part. After that come some askaris, and at some distance from them, the travellers themselves. After the travellers come armed men again, and drummers, and not until then, like the first of the bearers, the leader, *kirangosi*. This is a man particularly well-travelled, who knows the routes and is especially proud of carrying a very heavy load in the form of a *mdalla*, on which the sacred cock is tethered by one leg. This cock, which is given its freedom in camp, announces with great thoroughness with its crowing the coming day and is an important member of the caravan. The *kirangosi* is armed, clad in colourful, preferably red pieces of cloth and is richly adorned with a feather headdress. Behind him come all the *mdalla* bearers and in front of them those who carry the ammunition. After them come the bearers of the always necessary personal effects, then the long line of the others, whom women and children also join. The procession ends with a troop of armed men. Speed at first may not exceed 74 steps a minute, but after two hours' marching, this can be increased to 80–85 steps, and then towards the end of the march can again be reduced to 75. After two or three hours' unbroken march there is half an hour's rest, and after two more hours the same again, but afterwards no more until the goal of the day has been reached.'

Stanley takes with him eight thousand yards of denim, sixteen thousand yards of unbleached calico and over five thousand of blue and pink muslin – all in all, some eighteen miles of cloth. He has about a million dyed seeds and glass beads, and added to that a Persian rug, a bearskin, a bath-tub, silver cutlery and a bottle of Sillery champagne – in case he should come across Livingstone.

Stanley took particular care of a bottle of Worcester sauce. The Persian rug is spread out for visits from chieftains or Arab slave-traders. He has the Bible and some back numbers of the *New York Herald* as reading matter.

This was before the days of plastic and penicillin. Nothing is to be thrown away. The chances of surviving fevers are limited. All articles have a value, but also a place in the hierarchial order. They act as a surrogate for a way of life which will incur respect, a screen against chaos, a reminder of an inviolable civilisation, of the superiority of the white man.

In addition, some of the baggage is always lost during the rainy season at the various fords, so they are entitled to take overweight loads.

There are no maps of the interior of Africa for Stanley, and neither do sketches by Speke and Burton help him. He does not recognise where he is, nor rediscover what they have seen. He does not know where lowland jungle ends and becomes plateau. He relies on his compass, his interpreters and bearers, and keeps them in check with bribes, punishments and promises of better times ahead.

Wandering into the unknown, on a blank map, with a bottle of Sillery champagne in a padded case – it is a symbol of Victorian explorers, and was to be broadened to become an image of the wealthy section of humanity.

We are travelling towards an unknown future with a Persian rug and a bottle of champagne in the hope that western delicacies and superfluities will come in useful.

But who will listen to the pop of the cork and who will sit on the rug?

6. The Ivory Tower

Into Dar es Salaam from the house by the sea. The atmosphere is different, the turtle-pale air of fumes, the heat like a damp winter glove, the girls' glances which only town-dwellers allow themselves.

'To Rent' notices. An astrologist's placard two floors up; he calls himself Dr Path from the University of Madras, but how does anyone find him? A couple of White Fathers in long cassocks, followed by two Arabs in similar robes. Six Chinese crammed into a Land Rover. Mercedes cars with CD plates – the American ambassador has stopped cycling. The Russian ambassador never sank to such ingratiation.

'Diamonds & Jewellery' once stood on a shop window in gold lettering, but has been replaced by a strip of paper stating 'Printing and Copying'. Birth certificates and testimonials have become more valuable than precious metals. A family of pigeons living above advertises itself as Chiropodist. Alongside is the Hibernian Insurance Company: venetian blinds in front of a little room, a brown pole with clothes-hangers, an almost empty bookcase with a tin coffee-pot on it, a couple of bentwood chairs. Who voluntarily insures himself here? The other floors have been cleared – by the creditors, by the premium-payer whose house has burnt down or whose cows have been killed by bandits? Finally, on the corner, a challenge to try inexpensive 'fat dispersing Swedish massage'.

I see a group of hippies on the beach near the President's house. They have fled the superfluity of the west. They hitchhike their way, no one knows where. The boys hide behind beards and long hair, soon to be quite invisible. The girls in their long skirts at least fulfil the moral rules of the country. They look pale and disappointed. Africans have not much to offer these people searching for simplicity and origins, and would like to swap them for a tractor. But they are seldom told that.

I go out to the university, shining white and isolated on its hill, a true ivory tower. I discuss African literature for a couple of hours and in exchange am shown translations of Shabaan Robert the students have done from Swahili into English.

One student says that far too many Europeans deal with their literature. As Tanzania has not very much literature, he thinks outsiders appropriate research subjects. I reply that literature is a universal phenomenon, a way of understanding each other beyond boundaries of nationality and colour of skin. But they are tired of European literature. They want to study Swahili literature, i.e. Shabaan Robert, for there's not much more. They want to make him a national hero, a Tanzanian Dickens.

Robert was born in 1909 – when Shaw was fifty-three, for instance, and twenty years after T.S. Eliot was born – and when he died at fifty-three, he had carried Tanganyika's literature on his shoulders for two decades – epics, novels, essays and legends. He is the first author to write literature in Swahili and express his own ideas and thoughts, not those of the Koran or the Bible. So he became an originator, although his half-finished education kept him more firmly rooted in tradition than an originator ought to be.

The number of his works is greater than any other African author writing in an African language. There are fourteen fat volumes of his collected works, and more remain. He writes like a preacher, with a great many associations and allusions. Contemporary names such as Eliot, Joyce and Kafka were unknown on the east coast of Africa. What Robert read was what was translated into Swahili and on the school curriculum: Bunyan's *Pilgrim's Progress*, Swift's *Gulliver's Travels*, Stevenson, Lewis Carroll. His work shows their influence.

He was among the first to demand that Swahili should be the main language of East Africa. He compared the knowledge of Swahili with the milk from an African woman's breast and English with a tin of dried milk. He compared colonialism with a thin coat of varnish, easily scraped off. In that respect, he was all too hopeful. But he lived to see Tanzania's Independence Day.

When Robert is talked of today, it is as a man who lived long ago and achieved great things. That is not surprising when the living classicist of Africa, their Virginia Woolf, on whom new theses pour out every month, is the Nigerian Chinua Achebe, born in 1930.

Although Swahili has been the national language for some decades, Tanzanian literature has hardly moved on from the point where Shabaan left it at his death. His idea, a national literature representing the life and thoughts of the whole country, not just the Swahili coast, is still but a dream.

It is a matter of time. The reading public is small. The

ability to write is rationed. The forming of the *ujamaa* villages would be a subject for modern literature, but it is as if everyday life goes by unobserved. Robert is not without blame in that respect. There is nothing concrete or lively in his work.

I advise students to read West African and South African novels, and to study Nyerere's speeches. In them they will find unusually good prose, probably better written than that of any other living statesman.

But they distrust me. Nyerere is not radical enough. He has an honorary doctorate at the university and appears now and again to remind them that research and knowledge can never be an aim in itself in a poor country. The students must go out on to the land, into agriculture, putting their privileges at the service of the many. This is considered by some to be non-revolutionary and fussy nonsense.

In the evening, I listen to a discussion at the Overseas Political Society, mainly between white lecturers and foreign black students. There is no question of going out to help with illiteracy or in the *ujamaa* villages. The rhetorical extreme left dominates the meeting with its inability to differentiate between wishful dreams and reality. They resemble sectarians selling God on the promise or threat of the coming Day of Judgement – just like the revolution that is to happen tomorrow, shortly, soon. The belief in total revolution is such that doubters have to be eliminated: better a small faithful band than a large uncertain one. When a son of the country implies that a gradual revolution is going on in Tanzania – yet so thorough that it lacks any counterpart in most other countries – he is reproved for his ignorance. Another asks whether a sudden revolution would not put a lot of people out of work. The question arouses no approval from students who pay nothing for their education.

I am surprised at these people's fanatical optimism. They appear to be blind to capitalism's immense ability to adapt, the strength and flexibility of the multi-nationals, and the language of arms in the western world. They underestimate their enemy. They start out from regarding capitalist societies as a seething brew of discontent beneath a lid of bureaucratic control. The left will smash the lid, then a short and violent revolution will occur.

'The ruling class will be brought down... your reasoning is typically bourgeois ... a conscious counter-revolutionary strategy instigated by bourgeoisie in disguise ...'

The clichés leap into conversations here at the university as well. The bizarre idea that everything directed against revolution is consciously instigated by a master-mind and conductor of capitalism is constantly aired, whether registered in the Pentagon or Wall Street, the City of London or Brussels.

Two exiled students from Zimbabwe make it quite clear to me that Sweden is steered by the CIA, ITT and IBM, which through their subsidies keep social-democracy in power, as it would appear disturbing to have a right-wing government; what is decisive is that right-wing policies are carried out. I say that I hope that these Jehovah's Witnesses of Politics will soon be doing their stint at the brick factory in Dodoma. They reply – if not in these exact words – that because of their exiled status, they are excused contact with manual workers.

It is the students' phrases and mechanical choice of words that frighten me, not their behaviour, which is less threatening and less childish. Is it a need for faith, a profound disappointment in development in Africa as well as in the world, or what their elders call youthful intolerance? 'Every individual,' Nyerere has said recently, 'has the right to that maximum economic and political freedom which can be combined with the same freedom for everyone else.' He is closer to both reality and a productive utopia:

'We want to build a classless society for one reason. No nation has sufficient wealth to satisfy the individual's hunger for power and prestige. The moment wealth is separated from its purpose, namely the elimination of poverty, ruthless competition between individuals arises, and each and every one tries to acquire more wealth in order thus to acquire more power and prestige than his fellow men. Wealth becomes an instrument of dominance, a means of humiliating other people...

'But class differences are also widening in the socialist countries. No longer are there wealthy capitalist countries and poor socialist countries. There are wealthy socialist countries as well as poor socialist countries. I also think the socialist countries themselves, seen as individuals in the greater context of nations, are now committing the same crimes the capitalists committed before. On an international level, they are beginning to use wealth for capitalistic purposes, namely, to acquire power and prestige for themselves.'

But the students appear to be tired of the man who remains the wisest and boldest man in the country.

Afterwards I had coffee in one of the staff rooms with a woman translator and a professor from the Haya people, from Bukoba, west of Lake Victoria. I know them both from earlier days. He tells me he can no longer bear to go and see his mother, but sends her gifts and medicine instead. She refuses to believe the sea exists. She even doubts Dar es Salaam. When he shows her photographs, she is not impressed. When he went to the USA to study, he was declared dead by his mother and was ceremonially buried. She considered his letters to have been written by someone else. When he returned, it was as if he had been resurrected. Miracles such as that did occur occasionally, anyhow. But the sea remained impossible to believe in.

The translator is Czech and Jewish – there are many in southern and eastern Africa. She was one of those who survived Theresienstadt. After a few years, she left Stalinist Prague to seek a new life in Africa, where she met an Irish geologist in what was then Northern Rhodesia. She had friends who were sterilised by the SS. She was eighteen when she escaped and now she has one child. But she has told me about her dreams. They take the child away from her and she sees it disappearing into a great multitude. The child is stretching its arms out to her and she sees its expression as if it were much closer to her. She knows she can do nothing and she identifies so strongly with the child being taken from her that she feels as if she were literally being torn apart.

She says the Nazis have meant that she never feels at home. She has no roots, no childhood home; all security is illusory except that of the sea, the wind and the forest. She cannot trust anyone, because she dare not trust herself. At night, she is haunted by a past which many people in her present circumstances simply refuse to believe. She was taken into hot damp sauna-like rooms. She has been slightly claustrophobic ever since. So she loves the sea shores and the high African plateau. In her dreams, or when she is very tired, she becomes afraid time might just go into reverse and inexorably take her back to the painful death she thought she had survived.

It takes half an hour to drive home. A few fires are still burning outside invisible huts. I make a detour to avoid the real town, drive into a pothole and stop to see if the exhaust pipe has broken. My torch does not reach very far.

The African night sweeps the landscape into its invisible cloak. But there are so many sounds, it becomes visible again – to other senses.

This blackness when the small animals take over – crickets with their scraping fiddles, frogs with their croaking bells, mosquitoes with their tuning forks and the owl with its bass tuba.

And the other birds hiding right in next to the trunks, under green skirts of leaves, wild pigs grubbing away in their sleep, and water-bucks leaning asleep against blocks of stone.

Back home again, I find the electicity has gone off, presumably a fault in the transformer. The refrigerator has stopped humming. I say a polite hullo, should it be that some unexpected visitor wishes to make himself known.

Silent three-forked flashes of lightning illuminate the eastern sky over the sea, where the sun will soon rise above Zanzibar. I find a candle in the kitchen and quickly go to bed, thinking about nothing.

7. Sweden

There are days in Africa when I am so captivated by what I am doing that I don't give myself much time to think about people I like, about Sweden and the rest of the world.

Then there are others, marginal days, full of lacunae, pauses, distractions. I lie awake half the night, hearing the BOAC plane from Dar flying into a bank of clouds on its way to Nairobi and London. The gin bottles are beginning to rattle on the trays up there, the wagon of perfumes loaded with scents of distant cities, the foreign coins changing hands.

There is not a glimmer left of either fire or stars in the tropical darkness. Not a crack of light nor a glimpse of water.

Is it the sky or the earth which has retreated? I dare not take a step outside myself. I recall memories gliding across small scenaria. They have a special flavour, a scent, a feeling – they are quite private: an entire bakery of Madelaine cakes; memories.

Early Sunday morning in Heby. I drive down to the bus-stop in the square with the children to buy the newspaper. There is no delivery on Sundays. There is the fountain, the grey silo, the Salvation Army's faded wooden hut and the empty little shopping street that ends in a slope up to the church. It is an indefinite urban community which I seem to remember for generations: the smell of coffee in the lino-floored kitchen, old desks of oak veneer, the wet artificial ice-rink beneath sharp lights in the winter darkness, and Swedish comments – Ketchup or mustard? Both.

Images are released at random, like stills from a projector. The church park in Linköping one February day, the sky high, the sun on the limestone of the cathedral and mossy green trunks of limes. The children on the banks of Djurgårdbrunn Bay one muddy spring day, and the blue wing-flashes of the mallards. The light over Humlegård Park one afternoon in October, turning red towards evening. Sture Street's façades with lively window displays and the gaps towards Inner Östermalm. Striped survey poles in a cleared forest covered with powdery snow. A country auction in July, bending your head low in cramped rooms, drawing-pin marks in the wallpaper, a treadle sewing-machine, a mangle, a bread trough. A day of humming bumble-bees full of children's voices and crowds and recognisable things. The sticky buds of chestnuts in May: spring sugar. Cabbages being harvested in Bergslagen just as the frost leaves the first icy edge round the puddles.

In Africa, no resin stiffens in the cracks of the bark, and no water is so cold that it chills the liquor bottle wedged between two stones. But space, expanses, clarity, eternal banks of cloud, and lemur eyes lit up by the dusk, the swift-footed dusk.

Images and scents fasten in the boundaries of the seasons, in climatic transition. 'When summer comes, you can find an anthill has been erected round a dropped glove' (Artur Lundkvist). Living with the changes between snowdrop-spring and flaming maple-leaf autumn is a northern privilege, compared with the one-figure latitudes in which day and night are each other's opponents, drought deadly and the rains bringing floods with them.

This Sweden appears so seldom in literature in the way I think exact. The old-fashioned variation of photographic recognisability – bromide, brown but sharp – can be found in Sven Delblanc's series of novels, and in Sune Jonsson's books; the present day – black and white from photographic laboratories – of Birger Norman, in Jolo's and Lars Westman's causeries, and in Jörn Donner's *The Sweden Book*.

Sweden – object of my admiration and wonder; mazarine cakes and the Arts Council, the open television channel, liverpaste on white bread with wilting lettuce, Ingmar Bergman, the winter light over Gärdet in Stockholm, helpfulness when my car breaks down on the roadside, the opening of a housewives' sculpture exhibition in a Stockholm park, words like 'searching culture', the government declaration of the importance of infant schools helping children to be at the same time both creative and community-minded, pop-singer Alice Babs and actor Edvard Persson, Pommac and Grönstedts Blå, Gyldene Freden restaurant and ABF.*

This strange land where almost everyone sees the same television programmes, reads *Dagens Nyheter* and *Tips News*, drinks vodka and Lyckholm's beer and skimmed milk, with a blue and yellow flag, and where job security for public cleansing workers is greater than anywhere else in the world.

What can one think? Sweden, Sweden, commuter country...

8. Friends

One thinks one's old friends should stay like churn-stands along country roads. But in Africa, they move. They die, disappear, emigrate to other continents. Many whites are here on short-term contracts. The man who thought he had found a cave on the north slope of Kilimanjaro, close to the peak, the

---

* Equivalent of WEA (Workers' Education Association)

man who could plunder a car engine and make a separator and a crystal-set from it, the man who was a compositor at the mission printing works in Soni and drank himself to death while trembling more and more as he hand-set the *Epistles of St Paul to the Corinthians* in Kikuyu . . .

Where had they gone? My address book with all those box numbers – constantly out-of-date. The telephone directories list district officers and provincial commissioners from colonial days, and places with two thousand inhabitants still have only ten telephones. When the *Lucy Show* of 1948 is shown on television, you also expect the news bulletins to contain items on the Cuban crisis or Ghana's independence.

I leaf through old notes, memos and white papers. The Lutuli Foundation resulted in a memorial to Albert Lutuli, before it came to an end. Film projects shelved. Calculations for a radio transmitter in Botswana directed towards South Africa – considered politically too risky. Plans to send Scandinavian trawlers to the lobster-rich waters outside Namibia to show South Africa that according to international law, it could not decide Namibia's territorial boundaries. Correspondence with authorities and the Red Cross about a guard in Rhodesia who for the fun of it gave a political prisoner I knew twelve tablets a day instead of the prescribed three. The man died, the guard was dismissed, but the prison in Gwelo is still there, full of those imprisoned for thirteen years, but never sentenced.

The perpetual struggle for power within the African National Congress, constantly the same, communists against nationalists. The white communist party in exile, with its Moscow-faithful intellectuals, controls the London office. Oliver Tambo, ANC's leader in exile, hardly a born political leader, but he alone can balance the forces in the movement. He prevents the communists from being thrown out, but in exchange ensures they don't get the upper hand. Yet constant power struggles weaken and splinter the liberation movement and have afflicted some of its leading people, Robert Resha, Mazizi Kunene, South Africa's leading poet. ANC's treasurer, J.B. Marks, stationed in Moscow, withheld money from the disobedient and the unfaithful. Poverty-stricken, they applied to more dubious sources and so were finally damned. Now

Marks himself has been struck off the membership list – dead.

In the greatest secrecy, the Soviet Union once offered a considerable sum of money to free Bram Fischer, the white lawyer sentenced to life imprisonment in Pretoria's central prison, and who died in 1975. Huge bribes, disguises and submarines were involved. The Soviet Union made it clear they were only interested in Fischer, a leading communist. Nelson Mandela and the black freedom leaders were not their responsibility. Bram heard about the plan and said no, not without his friends. Nelson Mandela on Robben Island was told there was a chance of releasing him and Bram, but he also said no, not without my friends on the island. So nothing happened except that Bram got cancer and died, and Nelson went on breaking stones in the cold Atlantic winds. I think after all this time, I can relate this.

All those bulletins: MPLA's and FNLA's and ZANU's, SWAPO's and SWANU's, ANC's and NDP's, the Trotskyites', the militant-socialists' ... they seem to be written in water, but the press historians and political scientists would think differently. Who has time for all this? But the faces stay with me as I catch a glimpse of the reports or look through letters that happen to have been saved.

Joshua Nkomo in a basement in Gower Street in London just before he went back to Rhodesia and voluntarily chose eleven years in Gonakudzingwa camp, in the heat and isolation, so as not to betray his people. Broad and jovial as a wealthy merchant on his holiday veranda, in fact a shrewd and experienced union man. He is a negotiator by disposition, a discusser, but that does not entail betraying his people. But the lean and sugarless years of camp have given him an insatiable appetite. It is weird to watch him eating sweet things, desserts, cream. He is digging his own grave with his teeth.

Agostinho Neto in Luanda, Lusaka and Stockholm, with his careful smile, his unAfrican introversion which disappears when he talks about poetry. He plays with his cards close to his chest, enigmatic, afraid to give himself away, with a perfect memory of the past rather than vision ahead. He appears to have a great deal to reproach in life and does not appreciate jokes. Other African leaders who share his ideas say they have no idea who they are dealing with.

Holden Roberto, tall, handsome, untouched by war and guerilla activity, in a white Mercedes with a private chauffeur and a dinner jacket tucked into his black leather suitcase, Bakongo's uncrowned king, with his sceptical little smile when democracy is mentioned. He feels at home in chambers of commerce and rotary clubs, or in an old-fashioned operetta in which he can play the part of a somewhat worn male lead.

Herbert Chitepo and Amilcar Cabral, two of the best, one a lawyer, the other a teacher, but probably murdered by their own people, however much one would like to blame their deaths on enemy forces.

Benedicto Kiwanuka, who rose to be Prime Minister and after that Public Prosecutor. He refused to pronounce people guilty who General Amin wished to get rid of, so was executed by the General's bodyguard.

It was during the first years of de-colonisation, about 1960, when I got to know most people. All East Africa, Zambia, Malawi, Botswana, were still colonies. We met in a boarding-house basement in Bloomsbury, the bitter tea brewing from six in the morning, at the YMCA, at meetings in Euston Hall, in billiard halls with heavy green curtains, where much more was discussed than the rules of the game, and in an Indian cafeteria in Gray's Inn Road.

It was easy to reach them in those days, in clubs and hotels, in their homes in Africa, in union offices and the university. I got to know their habits, their wives, girl-friends and colleagues. Most of them lived a meagre, almost ascetic life. Then came power with its paraphernalia, its rituals and jealous courtiers, the security regulations which often arose at the thought of how many men had met violent deaths. Contacts became clumsier, more indirect. Every time, a wall of secretaries and officials had to be penetrated. It is only in the Scandinavian countries that it is still easy to meet ministers. No wonder bureaucracy fascinates the new countries. Tanzania is also becoming more and more bureaucratic – despite Nyerere's measures, and despite the fact that direct lines still go to the TANU cells in the villages. At the customs or police stations, I see the same stubby pencils being held like branding-irons to achieve eight copies, the top one being the most illegible.

A large proportion of humanity, not least in the underdeveloped countries, is occupied pushing pieces of paper around and loving it. The more copies, the happier they are, meaningless perfection giving gloss and structure to life.

In insufficiently industrialised countries, bureaucracy is the only career. Administration swallows all the educated, and with centralisation of power comes the misuse of it. 'The true delicacies are raw,' Paavo Haavikko says. 'Oysters, salmon and power.'

The wealthy world often hesitates to criticise the Third World and call corruption and bureaucratic excesses by their true names. Informed people fear that such criticism can serve as an excuse for them to do nothing for the underdeveloped countries. The gap between real aid and promises and the negative conservativeness which has hindered the flow of exports from the Third World should be a burden on the consciences of the rich countries. But at the same time, it is disheartening that the underdeveloped countries have given so little thought to the fact that the blessings of development can reach the truly poor, the people whose income per capita is below eighty pounds a year.

We know how they can be helped, and they themselves should have their eyes on the few countries who have wanted to help themselves (at present in Africa, Tanzania, Mozambique, Guinea-Bissau). Governments must concentrate less on developing visible objects of prestige and capital-intensive industries, because the poor live out in the countryside. But governments also have to encourage job opportunities in the towns, in the slums to which people flee in despair from an impoverished countryside. Hundreds of millions of people must be given the chance to be more productive, on their smallholdings, on the larger farms, in factories and family businesses. Only by producing more can they hope to support their families and keep hunger, disease and illiteracy at bay.

The élite of the Third World will not be forgiven, and maybe will not even survive, if it stands like a wall between the poor and the aid from the world outside they need so badly.

9. The Guerillas

I take out books Eduardo Mondlane studied before he was murdered. There is a work by Frantz Fanon, and I presume it is Eduardo who has written the exclamation marks in the margins. Unlike Fanon, he saw no antagonism between the poor of the towns and the countryside. There is a book there of Portuguese colonial history with an underlined quote by President Graveiro Lopes of Portugal, speaking in 1956:

'With God's help, we shall raise high the flag of Portugal. We shall tame the wilderness, build towns and make them flourish. We shall teach, educate and lead the masses of natives to a better life and suppress their dark instincts . . . steep their souls in the teachings of nobler Christian forms and see that justice is done with mildness and insight . . . we are moving towards a great, glowing and attainable future.'

It is this mysterious exaltation, this unrealistic rhetoric that stamps Portuguese statements to the last.

This is also evidence of the racial hatred that marked Portuguese colonialism despite all talk of the opposite. Mondlane saved extracts from lectures Mozambique's Commander-in-Chief, General Kaulza de Arriaga gave to his senior command and had printed in *Lessons in Strategy*, Volume XII:

'One must be very intelligent to be able to undertake subversion. It cannot be done by just anyone. The black people are not particularly intelligent. On the contrary, they are the least intelligent of all peoples. . . . The increase in the white population aims to keep pace with the number of educated blacks . . . As it is fortunately not possible to educate all blacks, it is possible, well, almost certain that we can place sufficiently many whites there (in Africa) that the numbers will keep pace with the number of blacks receiving education.'

Portuguese strategy in Africa is summarised by Arriaga: 'First increase the white population, then limit the black population.'

I remember Mondlane telling me what President Nyerere had said to him:

'You're lucky. You're fighting something you can see, and

then you will be able to fight what you can't see.'

The few occasions I had time to discuss things with Mondlane, it was on questions that had occupied many people. How far can the struggle for freedom in underdeveloped countries be compromised, that is, by accepting aid from countries with which they otherwise feel no solidarity? The realisation that neither the Soviet Union, China nor the USA had unselfish motives behind their aid. The triumph of China's peasant revolution. The question of how democracy could survive what is central to a socialist revolution – can it work in any other way apart from directly through workers' committees, village communities, peasant co-operatives, and avoid bureaucratic unions and omnipotent party organs? How much loyalty and unity concerning mutual aims was required to be able to carry out five-year plans without resorting to strong central rule?

Eduardo could look childishly sorrowful, and he could shake with a laughter which suddenly stopped. His impatience was disciplined.

'My sympathies,' he said, 'are not with those who keep order, but with those who see clearly what is arbitrary in that order.'

We once talked about how to spread information in enslaved Mozambique, how knowledge made its way to an illiterate population, and he said roughly this:

'When the scope of oppression is realised by people, it seems worse to them. The awareness that liberation is possible becomes a burden at the same time as giving hope. The truth is something that is discovered, a mirror which suddenly becomes clear. Then you have to live with that truth, a kind of double oppression, until you rise up and say that this truth requires action if you are to be able to go on living.'

Mondlane – like Cabral and most of the African freedom leaders – considered political education and organisation should precede armed struggle. Nationalism had to grow and unity arise between the educated and the uneducated. The masses needed convincing that guerilla warfare might improve their situation. Long before the fighting started, underground Frelimo groups were working to train leaders, who in their turn would instruct the people. A lengthy struggle is often a good thing. The unity of the people is decisive. The enemy cannot afford to wait, the property-less people have plenty of time. 'When the spider's webs are joined, they can bind a lion,' Mondlane said, quoting an African proverb.

That was why he turned so firmly against the school of thought favouring an élite group of devoted guerilla fighters, with a few well-planned military assaults, extracting revolutionary response from the people, despite the people's original lack of involvement and knowledge. He did not share Regis Debray's ideas based on co-operation with Che Guevara in Latin America.

Debray maintains the guerillas' contact with local populations should remain minimal. Rather than swimming like fish in the peasants' water – as Mao wrote – the guerillas should be self-sufficient. They must be organised so that the people do not notice the daily activities of the soldiers. Political instruction is not needed to win over a passive population. The actual struggle on behalf of the people serves a political purpose showing visible evidence of the vulnerability of the ruling class. The longer the struggle lasts – regardless as to whether military victories are proclaimed – the better the chance of convincing the peasants that the guerillas can win.

If a successful guerilla force thus liberates enough of the country to create an internal base, this has the propaganda effect that it denies government forces access to that part of their own country. A well-organised liberated area gives the peasants a lesson in how life could be in the future. – All this according to Debray.

On the latter point, Mondlane's and Debray's views appear to agree, but the difference lies in that Debray wants to liberate an area for the peasants, while Mondlane starts out from the peasants, after a period of political instruction, liberating the area where they live themselves, and after that, training guerilla soldiers who can go on and drive out the colonial power.

Many a time, I have had the opportunity of reflecting on the spirit of self-sacrifice. I have stood at a chasm and looked across at my friends on the other side, the ones who say they have nothing to lose. I have found that I do have something to lose. I do not want to do for them what I would do for my children. My egoistical driving-force is not that great, my ideological purity sullied.

They know it and so do I. They make no great demands on me; money, opinions and whatever kind of aid I can achieve. That is what they hope for from me, from Sweden, from outsiders. They expect no sacrifices. As long as oppression exists, as long as there are slaves in southern Africa and they themselves have succeeded in avoiding this slavery, they are incapable of laying down their arms. They reckon on the rest of us providing the stocks of bandages, dried milk, preserves and bicycles.

They are prepared to die. They don't do so on a heroic stage. They themselves won't hear their names called out afterwards or praise for their deeds. Their instinct is not to please a lord and master, a king, a god or a destiny. Men died like that before, and we find them doing so in chivalrous novels and schoolboy stories. They lie on the fields of Poltava, bleeding beneath their horses, and Field Marshal Lewenhaupt rides past saying 'May the Lord Bless You, old chap, you're dying for your king and your country.' And the dying man smiles proudly. His reward is that he has been noticed by the power he has served, and he knows he will be remembered in the Kingdom of Heaven as well as back in his home parish.

There have always been massacres, torture of civilians, and injustice with its superior grin. The few have exploited the many. But not until now, with new technical communications, has the majority become aware of it. There is no longer a way out for the oppressed. Before, there was a god and a paradise that might counter the misery. There were unknown areas to emigrate to, a fatalistic belief that people are tied to their caste, class and position, an assurance of spiritual values untouched by political decree. Many coped with their oppression this way, but those are growing fewer and fewer.

Those who find the world unendurable as it is prepare to die for it, and do so calmly. They are consumed by a realisation that the conditions of power must at any price be changed and no striving in that direction can be in vain. The price is death, torture, exposure and finally being photographed like Che Guevara in a circle of triumphant enemies.

The moral weapon of the freedom fighters, in the long run

stronger than the arms of capitalist or communist imperialism, is that they find justification in living solely within this struggle against prevailing unreasonable conditions. Without the struggle, life loses its value. They have nothing to lose, so cannot be corrupted or tempted with bribes and posts and prosperity on the other side.

I meet them, talk to them and think I understand them, sometimes as if in a fog, sometimes with such clarity that it seems that I myself am balancing on the sharp edge of existence. In between, I may close my eyes in fear of tolerating too much and becoming cynical and worldly-wise. Or I also witness so much degradation, contempt and mutual lack of consideration, so many of the neuroses of the exile, that it brings out narrow or superior defensive attitudes in me.

Mixing with members of the freedom movement can give rise to a hollow sense that I am an impalpable many-layered person, nothing in myself, a product of a humanistic way of seeing, of a society which combines social consideration with a cynical consumer philosophy.

There is an innocence that must be defended – concerned with the possibility of justice – and an innocence that must be lost – an expression of lack of experience, of a sense of alienation faced with the multiplicity and complexity of human behaviour. But the two forms of innocence must not be confused.

I dream of other societies only on behalf of others: if you go to Cythere, Utopia and China, I wish you luck, but I myself will stay here in the incompleteness, with confused humanism stammering and whimpering around suffering and guilt, around conditions of solidarity, compassion and empathy.

Enos – Guest-worker in his own country

1.

The football match is over, the referee has said his piece, the players' voices rise above the crowd's, and not until then is the night wind felt, as if it had paused briefly while the game lasted. The spotlights above the pitch are put out and a swaying string of stars appears.

I went there from a meeting and stayed because something was happening, but I was none the wiser. Kenya is a sporting nation, whose long-legged men keep on breaking world records. Football pitches and athletic grounds keep appearing round Nairobi – performances and occupation for the people.

I watch the movements of the players and hear the spectators cheering and shouting. There is so much to find out that I have failed to. Who had paid for the ball? Is there a match series they climb up? Are these men also heading for élite sport in the inter-African series? Will they be paid by the state, be interviewed for money, be treated, and gradually used, as chattels? Is that the dream of youth in a country with no film stars or aristocracy except the Kenyatta royal family?

I ask the man standing beside me. In the semi-darkness, he looks pleasant and sensible. I can't decide what his occupation might be. But he knows nothing except that Nakuru and Mombasa have good teams, and that's all he says in his reasonably good English.

Then the crowd leaves in scattered groups on paths and earthen roads, along which they seem to find their way with an inbuilt radar. Others jump up on to the backs of trucks with a bar in the middle to hold on to, where a great many men stand squashed together, just as they are taken to work outside town in the mornings.

We fall into conversation and I offer him a lift. His name is Enos. He is twenty-six and is a Luo from the northern part of Lake Victoria. He has been to Kamusinga for a couple of years, a Quaker mission school near Mount Kenya, and he has also worked for a year in a garage at Eldoret. He is now working on a building site in Nairobi, a hotel, standing by the cement-mixer and filling it up with sand. He can work a JCB, but many men like that job and they take turns.

To me, he could equally well have been a student at teachers' training college or an administrator at a mission. He replies in detail, but quickly, to everything I ask him, and as so often, I am pleased by the ease with which one makes contact with people on this continent.

Humour and openness are features which have impressed me most in the Africans I have got to know better. Naturally that's a generalisation, but I can't help that, nor the thought that there is a tradition of laughter in Africa – if it's not that we whites laugh at ourselves so seldom or only at certain things. The same laughter lives in Mozambique's and Angola's villages as well – while it is not so common in the élite of the French-speaking bureaucracy, whose sun-glasses filter and shut out the slums, the crowds and the suffering.

Enos is one of tens of thousands of East Africans who have left their families in a village in the country and chosen to seek their fortunes in town. In Tanzania, he would stay behind in his *ujamaa* village, but Kenya does little to persuade people to stay on the land that can feed them. Enos is a guest-worker in his own country. He has chosen Rastignac's community rather than his tribe's or his clan's. He says no one has to get stuck in the environment he happens to be born in.

A winding beam of headlights over a dark road into Nairobi – people plodding along the side of the road, a grass-fire creeping like a caterpillar across the plain farther away, frogs eddying round in the darkness, drowning all comments and engine noises.

I drive into a Drive-in to see part of a four-hour Indian film and to go on talking. It turns out to be a terrible story, with all the perfumed self-pity and powdered spirituality one has, alas, come to expect from India.

Enos is sceptical and fascinated. If he told them about this at home in the village, they wouldn't believe him – films with kissing going on so long you fall asleep, church music in the background and come-hither looks that would be more useful on an attacking mamba. The life portrayed in American and Indian films is remarkably unnatural, either enhancement of violence or tearful arrogance. There's something fatiguing and abandoned, detached and sickly-sweet about Indian films. I think Africans watch them with the same astonishment with which they watch American Tarzan films, in which the Son of the Apes behaves according to a gentlemanly British code and looks down on the real savages, the blacks who have neither the advantage of being born white nor of being brought up by the apes.

Enos tells me why he came to the city, to escape something rather than to get something. In the village he has left, nothing changed except people grew old and died. An exhausted agricultural inspector might come by and talk about sowing and manuring, but unemployment was the same. There was no job for him, either. He wanted to start up a garage, but there were no cars. A carpenter's workshop – yes, if he had the capital. But no one has any money to pay for his services.

To Enos, the village is stagnation, the worst aspect of underdevelopment, a living death, uneventfulness. He has been through several years of drought and crop-failure. He has seen children slowly withering away and dying of hunger. To escape from this, he is prepared to do anything. He says goodbye to those left in the village. He knows them all, and he knows that some will be dead when he returns, and others will have left but perhaps not gone to the same town.

It is a kind of emigration, external and internal. He will face different values and greater dangers. For whoever loses the match in town drowns in its waters and is never seen again. Only the elders in the village will ever mention their names, asking what happened to them and waiting in vain for an answer.

He could have become one of those ragged tramps on the road I have seen many a time in northern Tanzania and southern Kenya. They drape themselves in shabby Second World War great-coats. They wear woollen socks with holes, shirts with no backs, an indescribable shawl wound round their heads and sometimes a crash-helmet. I imagine the Germans left supplies behind from a distant epoch, some store abandoned by the Prussian quartermaster, now plundered and distributed.

He travelled to the city by bus, because that symbolised openness and freedom – just as cars, watches and tailor-made clothes do. The horizon is rarely visible in town. That doesn't matter. The world is extensive anyhow, and that is where everything is. At his departure from the village, he gave orders for how things were to be looked after, his animals seen to, the land tilled – as if he were to be away for a month. But he knows and they all know he will be away a long time.

A revolutionary party would have told him to wait – the land is the most important and cities have no solution to offer. Or join us, join the guerillas. But there is no such party, so he saw no hope but to leave.

Kenya is peaceful on the surface, apparently stable, with an independent judiciary and a reasonably free press. But it is heading for violence – because Kenyatta allows less and less opposition and because the land problem has not been solved. The whites' land which was to have been distributed among poor Kenyans has gone to the royal family, which receives free goodwill supplies from the large companies.

Josiah – called J.M. – Kariuki, once secretary to Kenyatta, long-serving cabinet minister, talked about a Kenya with ten millionaires and ten million beggars. 'Our people who died in the forests died with a handful of earth in their hands. They believed they had died in a noble battle for the return of our country . . . but we have been pushed aside by selfishness and avarice.' On 2nd March, 1975, Kariuki was driven from the bar in the Hilton Hotel to be killed on a garbage-tip in the Ngong Hills.

Parliament investigated the murder and the results were aggravating for people surrounding Kenyatta. Then the President took to persecution. One member was imprisoned on the pretext that he tormented his ex-wife and stirred rival tribes up against each other. At a burglary and assault on the Minister of Co-operation, considered less faithful to Kenyatta, it turned out the perpetrators were the police. The security chiefs and police indicted in the Kariuki report have been assured from the highest quarters that they can rest assured in their posts, and instead the investigators are to be dealt with.

A revolutionary situation should be considered to exist when the majority of people have no chance of acquiring land to cultivate, when the majority of peasants can scrape up at the most five pounds a month, when leading politicians, officials and business men have suits made in London, have Dior dress their wives, and acquire mistresses from the international world of mannequins. Kariuki saw this – although he himself put on playboy airs – and he was not alone in seeing it.

Kenya is seething, simmering obstinately in the pan. Cautious conversations go on in the huts, with more grim humour and exhilaration that at the university. There are still a few unafraid critics and social reformers. East Africa's leading poet, Okot p'Bitek, originally from Uganda, is there and he finds the injustice and false promises unendurable. When shall we drown the clink of glasses at ambassadorial receptions? he asks. When shall we be heard above the rustling of the wind in the forest of office files?

'Our leaders wear top hats and tails when they get married,' Okot says one day when I meet him. 'They cover their wives with mosquito nets. At the altar they repeat words no one believes in – never again in my life will I look at another woman. The newly-weds cut a cake and the husband helps her cut it. Are these married women so weak they cannot even cut this soft thing without help? Mimicry, 'apemanship', borrowed European clothes – they inhibit creation in Africa. Uhuru, freedom, mostly means the rule of strangers is replaced by a native dictatorship.'

I think about this at the outdoor cinema, where a fat girl on the white screen is moaning out into the African night:

'I want to faint. Open your arms for your darling!'

She has just been told her rajah has been disinherited, and she falls like a cut rose into his embrace.

2.

Enos and I talk, only now and again putting the earphones to our ears.

I think about what the poor in town say: you must move to the country to manage. Where there's soil there's bread. But it's a mistake. Nature does not give much in itself. It must be coaxed. The greenery is deceptive. But the town is deceptive too – there it can be easier to find a wristwatch than fresh fish.

After a couple of years as a guest-worker, Enos knows this. Why doesn't he bring his family to town? Because he is working on a short-term contract, with no security, and the few acres of land near the borders of Uganda are his guarantee against failure. The city refuses to open up for him and become a home.

This has nothing to do with the slums as such. I have known men in Johannesburg who regard the city as a hiding-place in a tough existence, a constant surprise when one finds a silver coin in the gutter, and everyone, because of apartheid, is in the same boat, from ping-pong-playing priests to brilliant undiscovered painters. But those men were born in the city and existed only in its rhythm. To Enos from the country, Nairobi seems more of a monstrous ant-heap, as Wordsworth described London a hundred and fifty years ago.

He longs for his village. Sometimes a friend from the district comes and brings a coconut with him. Enos knows exactly which tree it has come from. Comradeship is to be found in Nairobi, too, fragile but necessary. But everything tastes artificial – beer, sex, the air and the smells. He knows that he himself and his blanket smell differently. He shakes it, but that doesn't help. Sundays, too, when the men are in the slums, the children yelling and church bells ringing, have an atmosphere which is quite unlike that of the village.

The village he comes from is small and scattered – at most a hundred families, he says. Is there any real return to it? He sends money to his family, but who has any use for his advice and knowledge? The things he has acquired and the job he does – the cement-mixer and the JCB – are objects of admiration, but they testify to a life which would be impractical in the country. The question is whether he has become too grand to drive the cows out to the fields – not in his own eyes, but in theirs.

Enos describes his wife's rural routine, crushing cassava, fetching water, lighting the fire, gutting fish. Out to the shamba and turning the soil with a hoe. Drinking water, eating a papaya, home to mix cassava flour and water . . . she has had no education and needs none, he thinks, but his daughter is to be allowed to go to school, even if she then gets married to some liberated young man who refuses to pay his father-in-law a dowry.

Enos has plans, which vary – starting a photographic studio, taking goods from the town and selling them, becoming a stonemason and house-builder, showing them how to make bricks and use straight branches. Putting his knowledge at the disposal of the village, sharing, yet being a little wealthier than the others. He paid for these years with his experience, and he wants some return on them – working-time transformed again into time to live.

He has become a dreamer. The longer he stays in town, the more alien it becomes to him. He learns to exclude the present. He drifts between a football match, a cinema, a bar and a political meeting. He thinks his children are where he left them, the same age, and is surprised when he gradually hears that the one year-old is talking and walking.

He resembles a prisoner who does not want his family to develop in his absence; what does not exist for him now may not exist for them, either. The moment he is free, he thinks his old past and his future will be unnoticeably united.

We watch the film for an hour or so. The heroine is lying in her saris and wrappings, like a disintegrating jelly-fish, on the rugs in her home, and her mother curses her because she has followed her emotions. I drive Enos to Pumwani Road. He doesn't want me to take him all the way. Someone might jerk open the door, throw me out and drive on. Lights from hurricane lamps shine from the huts, and here and there fires are dying down outside the houses. Dogs run around like lost shadows in the beam of the headlights. Hens cackle. A street vendor is offering wood and charcoal. Children yell and shout, but I hardly ever hear them crying.

I leave Enos in the dark. His only leisure shirt shines white. I drive through the long slum and the area of Indian shops linking it to western Nairobi. I see the silhouette of skyscrapers, the towers apparently trembling beneath the stars. Long cars are being driven along in a torrent of steam and fumes. Goods are being delivered, marble glitters, the concrete numbs ... the buildings become bigger and bigger, though no one lives in them except temporary safari-hunters and corporations disguised in initials.

3.

Nairobi grows before your very eyes. The town I went to at the end of the 1950s is unrecognisable. It fills out the empty space and starts pulsating and panting. Tomatoes have become bigger, but more tasteless. Potatoes are larger, but softer. Something immense is happening – growth. Photographers run round recording the present so that it can swiftly be transformed into the past.

Growth – that mystery word. Every ruler's justification, motto and banner. He kills, tortures and oppresses for the sake of the great dream of growth. Mineral rights are sold, oil drilled for, coffee grown – the drought lies in wait and rebellion threatens. How much will the people understand? Can growth be sold like Coca-Cola? Before it was uhuru, freedom, that had so many names. Now it's growth, the standard. To most people, both concepts are as invisible as the gods stalking the jungle, glancing under a leaf occasionally, wailing laments at night, screaming with the hyenas, creating an ode to industrial culture on a notice board or in a bright newspaper advertisement.

The silence of the plateau has been broken, the soundless hooves of antelopes confusing no one. Sledge-hammers and machine-hammers, the roar of traffic, planes landing full of people who seem to have spent their lives on charter flights ... dollars, yen, metals transformed into steel skeletons of buildings and straight new asphalt roads.

What part in this does Enos have? Prosperity is for those who have already shown that they can administer and improve on it. Though it has not yet gone so far as it has in Brazil, where anyone moved by compassion must be destroyed by military will, and where human sacrifice has become a profane purification rite practised in the name of progress and investment.

At about six in the evening the following day, I drive out to Enos', just before the swift dusk of the equator. He lives in a long low hut, a corridor down the middle with six rooms opening out on to it. He has a bunk and a suitcase. He has been back home for an hour or so. He works from eight to four with a half-hour break. He is lying on the bunk when I make my way in – another of the city's guest-workers shows me the way.

He is tired and looks different from the evening before.

He is wearing the remains of a working shirt, the same kind nearly all the poor wear. At first the material splits under the arms, then rents appear across the shoulder-blades: acid sweat eats into it. The rents are cobbled together, patched and mended, darned, odd rags added to the whole. When the shirt no longer has an original part left, when it is all seams and patches, it can suddenly fall into a thousand pieces – like a protest of atoms. Then it's a matter of finding someone with a treadle sewing-machine, a pattern, and having a new one made. But Africans do not to my white eyes look naked. Black skin is a kind of clothing, though they don't think so themselves.

Enos has one of the better worker's dwellings in Nairobi. I look right through the house out into the yard, where washing up and washing is being done. The yard is bordered by a hut with three rooms – latrine, kitchen and store. Enos' room is twenty-seven square feet, windowless but with a hatch in the wall. Low voices cannot be heard through the clay walls. A piece of sacking hangs over the open door in the daytime so passers-by cannot see in. The house has a concrete floor, painted clay walls, a corrugated iron roof. Each man has a paraffin lamp. Water is fetched from a communal pump many blocks away.

For the moment, Enos has his room to himself. Otherwise, a family lives in each room, the rent four pounds a month. Of the five women, four are illiterate, Enos tells me, but the children go to primary school or Koran school and are learning Swahili. The owner of the building is a retired East African Railways fireman. He doesn't live in the house, but is a permanently present father-figure, in his own eyes functioning as a caretaker, in other people's as a controller. He can mend bicycles, set rat-traps and settle quarrels. He hands out yesterday's paper for circulation round the house. He has two grown sons, one a hotel baker, the other a compositor on *The Nation*. Their first names are Byron and Wales (after the Prince), but they have changed them for African names. Otherwise they are modern city-dwellers and men of the world.

The cost of building an eighty square-yard house of concrete and metal sheeting is about a thousand pounds, i.e. four years' rental. No one has stayed in this house for more than a year. The plumber is on his way out, to be replaced by a laundryman, and the worker at the bicycle factory is to give way to a truck driver. When I ask for the reasons for these constant moves, the most common ones are that the landlord wants to lock up at ten o'clock, does not like parties, does no repairs, and wants the rent on the day. Many squabble over who shall clean the yard and the latrine. The women squabble over wood and salt. The husband suspects his wife of being unfaithful with some unemployed man or a shift-worker. Lack of privacy lies behind most of the discord.

I ask Enos whether the friends of the people in the building are mostly from their own tribe? No. Their closest friends are workmates. Some have met their friends where they first rented a room. Several prefer to live anonymously, otherwise cousins and aunts from the village will come and want to live with them and be supported. Relations have the right to beg, but they also lend money if they have any. No one likes borrowing money from friends.

Naturally the slums are not always what they appear to be, a mess of incoherent hopeless poverty. It is hard to get out of them – like getting out of a bog into which you sink even deeper for every step. The sun is hot, but hunger bites deeply. The fatherless do not find their fathers, only other fatherless people. They are many, and when they see each other, a sly laugh is born. A stranger goes through and says 'Slum!', because he sees nothing else. But people who live there see a street on which no one is like anyone else.

Life in the slums would be impossible without group solidarity. It's a hard life, with a great deal of competition and rivalry. But there is also fellowship, otherwise it would be sheer hell. It is mostly fellowship between the women, including the children, but excluding the men, who are regarded as hard, importunate and sex-mad. You can sense the fellowship of the women round the washing-places and the wells. They talk there, carrying their buckets of wrung-out clothes back to hang up to dry and balancing pails of slopping water. They wonder about the water, which contains worms, parasites and amoebae, three species wanting to share man's satisfaction and transform it into hunger.

Living in the slums... perhaps for a few years, perhaps for a couple of generations. The difficulties are enormous. The slums promote apathy, inactivity, hanging about street corners, hooliganism, day-dreaming and a tough illusionless view of life. The children live so close to the adults, their money problems, quarrels, rows and sex, soon out into earning a living, learning the tricks very quickly, for there are always others willing. Hands tremble with hunger and minds find it hard to concentrate, owing to malnutrition, but neither employers nor machines take any notice.

So life appears to consist of toil, a few parties, then at some time or other being carted away like garbage. At best, to be buried between huts in their own village in a close-knit community not yet destroyed. No social security except the solidarity of the family. God waves his hand up in the clouds and ancestors call from the depths of the soil.

Enos' suitcase is his bridge to the past. In it are his memories, his talismans, sacred objects that seem like rubbish to other eyes, or simply ordinary – a jersey, a carved stick, a calabash tattooed with a sun and an eye. He lets me see all this, and a photograph of his mother stuck inside the lining. He takes it out when his friends start talking about their mothers, and then it often turns out that they also have a photograph.

They talk a lot about the places where they come from. Those living in the huts are not city-dwellers. The married ones are here for a few years to earn money. Then there's the possibility of buying more land in their home village, or bringing the family to town and settling down there. This bachelor time is an intermediate period, a kind of hard-working pause in life. Enos knows that later on they will seldom talk about this time as it really was, but they will falsify and gild it, because there is no point in talking about something that appears to be worthless.

A dusty Japanese transistor captures a passionate pop-song in which screams of pain and suffering glide together into a fierce racket, and at the same time a harsh educational voice from another station comes through with something about intestinal worms, drinking-water and breast-feeding.

There is a café on a corner of Pumwani Road, and we go there for a beer. I am the only white in the place. I don't know what the others think about me, for Africans with white friends are usually found in other parts of the city. I notice that I can scarcely enter into Enos' experience. I might if I think in terms of sharing it for a week, a month, as if sent on an assignment from another world. His gestures at the machine – sometimes physically arduous, probably easy to imitate, but it is the repetition that is frightening, the gestures increasing minute by minute throughout the working day.

Can free people understand slaves, or the well-fed the undernourished? Standing in a supermarket without any money, having to look as if you had money, and getting yourself out with dignity intact, without being taken for a thief. What separates us is mostly the economic factor that for so many people limits choices in life to almost nothing.

4.

In Kenya – as opposed to Tanzania and Mozambique – Enos is faced with a western society, based on a division between body and soul, manual and cerebral, low and high. As a guest-worker in the city, the lowly jobs are open to him. They ought to be well paid, then the hierarchy could collapse, and the under-employed already living in the city could have them. But that doesn't happen. There are always unemployed from the countryside prepared to do the most wretched jobs.

Enos himself has been fortunate. His job is relatively skilled and well-paid. He can put money aside, but at a cost of solitary barrack life, and he can be dismissed at any moment without the union thinking it worth reacting. He will then look for another job, or return to his village, if his manly pride can tolerate that. For they will ask him what he has done and experienced, and if he replies nothing, he is afraid he will seem nothing in the eyes of the villagers.

Enos is building a hotel, because his country earns more from tourism than from agriculture and minerals. The multinational group constructing the hotel won the contract in competition with many others, probably because it has bribed a number of highly placed people in the most appropriate manner – champagne or cars, shares, or some houses built free with ignorant and cheap labour. One fine day it will come out how it happened. Kenya is a country with little honour and a great many scandals.

Enos is a victim of the system, but he is aware of it and keeps his own counsel. He reminds me of many others I have met in Rhodesia, Angola, Lesotho... open in an almost innocent way and his gifts shining through the layer of fatigue. His broad strong hands seem to be made for building the straightforward huts he dreams about, or for yanking out all kinds of humbug by the roots. He talks about replacing earthen floors with concrete ones which are good against damp and rats, about white-plastered clay walls with a gap between wall and grass roof for smoke and ventilation.

Equality has nothing to do with knowledge or usefulness. Equality is to admit man as a whole creature. Enos knows how to do things that I don't. I know a great deal economically more valuable in western society. I am a human being who costs more and receives more and am therefore 'more precious'.

Only a *principle* of equality can maintain our similarity beyond hierarchies. To accept equality as something *natural* – regardless of the fact that different people are gifted at different things or simply lack most talents – that is to be fragmented. You are appreciated for something considered of value or brilliant, but not as a whole person. You are forced to see yourself as the sum of certain knowledge, skills and needs.

When I meet Enos again a few days later, I tell him about Amos G, whom I met at a lunch at the New Stanley Hotel. He has a haulage business and owns a number of buses. He is a black capitalist who has succeeded. He makes no attempt to hide the fact that he has partly achieved his position with the help of advantageously placed acquaintances. On the other hand, he has worked immensely hard, paid interest on considerable loans, and gradually got his head above water.

Now his own private take-off is long in the past, and the result is trucks moving people and their possessions hither and thither, and for himself a house with a swimming-pool in a previously all-white suburb, his children at the best schools, a Diners Club card, an American Express card, a Hertz card.

So Amos belongs to the new African upper middle-class, who over a period of a few months replaced the Indians in Kenya, and of which there is no corresponding group in socialist Tanzania. At lunch at the New Stanley, where business men drink white Bordeaux with their turkey and broccoli, he says he is sorry for his friends in Tanzania. Equality madness is an obstacle to progress and makes work meaningless.

I ask him whether we are to work just to earn money and not for our fellows. He considers my question misplaced and smiles broadly and convincingly – the more money he gets, the more good that does to others. Taxes are low, so I don't understand what magic he uses for others to have a share in his income.

One thing is for sure, however – his trucks run a shuttle service, society is moving upwards and sideways, some can afford to and have the opportunity to move to better housing, and this occurs within a limited circle of uninterrupted social change. Amos is himself one of many who in one generation have moved from peasant level to the middle classes. But for most people, poverty is the same, the countryside equally monotonous, and in Nairobi the dark strangers, hidden behind dark glasses, have become as numerous as the whites.

I ask Amos whether he isn't frightened by this free-running capitalism which gives those who are stronger and temporarily more powerful rights over those who are weaker. They may hit back and afflict him with bankruptcy, poverty and exclusion from the succeeders. He says he is not afraid. He has helped many people and is counting on their gratitude. He is safely anchored.

I see Enos' shirt in front of me. Won't Kenya's present system, based on free-running foreign investments, begin to split at all the seams, leaving nothing but the need to acquire a new shirt?

Telling Enos about Amos G, it turns out that Enos has tried for a job with him and has been promised to be allowed to come back. He says he is hesitant, but doesn't know why. He appears to admire Amos G, a village man who has succeeded, one of the few. But that may be due to the fact that he is a Kikuyu and comes from the same district as the President. Guest-worker Enos does not wish to judge guest-director Amos, for that would mean he was disassociating from a part of himself.

It is hard to know best how to part – not only in Africa. My close friends embrace me. We hug each other in the Russian way. I take Enos' arm. He punches me lightly on the shoulder. Traditionally, Africans meet almost unnoticeably. I have seen a girl waiting at the bus-station in Morogoro, and a young man jumps off the bus, his cloth-bundle under his arm, for only women use their heads. Neither of them brightens. He goes swiftly across to her, their hands touch for a moment, and they turn round to go. But there is no doubt they belong intimately together. That can be seen from their faces, though their expressions do not resemble ours.

Some time later, I try to get hold of Enos. He is no longer living in the hut, and he has stopped working on the hotel, which is nearly finished. His friends give me a variety of information. Someone thinks it's something 'political', which is why he is not working there. Another guesses that he has started work at Amos' haulage firm – which the latter eventually denies – and again others seem to think that in his longing for his family, Enos has returned to his home village north of Lake Victoria.

I find I can't induce myself to make further enquiries. I cross his name out in my address book. He is one of many meetings, and I am the same to him. It is easy to imagine him appearing again in a new incarnation – one of Africa's millions of guest-workers – just as he will see me in another form – one of Africa's strange visitors and interrogators, so numerous that they have to be tolerated so that yet another minority problem does not arise.

Pula – Give us water

1.

I catch a glimpse of a human head deep down in a hole in Botswana's red soil. I call out to him. How far has he got? Sixty feet. Any sign of water? No. He thinks at a hundred feet. The sand trickles down on to his hair. He does not give up.

In the dust of the bush steppe, lizards crackle like newspaper. The cows appear to live off thorns, off invisibility. The ground is all scored marks and folds, a record about to be decoded.

Far down there in the hole, another Botswana is greening.

The old village woman – one of the few I have seen with white hair, for most don't live that long – takes my hands, twists and turns them, looks at them, shakes her head, either troubled or dissatisfied. She mutters. I don't understand.

A young man glances indifferently at us. He has a mourning-band on his arm. A little rain has at last come, and that means joy, the countryside open and newly washed. There is a smell of wet earth, but never the autumn scents of dead leaves and frosts to come.

Then she says something, suddenly smiling and apologetic, so I have to call to the man with the mourning-band to come and translate.

'White people don't look well. They look like upside-down turtles, pink and floppy . . .'

He stops:

'She's just talking nonsense.'

Typhoons swirl across the plain. Tall water-pumps look like withered aloe trunks at a distance. A grass fire snakes along like a bright train, goes out, then receives new nourishment. The Land Rover is a slow creature, especially when driven on four-wheel drive over miserable terrain. The African driver clearly regards the internal combustion engine as a slightly hostile servant who has to be kept under strict control. Uphill, he allows the engine to grunt and struggle, until the thumping begins to sound like the thunder of church bells. At the last moment, he changes down, reluctantly, as if made to give way to some absurd mechanical principle.

He is at home here. This is the territory he is supposed to know like the palm of his hand. Yet he is more hesitant than we are, afraid of the wilds and unknown roads. It is always the same, and it is irritating.

I have the map spread out on my lap. There is the only road with a strip of asphalt down the middle, there are the yellow ones which are gravelled, and the thin black ones often only visible from the air like the shadow of a snake in the grass. The driver wants to stick to the asphalt and gravel. He suspects there is something apart from what I read off the map, which looks ordinary and European.

Perhaps it is the contradictions which are frightening. On the road, in the Land Rover with its diesel engine and dashboard, present calendar years reign, and you are within reach of the civilisation produced by Coca-Cola, *Newsweek*, radio sports commentaries and Kissinger as the Flying Dutchman.

But two steps off the road, every link with that life appears to cease; thorn trees and termites, porcupines and hyenas reign there. Above, kites hover in ever decreasing circles, like radar waves, signalling the spot that is death. I sense the place, quite close to, yet totally inaccessible in the undergrowth.

Where roads are marked on the map, there are no roads, the driver says. They are planned roads. But there are cattle tracks, I say. Follow the cow-pats and we'll come to a village. The Land Rover's bumper mows the grass on the invisible pathway. We lurch along with the engine thumping like a present-day melody in timelessness, and we come to the little village, where the women are selling vegetables beneath the dark-green mango tree – but to whom?

The village appears empty. The huts are of mud held

together by crooked unbarked branches. These branches gradually dry out, the wall cracks and has to be built again. The huts stay up for at the most four years, for all this crooked darkish material is alive, aging and changing, in contrast to stone and bricks. The trees are too short to become poles or timber. What is irregular and distorted becomes the architectural norm. It is as far from the modern centre of Stockholm as anyone could come in our planetary system, and so both frightening and attractive.

Children and old people emerge from the shade of the huts. People are returning from the maize fields, plots hacked out of the bush and resembling pale patches of cloth laid out to dry. They stop in front of the vehicle and look at it rather than at me. We exchange greetings.

Some dogs are acting dead on the sandy patch in front of the huts. Part of the village is surrounded by prickly silvery thorn bushes placed like rolled-up barbed wire, and some small humped cattle push their way through the spectators.

A farmer shows me a brochure. It tells you how to send for an Alfa-Laval separator from Tumba, via an agent in South Africa. I explain how the cream is separated from the milk. He very much wants a separator. He might get together with some others, but it's a long way to the next village and money is something no one has. They live outside a money economy. Someone thinks you have to buy money.

Shashi River School lies in the wilderness a few miles outside Francistown, a collection of huts in a green and thorny world, with islands of stone cairns that appear to have been stacked up by an Ice Age man.

A single toilet and shower for ten or so teachers, idealistic youngsters, mostly Americans in rebellion against prosperity. They appear to me to be living in a simplicity so extreme that is becomes impractical, time-consuming and expensive. Yet perhaps it is justified as a model.

I stay in a round hut with a concrete floor, straw roof, and no furniture. The pupils eat maize porridge with their fingers out among the stones. We elders gather in a long hut with a simple gas-stove and a small paraffin-driven refrigerator, shovelling into ourselves the communal mixture of maize porridge off chipped enamel plates. The coffee is chicory from South Africa. The tea is crushed leaves from a South African tree, twenty times cheaper and worse than ordinary tea.

The diet is as simple as it is unhealthy, its awfulness as monumental as unnecessary. It would be so easy to acquire fruit and cheese, knock up a rough country table, and pour enamel paint onto the concrete!

The children learn *tswana*, natural history, evolution and in between they do practical work in the fields with maize, beetroot and spinach. Their first names unite the weekly magazine dreams, the Bible and tradition – Beauty, Lovemore, Desire, Cornelius, Philimon, Genesis, Job, Osenotse, Tsokonombwe (grasshopper), Chigupwana (surprise).

As the only truck has collapsed, I leave Shashi River School on a green cart behind two mules, the shaft a crooked branch. The cart almost tips over on the dry thorny river-bed. This is what it must have been like for a Russian landowner of the lesser nobility being taken to the train across Chekhov's steppes.

Suddenly we catch sight of the white plastered station building, like a mirage of the New Jerusalem. The mules snort, while the station-master, appointed by Rhodesia's railway management, taps on his little morse-key and the goats forage along the sun-hot rails.

2.

Patrick van Rensburg, next to the President, is the best known and most discussed personality in Botswana. We worked together in London on a world campaign for the boycott of South Africa. At the time, he had recently fled from his country. He comes from an old Boer family. He settled in Botswana and became a pioneer in the educational system, not just there, but through practical example, all over the world.

He is a quiet man, large and much bewhiskered. He speaks far too quietly, as if wanting to mask his strong will and stubbornness. His kind can be recognised in Peace Corps and church aid organisations – healthy, indifferent to bank accounts and fixed addresses, greying when young, shabby wind-cheaters, leather elbow patches on the finest blazers and baggy trousers. Uninterested in what things look like as long as they can be used.

He is an experimenter who dares to admit to mistakes and to start again with quite different attempts. His instructive book, *Report from Swaneng Hill*, is a machine at work, with the heads taken away so that we can see what's happening. He hints at answers and asks new questions.

Swaneng Hill, the starting point of his experiments, was opened in 1963 with twenty-eight non-selected pupils. After a week, one boy asked for a sports ground. There was no money. The pupils agreed to make one themselves. That kind of voluntary work became the core of Rensburg's views on the relationship of secondary school pupils to the community around them, a serious problem in the new Africa.

Very few get into secondary school and they aim at senior posts in the administration. They don't waste time on voluntary work and do not want to stay on the land. Their parents mind less about what their children learn than the way they behave, eat and live. The government also demands better housing than the cheap airy huts the pupils themselves could make out of the materials on the spot.

Patrick founded the work brigades, because many pupils finishing primary school were not given places to continue theoretical studies. So they could go in for the practical professions Botswana needs more than anything else. The brigades are groups or patrols of budding building-workers, masons, mechanics, tanners and weavers, who are at the same time trained in elementary book-keeping, work-ethic and administrative co-operation.

One aim of the Swaneng Hill experiment is to break the rule that the countryside takes its raw materials to the town and then purchases ready-made products there – a kind of indigenous colonialism.

On the school farm, they have pigs for bacon, soap, gelatine and hides. The goats provide meat, milk, yoghurt and cheese. Their hides are placed in unslaked lime to remove the hairs, then softened in beer and turned into bags, sandals and briefcases. Jackals shot in the area are used in the same way. The sheep provide them with jerseys and hand-woven blankets, and the local clay is made into dishes and vessels. Chalk is made for their blackboards.

A building brigade constructs a co-operative brewery. The boys work without wages and learn techniques from instructors as they build. The brigade also keeps together later and can be paid to build a bus station, a house, or a shop. But many of them get no paid jobs afterwards. They use their skills within the framework of self-sufficiency.

The practical starting-point for Patrick van Rensburg is that education shall be paid for by the productive work of the pupils, which in its turn is an important part of their education. The school should be self-supporting and as far as possible independent of imports from outside. In this way, the school becomes a model or a miniature of what society should be as a whole.

If the secondary pupils, too, not only the work brigades, take part in agriculture, crafts and simple industry, the school is tied closely to its environment and doesn't become a citadel, but part of the life of the underdeveloped countryside. By not creating privileges for the few, this avoids creating hostility in the majority burdened with work and with no advantages.

Rensburg sees poverty-stricken Botswana as a number of Robinson Crusoe islands, in which most people should be able to do as much as possible and not rely on salvation lying in the cities, foreign experts or superfluous imported goods. He has been met with distrust and adversity.

The secondary schools in Botswana – as in most under-developed countries – promote élitist attitudes, and separate book-learning from the practical. The pupils are isolated from their villages, escaping home chores, and they learn to think and behave differently from their families. For very little money, they receive good food, water and light. Many of them demand an increasing standard of living from society and are less worried about how it is to be shared.

Many students loathe physical labour, although they devote many more hours to demanding sports. They can make a radical analysis for society in the morning, only to refuse to live according to it in the afternoon.

Alongside the fortunate few are the innumerable who finish

basic schooling with false or exaggerated expectations of work. The unemployed are the greatest unexploited asset for development in the Third World. In Botswana, half of the population is under eighteen years of age, and hardly any of them have a paid job. But the prosperity that is slowly approaching is not measured best by GNP, but in the growing self-confidence and strength, following the contributions of those such as Patrick van Rensburg.

3.

Botswana, 650,000 inhabitants, one and a half times the size of Sweden, deserts and savanna, squashed between South Africa, Namibia and Rhodesia, and with a northern life-line in the form of a road and a ferry across the Zambezi river into Zambia.

From the very earliest settlers, the bushmen, Botswana has been populated by people fleeing from tyranny. We didn't choose to live here, people in Botswana often say. We were driven here by stronger and more war-like people. The hunted still come to this nation – from Angola, Namibia, Rhodesia and South Africa. Refugees have been kidnapped on Botswana territory. President Seretse Khama can protect them only by assuring his neighbours that he will not permit guerilla bases.

At the end of the last century, what was at the time Bechuanaland saw the threat from the Boers, and put themselves under the protection of the British. Missionaries such as Livingstone and Moffat had given the people faith in British justice. Of Cecil Rhodes and his companions, Khama III wrote to Queen Victoria: 'We fear they are intending to fill our country with wine stores as they did in Bulawayo.' And to the British government: 'We beg you not to cast us aside as if we were naughty children refusing to listen to their mother's words.'

The people of Botswana avoided being thrown to the wolves. They survived on the desert's edge. To conquer an area and die of thirst was not tempting, and also South Africa did not dare annexe it for political and military reasons. On the other hand, able-bodied men and valuable goods were driven south. That traffic has gone on for a long time and anything stopping it is a way of fighting apartheid.

Botswana is an imprisoned country, 'landlocked', an expensive and lonely experience. People stay at home. Few can travel to neighbouring countries, where the rights of the individual are not respected. A successful life-style, an alien ideology of materialism and contempt for human beings casts its shadow across the border. South Africa's and Rhodesia's radio stations are heard all over Botswana.

'We realise,' said Seretse Khama, 'that there is little Botswana can do to achieve change in South Africa, except through the power of persuasion and example. On the other hand, Botswana will never in deed or action make it any easier for those who advocate racial superiority.'

Anyone meeting Seretse would be struck by his calm, friendliness and tolerance, and yet he has a stormy background. In 1948, he secretly married an English girl, Ruth Williams, at a registry office in London. She was a twenty-five year old daughter of an officer. He was up at Oxford reading law. He was the heir to the chieftainship of the Bamangwato tribe.

It is hard to imagine today the uproar this marriage caused. South Africa protested that it was impossible to have a white woman married to a kaffir so close to the border. The old chieftain thought his heir should marry within his own tribe. The couple were the scandal and romance of the year.

Attlee's Labour government deported Seretse and his family from Bechuanaland to England, where they had to stay for six years. It all seems a long time ago now, and their elder son has been to Sandhurst. But Ruth Khama still complains:

'All journalists say they want a serious interview, but all they really want to know is what is it like to go to bed with a black man!'

Anyone who happens to meet the three presidents and friends from Tanzania, Zambia and Botswana would be struck by their mutual dissimilarities. Nyerere is a bold visionary, who then patiently teaches his ideas and adapts them to reality, intellectually a statesman with no counterpart in his generation. Kaunda is touchy, restless, hot-tempered, impatiently finding fault with sluggishness around him, burning with desire to carry out things that turn out to be possible in

Tanzania but difficult in Zambia, and more personal in his rancour and evaluations of friends and opponents. Seretse is secure and pragmatic, with something of a wise manager's sense of the art of the possible on the border between black and white in southern Africa.

So his country also succeeded in achieving appreciation for its independent policies for Black Africa and keeping a *modus vivendi* with her white neighbours. She has avoided becoming politically subordinate to South Africa, although South Africa exercises economic pressures. There are suddenly no refrigerator wagons for the abbatoir in Lobatse, since they are needed for the vulnerable fruit exports of the Cape Province. So the carcasses rot. Suddenly no one can telephone outside the country because of a break in the cable. So conversations can be controlled by South Africa's telephonists.

Seretse is outspoken in his criticism of apartheid, and has frightened South Africa by introducing diplomatic links with China and the Soviet Union. His fearlessness is directed in various quarters. He was the first to declare that he would not send a delegation to the 1975 OAU meeting in Kampala, because General Amin was an untrustworthy murderer.

Since 1976, parliament has brought in a national currency instead of South Africa's rand. The currency is called Pula, the key word in Botswana – give us water. For this is a country threatened by drought even more than South Africa. The Kalahari Desert is strewn with bones of cattle which never reached the modern abbatoir outside the capital, Gaborone.

When Botswana became independent in 1966, it was one of the poorest countries in the world. In about 1970, prospecting seemed to confirm that this new nation possessed an almost unique wealth of minerals, the largest diamond finds in the world, immeasurable coal fields, huge quantities of copper and nickel. The multi-national companies poured in. Competing interests tested the government's ability to uphold national integrity.

But the country was soon to be declared poor again. South African and American companies began to have 'technical difficulties'. Production costs were high and the half-profits the state was to receive never materialised. The raw copper and nickel were exported to the USA, refined by one of the

American owners, and the metal then sold mainly to the West Germans with a co-interest in the mines. Botswana, having undertaken building the small towns round the mines, the road networks, health care and schools, was left with unexpected debts. Does the thought of Botswana as an economic hostage to South Africa and the USA lie behind this?

Seretse emphasises more strongly then ever that Botswana is an agricultural society, that cattle is the people's way of life, and the country is one of the world's largest natural grazing grounds. With modern irrigation techniques, the cultivation of vegetables could be developed enormously, and there are also Swedish experts there. But neither has this gone so well as expected. The Common Market has banned the importing of meat from Botswana and taken her best customer, Britain, for itself.

4.

What I find in Botswana – though I hardly like to admit it – is a kind of idyll, the idyll of poverty and effort, the first pages in an infant primer; a tolerance mixed with a sense of morality, and up to now no noticeable corruption. Colonial symbols remain without offending: 'Galloping Strictly Forbidden' a notice still says among the market stalls. Angry South Africans shout at the boy at the petrol station, calling him an idiot kaffir, and receive the quiet answer:

'We don't talk like that in Botswana any more.'

No idyll is ever quite real. There is criticism concealed by Seretse Khama's immense popularity and his party's dominance at one election after another. Higher education has become chaotic since Lesotho nationalised the university in which Swaziland and Botswana had equal shares. Yet the calm is palpable compared with neighbouring countries, and that feeling is reinforced by the absence of mass media. No television, one single newspaper which is nothing but a few pages published by the Office of Information. I am cynically relieved to escape Israeli bombing raids, torture in Chile and guest-workers in the Ruhr.

I relax in the harsh thorny countryside, where the rocks appear to have been polished by an antarctic Ice Age. The low hills extend in waves, the grass like a Gotland orchid-meadow. But it is harsh to touch. Africa is cruel to the senses.

In the clear air round the tropic of Capricorn, I often think of late autumn in England, and its mists between the hills remind me of those in Botswana. The smell of damp earth, the grass short and green, darkness falling slowly, and at last it is time to go to The Plover and talk about the constant decline of England. Put together, I have spent several years of my life in England, an experience which never leaves me. I know the heathland beneath my feet round Corfe Castle and what it is like to come home after the rain. I have sat in August thunderstorms in a decayed vicarage on Dartmoor, with all the Brontë sisters, and Mrs Gaskell and Mrs Humphrey Ward around me in worn skirts, no, in worn volumes.

Yet there are moments here on the savanna when Europe seems as distant as some future century I shall never know. These plains which have seen so much, sandstorms, fertile soil, exhausted animals and people. And I – what kind of animals and people are they I will never see? They await a galactic future the contours of which I cannot discern.

Here I am, sitting on a pinpoint of time, imprisoned in a cramped dimension I cannot escape from, the cells of my brain disintegrating instead of helping to free the imagination.

How little one manages to see in a lifetime, how little one learns of all that one wants to learn. You join the caravan for a few miles and are left by the path, the wind blowing away the traces.

Everything seems to be chance occurrences, the fact that I was born at this time, or that we human beings have hands, not fins or hoofs; that was something that happened on the savanna many millions of years ago, a crossroads, a choice. And it became hands, those instruments which have shaped the world, which is our everyday life and our mystery.

Night falls, speckled as an egg, bright stars in the darkness. The frogs croak come to me, listen to me. A night bird sings a song, or an alarm call.

It is like existing at the start of a development. I seem to hear the lark singing inside its egg, gaining nourishment from the vaulted shell of space.

In a lizard foot, I see myself passing. Some part of me is unexplored and unrealised in the guise I inhabit.

Snails in Tanga

1.

'Are you writing books again this year?' says Joseph, TANU secretary in Tanga, with ill-concealed sympathy – a moment later pointing silently at a bundle of schedules and brochures, all in the process of obvious disintegration in the heat and the damp.

That books should be part of life must be a proposition of almost metaphysical significance here on the east coast of Africa. Marmalade goes mouldy, Coca-Cola bottle caps rust, houses peel in the salty wind. Books are devoured by termites or are dissolved by the humidity of the monsoon. Nothing seems to last here. The soil is eroded and blown out to sea, and monuments of past explorers and governors decompose. Governments are brought down and creative minds devote themselves to radio quizzes.

'Sometimes I write books,' I reply. 'When I have the time.'

He understands, although I have given him an evasive answer. Those who think it more important than anything else to keep writing, do so, and they always find the time. Others easily find excuses. 'I haven't had time to go to work for a month,' is an inexplicable explanation, but everyone understands that you haven't had the time to write a line.

'Is the sisal crop as bad as last year?' I ask.

'Very bad. Lots of the unemployed stay on the plantations. They think something will happen. But we're beginning to have doubts. It's the fault of the British. They wanted to make Tanzania into a country of groundnuts and sisal.'

We set off in a Land Rover along the dusty red roads. Miles of stubble fields with nothing happening in them, drying-sheds of corrugated iron, ninety feet long, thirty feet high, like empty cathedrals. They could be used as schools, workshops or assembly places. Men and women could be organised into work-brigades to clear up. But using this dry land for anything but sisal appears to be difficult.

The unemployed sit quietly in the shade of the mango trees. Pineapples grow here too, and are exchanged for dried fish. It is TANU's task to convince them of a meaningful alternative.

Most of the Greek sisal growers have gone. They had sat in a hotel in Tanga playing poker and roulette with whole plantations as stakes. That was before the world went over to artificial fibres and the factories closed.

Today, Tanga sleeps as if in a novel by Graham Greene. The harbour is dead. The few Europeans drink gin at the club and try to beat the fishing records recorded on silver plaques.

Glimpses of merchant ships on their way between Dar es Salaam and Mombasa can be seen on the horizon. They no longer come in to the rusting cranes on Tanga's quays.

Tanga seems like the end of the world. After hectic uneasy days with bureaucrats, lawyers and guerillas, I am overwhelmed by the heavy stillness of a place developments have left in the lurch.

I am living in a guest house run by an Indian family. I have dinner with them. My landlady's upper arms are abnormally large and wobble like jellies. She talks about the simple life everyone should live; vegetables and meditation, a glass of hot water with a little salt in it every morning . . . though that would not be good for business.

'Have some more curry,' she urges me. 'When we were small, we were warned about it. Hot food creates hot desires. I don't believe it any longer.'

'Is that from your own experience?'

'Yes,' she says, with a resigned smile.

Her husband eats greedily. He has a draper's shop round the corner, and the children help in it. At the end of the table is my landlady's white-haired father, his profile thin and chiselled. He says nothing and smiles inwardly, as if he had seen something beautiful within himself.

Later that evening, Joseph comes and takes me to a bar in a tin shack built onto a mud hut. Two unshaded bulbs, beer in large mugs, fly-papers and dogs slinking about. Men only – and no one seems worried about having to get up early the next morning, as the women do. We spend most of the night discussing conditions of life in Tanzania; politics, politics.

In a newspaper I find in the guest house, I see a report which says that after many years, a diver has gone down to the *Andrea Doria*, eighteen hundred feet below. He found the huge Atlantic steamer ready for a new cruise, the brass polished, the railings shining and without algae, sailcloth stretched out to protect the deck-chairs, and jingling keys to one of the double-cabins on A-deck.

The extraordinary fascination of environments bearing hardly any traces of the people who have abandoned them – frozen ocean worlds, silver-mine villages in the drought area of Mexico, where when you open the door, newspapers of the thirties rustle and carbon dioxide still bubbles in a bottle of lemonade.

Is Tanga – owing to new discoveries and consumer habits in the wealthy world – also on its way to sinking into the world's aquarium?

2.

In Tanga in 1971 . . .

I was living at the Splendid View Hotel, a low decaying ten-roomed shack with a view across a pot-holed road. I was travelling in Tanzania with Günter Grass. We were involved in a German-Swedish-Jugoslavian project Grass had thought up, and I and some others were to be part of the practical aspects of it. If it had come off, he and I were to live in Tanzania for one or two months every year. It fell apart over antagonisms between West German and Jugoslavian trade unions, a whole lot of work was wasted and Tanzania's trades union council was cheated of a good thing. All that remains is a few lines in *From the Diary of a Snail*, which Günter was writing the first version of at the time.

Trying to find a compromise between common kindness and uncommon imaginative force – Günter has a taste for central

European cuisine, hissing and bubbling in his sooty pans, ribs of pork and tripe with caraway, tomatoes and garlic, green eels from the dirty Havel lakes, ox-heart stuffed with plums, pheasant with pickled cabbage, minced-meat and wild mushrooms and peppercorns. That's what his novels are like – soup made from many bones, with occasional vegetables and the remains of previous meals.

In his novel on the social-democratic snail, Günter shows how the soup is made – all the ingredients are laid out for our inspection.

He says about the sister of melancholy, Utopia, that she is always on the move, thinking everything can be changed, a new human being born, all obstructive hands and spokes in the wheel swept aside by the power of abstract ideas. Sister Utopia is the guardian angel of those 'who want to carve out a track for the blessing of mankind'.

Against dreams, absolutism and puritanism Günter sets grey circuitous routes, which without honour, through disappointments and reverses, slowly move towards a goal.

There are also glimpses in the book of Czechoslovakia the year after the Russian invasion, of the innumerable people who chose not to compromise and sacrificed everything in order to say what they thought. Later, a year after the novel came out, Allende was brought down in Chile. He was a snail. He didn't move fast enough, and wild animals fell on him as he crossed a path. The workers barricaded themselves in the factories round Santiago, but they were also inside their shells and were crushed. The left-wing which Günter scorns in Germany, students, middle-class boys and girls and the leftish tennis club, they all fought and died with the workers during those days.

Utopia, Sister Melancholia in the etching by Albrecht Dürer Grass writes about, is an angel with folded wings, deep in thought. One day, perhaps tyranny will be so strong somewhere that no snail can defeat it, and only that angel will be able to, by ceasing to ponder and taking to the sword.

We waded through shallow water along the sandy shores south of Tanga, I helping Günter collect shells. He blew into them, examined them thoroughly and brushed them clean of sand. He had drawn hundreds of snails and shells. He is obsessed by their link with primaeval slime, with something slow and enduring, surviving, and in his etchings they resemble reproductive organs swaying in sea-grass beside an endless sea.

Grass is a centre-man. He has experienced Nazism and Stalinism. He sees how the extremes touch each other, violent left-wing activities followed by right-wing calls for the death sentence, and that has to be avoided. He has gone the way of social-democratic compromise between CDU and Rudi Dutschke, between the Springer Press and Baader-Meinhof. That way, so multi-laned and broad in Sweden, is very narrow in West Germany.

But in his prose, intoxicated by words, he is drawn into divergent and singular characters, who behave in the strangest ways.

'Fiction is no mapper of reality,' he says. 'Some people think the world around us is the writer's only employer. But we're not colonised. We would have thrown off such oppression. That's what the Africans in Tanzania have done.'

Günter tells me about a young Romanian poet who lived with him in Berlin. The shortage of housing was great in Romania, and he had wished all his life to escape having to share a room with other people. At Günter's home, he had a room of his own and he didn't really want to leave it. He loved his solitariness and worked all day.

To the young people in the house, Grass' twin sons, the nursemaid and their acquaintances, the Romanian's behaviour caused dismay. They were agitated. What does he do all alone in there? What's he really up to? What kind of Kafka is he? He was thinking: and writing. Does he have to do that all alone? they asked. It shows lack of solidarity. I must be left in peace, the Romanian said quietly. I don't want to disturb anyone.

That was it. The others could not be alone. They sat in the kitchen discussing things as soon as they could, quite without any desire for a private life. People can think things out together. What the Romanian poet called not disturbing anyone or intruding upon anyone, the young people thought was betrayal and withdrawal of fellowship.

They demanded that he should show them what he was writing. Everyone in the house should have the right to erase and change things after discussion and mutual agreement.

Nothing could pass without being thoroughly argued out. Censorship, complained the poet bitterly, just like at home. My poems are my own. His West German friends replied unmoved: democracy. We can all do as we wish, but we decide together what our actions are used for, as we all live in the same house.

Sickened by the sight of luxurious consumption, and having fallen asleep during several big meetings, the young Romanian poet said he was feeling slightly schizophrenic. He even confessed to a longing for the little town in Siebenburgen where he had lived in an obligatory but considerate collective while writing his difficult allegorical poems on lingering Stalinism.

Two German electricians – in Tanga to set up ammonia-cisterns for an artificial fertiliser factory further inland – rode a motor-cycle round the town's five bars to see what was happening. One of them turned cautiously to Günter.

'Are you by any chance the fraudulent Herr Grass?'

Günter admitted he was.

In the documentary spirit of the day, we interviewed the two bar girls at the Splendid View Hotel. One was twenty-two, unmarried, with two children. She very badly wanted to go to Nairobi, just as others want to go to Paris. She worked from seven until midnight for about eight pounds a month. After that she worked at a night-club for four hours and was at the disposal of customers for one to three pounds according to appearance, status and period of time. The other woman was thirty-eight, had fifteen children and had no wish for any more. She came from an island in Lake Victoria and was thinking of returning, but the children had a better chance of schooling in Tanga. People on the island were proud of those who lived in town and earned money, no matter how. She was very open-hearted about this, and also aware of one thing – it was dangerous to feel anything for a customer, because then you gave him the power she herself had to have over him, and then she lost her protection, her integrity.

At night the temperature in the room rose to 35° Celsius. Every bulge in the lino concealed unknown creatures. Small lizards swirled round the bed's legs. Günter pulled his bed out under the ceiling fan, and I switched it on. It began with a weird groan, and something large and black fell off it on to Günter's eyelids.

The first light gradually crept like a snake across the crack under the door. What to do if it was a cobra? Advice I had been given was to set fire to some paper – one of Günter Grass' manuscript pages – to dazzle the death-dealing reptile.

3.

Go to the town's only cinema, because it is air-conditioned. An Indian film with squeaky flute music and banging brass. Two pale teenagers seeking each other's mouths in the last frame. Swedish films have never been that romantic and chaste. If all Indian films were like that – and I have no wish to be asked to find out – and if the behaviour of film actors influences people as much as is sometimes maintained back at home, then the problem of over-population in southern Asia would be one step nearer a solution.

One row is full of a group of Goanese musicians – half of them Portuguese, half Indian – whom I recognise from other places in Tanzania. They left the Portuguese colony when it was taken over by Nehru, and now they take out-of-date tunes from Hollywood and the Empire all round East Africa. They perform in the evenings and on social occasions such as bazaars, cricket and baseball matches, and openings of monkey houses and hotels.

Otherwise they prefer to spend the day going to cinema matinées, if they exist. There can be long distances between cinemas in the regions they are travelling, and they have to make the most of it. They watch anything, preferably several performances in a row, even if it is exhausting. They seldom have time to eat.

They talk about their insecure life with its indefinite seasons and no guarantees. There are no people's parks or community organisations, nor any musicians' association. We leave the cave of the cinema together and come out into broad daylight, hard and prickly, although it is filtering through green screens of acacias.

Joseph of TANU has a daughter of nine.

'I'm so glad Mwalimu (President Nyerere) exists,' she says. 'He makes sure no enemies come. I'm going to go to Dar es Salaam to see where he lives.'

Her father looks unexpectedly proud.

Modern Africa rejects Carlyle's view of world history as biographies of great men. But at the same time, illiteracy makes it almost necessary to have one or two constant faces to embody history, development, and hope for the future.

I preach a little sermon.

'It isn't just Mwalimu who stops the enemy. It's all of you together deciding what Tanzania will look like.'

'When I'm grown-up, I'm going to be part of the deciding. Now I'll show you how I can draw the flag of Tanzania.'

The child's untroubled patriotism is the same everywhere. I have seen it in the Soviet Union and the USA. King and President, heroes and a few famous names at the top will cope with everything. They are better than others and will make quite sure we live in the best of all countries.

But what if the little girl is right? Perhaps it is Nyerere alone and a few others doing the deciding. In that case, this place is much like most places in the world.

Resting place in Zambia

1.

When Sven Hedin set off on his fourth journey to Asia, intended to last two years, he took with him a crate of Liebig's meat extract, musical boxes and Eskiltuna knives for the natives, fifty-eight pairs of spectacles, an Assman psychrometer and a great many other things. His collection of books was surprisingly small: the Bible and the Prayer Book, Watchword of the Day, a History of Sweden, a paper on the Ice Age, a meteorological textbook, and some works by major Swedish poets.

Aldous Huxley travelled through India with the whole of the Encyclopaedia Britannica in crates – so that he could check the truth of what he saw, and flee from the obscure shimmering of reality to exact lexicography.

Without access to Hedin's and Huxley's teams of bearers, I have contented myself with fewer books, and they usually remain unread. My evenings are marked with fatigue or an indolence which according to Nyerere is the opposite of freedom.

But there is a book I have taken with me for almost twenty years now, as a trophy, a mascot, with the view that one day I'll be so hopelessly isolated that I'll *have* to read it. It is Henry James' *The Ambassadors*, in a cheap bound volume, a famous novel, part of the required reading for Anglo-Saxon higher education.

I have often imagined the situation – a desperate vacuum somewhere in a hot country, on a dusty verandah of some recently nationalised club, not yet taken over by new officials, the floor boards half up, hairy brown insects coming out of the taps when you turn one on in an attack of absent-mindedness, a floor-toilet you risk falling into and getting stuck in for ever, a bed standing in cups of water to limit the assault of cockroaches, grubby sheets which make you want to lift them to examine the mattress in all its repulsiveness . . . a place of existential desperation, ominous intrigues and ruined hopes – the landlord resembling Humphrey Bogart, rigid with boredom but for some obscure reason bound to this distant corner.

Hitherto this has never happened to me, but that has not prevented a fleeting acquaintance with the novel. I usually ask other people about it and listen with sceptical delight to what they say. So that's what awaits me, I think stoically. Oh, well, there are worse fates. And better ones.

One evening in western Zambia, I say to myself that the time has come to try Henry James. I clock into a Government Rest House, a leftover from the British Empire. In regions where there are no hotels or missions, they are available to mobile officials and other serious travellers. This one has room for five guests, but hitherto I am the only one. It is five times as cheap as an ordinary hotel, but the service is limited.

On my assignment, as well as for other reasons, I have stayed in Lusaka, the capital of Zambia, where several liberation movements have their offices. Lusaka is full of violent political intrigues plus a gloom and architectural ugliness which fortunately makes it unique among African cities I know. SWAPO's training camp for Namibians, what remains of ANC-Zimbabwe and its educational centres, and the prison for ZANU rebels have all been moved out into the countryside, sometimes deliberately to distant battle-zones.

Escaping from this snake-pit of slander, accusations and politically uneasy equilibrium, out into the countryside, out towards Simua and the upper reaches of the Zambezi river is a relief, although the Zambian landscape is less beautiful than that of most African states; flat plateaux, bush that has been compared to a chaotic abandoned nursery and shapeless low forest where the trees never grow straight.

The bush makes you long for African forest, heathen, full of unbaptised nameless creatures, simmering with the terror which later becomes myth and legend. The trees stretch out for you, capturing you in their green caves. A liana gets caught in the fork of a tree and screams like a crushed owl.

It is like an old pumping station inside the African high forest, everything damp, a machine pumping up and down like a worn muscle. The tree trunks are wet, the sun breaking through layers of foliage and just visible high up there, while at ground level it is as dim as in the eclipse of the sun. There is never a still moment, but sounds are hard to localise, like in an echo-temple.

I drive through twenty miles or so of Zambia's bush with a Swedish health worker, whose main task is to keep the different district stations happy and provide them with appropriate equipment. He is one of several hundred Swedish Peace Corps members and experts in Zambia. They are to be found everywhere, demonstrating how to grow lettuce, the care of tomato plants, repairing the co-operative's maize-mill, taking timber of the right lengths and thicknesses for the sawmill, making wells, choosing anti-insect remedies that are not dangerous, connecting cables, and looking after clinics for mothers and children. When they have passed on their skills, they move on. Some break down, especially women who haven't managed to get a job and have had to stay back at the SIDA house, but most of them are both capable and admirable.

Why do white people go to Africa at all, now more than ever before, though they are to some extent different kinds of people? Paul Theroux, a writer who was for a long time a teacher in Uganda, gives five reasons in an article in *Transition*, called 'Tarzan Is An Expatriate': a vague sense that Africa rewards her visitors, an aversion to the anonymity of industrial Europe, a wish to be someone special, an unconscious desire to stop thinking and let the body take over. To these selfish reasons can be added a wish to do something good, to help in some way, though that is perhaps less a reason for going than an excuse to do so. Africa remains a geographical and psychological jungle, in which they all test out their hopes, their anger, their tolerance, their prejudices and their imaginations.

Black Africans are often speechless with amazement at the number of childless families their governments appear to borrow for a couple of years; anxious and fussy, with an obvious desire to adopt, i.e. kidnap, black children, clearly impotent from all that dissolute living in the West . . .

Göran, my companion in the car, is bright, blond and direct, a pacifist up to a point, based in several adult education colleges before going to Uppsala university to read theology and becoming a radical priest, like the many in Latin America, though not in countries where SIDA has aid programmes. So he changed, took a course in health care, and came here.

He eats what he is given and appears to have no phobias. He slaps his calves impatiently and keeps a look-out for characteristic information. He points at a calabash upside-down by a path running in towards a village. That means 'no maize-beer for sale', and then you don't have to make an unnecessary journey. He tells me that once when he was just about to enjoy his afternoon coffee, a puff-adder came wriggling towards him. He drew up his legs and sacrificed the scalding coffee on the snake's head. Violence against serpents is sanctioned in Genesis, the First Book of Moses.

After we had been travelling for a few hours without the landscape changing noticeably – acacias swaying lightly like spring winds above the greyish yellow grass are most beautiful – Göran is seized with such homesickness for the mildly exegetical atmosphere of Odinslund that he tries a verse:

All is so silent. A mallard
Can be heard chattering in the marsh.
And from a pine an occasional
Squirrel-tooth crunches.

I stop him before he is ensnared by *The Master's Spring Fantasy on an Apple*:

And when the steamer comes, brother mine
There's smoked fish on board I find . . .

I know he has pickled herring and Swedish hard crispbread back at home in Lusaka. Half his salary goes into a savings account for a house in Tunabackar, and he has God in mind.

He jumps out at a small Baptist station. While he is busy with the inventory of stores and questioning a Swedish Nurse and two Africans, I fall into conversation with a white-haired old lay-worker smoking a pipe. There is more health care and less baptism these days, he tells me. He was converted by a Moffat at about the turn of the century. When he first came across the Holy Scriptures, he was surprised about the serpent tempting Eve. Why not a humming-bird? Who ever is tempted by a snake? He also wondered why the Devil was black. Evil in African folk-lore is grey, colourless, or as white as a dry skeleton. And Africans would never be so arrogant as to call themselves the Children of God. They regarded themselves as ants who together made an anthill in honour of their ancestors and the Almighty.

I fill our reserve tank, clean the carburetor with the same indispensable sewing needle I use to unblock shower-heads, and drive on alone, for Göran turns out to prefer to stay overnight and wait for another car the following day.

I have gone no further than ten miles or so when I run into a rainstorm. The clouds fall perpendicularly, the sun illuminating them like a stage backcloth. For a moment, the whole countryside falls silent. Then the skies open their artillery fire. Lightning like rods. I remember Johan Fredrik Victorin's comment in his South African diary of 1863: 'The thunder here is to some extent different from what we hear at home. The lightning does not zig-zag, but is straighter, with only small hooks.'

I have time to see the heart-shaped droppings of antelopes being washed off the road. I hear branches breaking, unripe fruit dancing down on the radiator, and the clouds are as sharp and jagged as splinters of stone. A pause of a minute, then down comes the hail. Ant-eggs bounce on the ground, the trees hissing like kettles. I am in Frankenstein's laboratory, flasks bubbling, culverts roaring, the elements combined in new constellations.

Then it's all over. The road has become a muddy pool, but the countryside looks freshly cleaned and green, the air shimmering clear. The thunder has gone, the God of our ancestors has stretched his legs, cracked his joints, and has now returned to rest.

The air in Africa is an element you are aware of like the shifting sea. Far away on the plateau, the sun is reflected in water, but if you look through the binoculars, the surrounding trees come closer, but the glitter remains equally distant. You are constantly deceived by clumps of trees hovering in the air, by glistening roads, and I have even seen a herd of gnu come galloping across the horizon, but a hand's breadth up in the air, as if they were the bucks of Thor leaping along the equator.

I am installed in the Government Rest House in good time before darkness. The flagpole outside is bare and unpainted, as if the traveller should have brought with him a national emblem and a rope in place of the one the mice have gnawed away.

I have stayed in these places before, in Uganda, Malawi and Ghana. The standard is simple and varied, but they have certain factors in common, thumbed issues of *Punch* and a bound copy of the weekly edition of the *Daily Mirror*, and mouldering books by Angela Thirkell and Somerset Maugham. I find a bundle of quarantine flags in a chest, tattered by the wind and spotted with bird droppings. They remind me of another era, when the long-distance traveller was informed with a flag that foot-and-mouth disease was raging, or something even more terrifying.

I lie down on the bunk in my room. The thin white mosquito-net rises in a cone above the bed, and a faint breeze moves through the room, purring like a cat. The door into the communal dining-cum-sitting-room is made of slanting slats to make the most of the draught. Through the window hole, I can see weaver birds clearing out hibiscus flowers and a sparrow-hawk's family nesting in the mango tree, its flowers exuding an odour of decay.

The man in charge of this rest house summons me to dinner, but when I arrive, he asks me to wait in a shabby chintz-covered armchair, with creaking springs. I open the *National Geographic Magazine* with its pictures of satisfied Buddhas and temples in Thailand. I ask myself whether there was a moment, about five hundred years BC, when archaic smiles faded and art became warlike. They are fighting on the Parthenon frieze. Not until two thousand years later, in Holland, did Madonnas start to smile. That happened in Europe. In Indian art, there is always a smile, often sinister, full of superior knowledge rather than surprise and joy. African art is a grin, a caricature. It has something to do with the resistance of the material, the hardness of the wood. In reality, I hear black people laughing almost incessantly.

2.

I am just considering giving Henry James' *The Ambassadors* another chance, when I hear a car driving up. An African in a well-pressed khaki suit steps in with a suitcase and says good-evening to me without surprise. Henry James remains unread, the manager lays two places at the table with unexpected eagerness, and the newcomer and I sit down opposite each other for vegetable soup, stew, fruit and boiled bottled water.

His name is Mark, his surname unusually long and sounding like the wing-beat of a tired bird. He is a state-salaried veterinary surgeon, travelling round for six months inspecting cattle, their condition, number and health for a special office under the Department of Agriculture in Lusaka, where he lives. In between times, he is a desk-bound official.

'I haven't been to this district for a year. From tomorrow onwards, I'll smell of cattle. Rather troubled tracts, actually. Thinly populated, poor, far from Lusaka and the copper belt. The President's humanism and nation-building is not really taken seriously. And then there is the proximity to Angola. MPLA came through here on their way to their liberated areas.'

In south-western Zambia, South Africans and Rhodesians have crossed the border on several occasions, laid land-mines and killed villagers. Zambia's defence is limited. She can scarcely answer back. Zambia would need a military guarantee – preferably from Britain – to frighten off Rhodesia from attacking. No country has suffered more from the sanctions against Rhodesia. Zambia has no coastline and for historical and geographical reasons has traded mostly with the racist countries. Oil came via Mozambique, coal for the copper mines from Rhodesia, until the border was closed. Now imports from the south have decreased in ten years from sixty per cent to seven.

Zambia produces and sells at a loss in order to acquire foreign currency to buy necessities, fuel, tools, food, clothes and spare parts. She mortgages her copper resources to avoid giving in to Ian Smith. The Rhodesians reckon on the collapse of the Zambian economy giving them breathing space. The country which has sacrificed most by isolating Smith should be guaranteed foreign credit.

More than most countries, Zambia will probably influence the fate of Africa in the years to come. She has to overcome the threat from the south. She gives refuge to and encourages (and imprisons if necessary) some of Namibia's and Zimbabwe's splintered guerilla forces. Copper provides ninety per cent of her income, but the price of copper is decided on a world market controlled by multi-national companies. The decreasing profitability of the mining industry may bring with it some good, in that more and more people realise how necessary it is to invest in a balanced economy and increased food production. But there is no thought-out strategy for mobilising the small farmers. Since copper has lost its stranglehold, in principle the way is open to changes, difficult for the top layer, but at the same time their best chance of going on living with their honour intact.

'What's made Kaunda lonelier than Nyerere,' says Mark, 'is that he has never had an inner circle of trustworthy and intelligent advisers. Some have deceived him and some have looked after their own interests too much. He himself is too touchy. He has a magnificent great vision, but he's a prisoner of economic realities he has no control over.'

Mark is a critical patriot. My criticism hurts, but he delivers his own. It doesn't cost Tanzania much to be a moral pattern for African small farming communities. But Zambia – with her minerals, her foreign experts in the state copper companies, her class differences, her lack of agricultural reforms which everyone talks about but no one wants to tackle – it is a typically African country.

Typically African, too, because import prices have risen since independence by fifteen per cent, while prices of African raw materials have stagnated or fallen. The rich world retains its hold on the poor countries, and that is made easier by Africa's lack of educated people and it is hard to make conditions for foreign intervention.

No continent is richer in coveted goods. No continent has a

lower standard of living. How long will we want to go on living with this paradox – or they?

Mark seems almost proud of living in a complicated, divided society with hugely unexploited assets. He comes from Ndola in the copper belt. His father was a miner and ended as foreman of a team, 'boss-boy'. He was among the best paid Africans in colonial Northern Rhodesia.

'Communications, education, health care, we've done quite well in those fields,' Mark says. 'We have achieved an egg a day for every Zambian. But otherwise the farmers and cattle-owners are scarcely better off. We lack educated people. We have a small coterie of highly qualified people with long administrative experience, tough and efficient, tired of tribalism and idealism, and anything that doesn't show results. We can't manage without them, but they're dangerous as models. They arouse envy and cynicism. They keep to old tracks. Real reforms would be against their interests. But they don't say so. Their election speeches are very radical.'

But the President isn't like them, Mark says. He is unique, but he has neither the time nor the staff to reduce the power of the élite. In his code of leadership, Kaunda has decided that by 1977 at the latest, all national leaders in various fields must have disposed of all supplementary incomes and investments, and will have to live entirely off their salaries, and they will have to replace their Mercedes with Fiats assembled in Zambia. But there are many loopholes for large cars.

We must learn to behave like a poor country, Kaunda has said, pointing at the insanity of scarcely five per cent of cultivatable land in use, while Zambia imports most of her wheat, meat, rice and dairy products.

For in Zambia, where the average income of black workers is considerably higher than that of South Africa, between three and four children out of every ten still die before the age of five. Of those who reach school age, many have to walk at least three miles to their classes, sit through the lessons and walk back in the afternoon without having had anything to eat. A man who has little to eat works badly and earns less money, so his children also go hungry, thus closing the vicious circle.

Zambia's profile is hard to discern. I hear younger people complaining about no one spurring them on and pointing out the way ahead, as in Tanzania. Humanism is official ideology. But does that mean showing consideration in traffic, is it socialist philosophy in the interests of the powerless – as it makes itself out to be – or is it a correspondence course in state capitalism for the new bureaucrats and party ombudsmen?

In Zambia, the rift between ambition and ability is great. The one-party system has not united the country, and nationalisation of the mines, the banks and some of the land has not led to greater equality, but has reinforced the bureaucrats' position towards those with capital. People's interest in Kaunda's 'participatory democracy' has been waning year by year, the numbers voting at elections growing smaller and smaller. It is an ill omen that so much energy is used to depict students, Jehovah's witnesses and alcoholics as enemies of the state.

Mark is an ordinary official, and when I meet him, I think: I have confidence in many Africans, but seldom in their leaders. I ask him whether he ever wanted to be a politician. Yes, but he realised he lacked aptitude. What kind of aptitude? Perhaps the ability to promise something without having to keep that promise, because nothing concrete has been promised. Perhaps the art of using grandiose words such as revolution, reaction, exploitation, solidarity, fellowship, humanism, foreign agents – and thinking they say as much as everyday words such as milk, worms, water, fire. Perhaps the temptation to identify yourself with the Party and the Movement (UNIP) and allow every criticism of yourself to become an insult to the Movement, so that you become inaccessible and infallible.

He does not deny that as an inspector of Zambia's cattle, he plays an important part. Vaccination, methods of slaughter, de-worming, pasteurisation of milk – all are important to the position of farmers and the economy of the country. Officials like himself, out among the people for six months of the year, acquire experience and knowledge of local traditions and ways of looking at things, and can contribute with creative impulses, each within his own particular field.

'The politicians I know are bitter men. They have a hole in them which has to be filled successfully, to enable them to use their talents. Without success they are more dangerous than all the others.'

Later that evening, Mark tells me of his childhood memories from Ndola. A circus came to town. He was a town boy and hadn't seen many animals. Bears danced, lions leapt through burning hoops, elephants stood on their hind legs and waved at the audience. A divine woman in a glittering costume flew through the air and twirled like a flame between trapezes. Horses danced, plumes extending their manes. A huge square man with vast arm muscles swallowed knives and slivers of glass, the music pounding away all the time, a blaring introduction to a different life.

Then it had all gone, the circus, tents, wagons, the whole caravan. No sawdust, no droppings, leaving behind it a dismal British Sunday that was enough to make the urbanised heart of Africa stop with melancholy and emptiness.

'Everything centred on copper in Ndola. You drank beer. You sat outside the house. You had nowhere to go. But I think that circus tempted me to become a vet and get out into the country.'

I ask Mark what he considers the predominant characteristic of whites and he replies – impatience. He went to a mission school, and they had a print of a staircase of age. All that climbing to achieve a number of heaven-only-knows-what good deeds seemed to him hectic and laborious. He learnt that being clever meant doing a lot.

Africans learnt that they weren't clever. Mark told me with the usual smile – God started by making man out of light-coloured clay but his hands gradually got dirtier and dirtier. The longer he went on, the blacker people became and the more tired God grew. So black people are the least favoured. They lack both weapons and books.

Mark has been to white countries and gone on courses. From America, he remembers small pastel-coloured Baptist chapels and church bells every Sunday, an unusual sound, and from London, double-decker buses and bowler hats.

'The real war starts there,' he says. 'Among those lovely chapels and peculiar hats. Is that your war culture?'

I think about European tribalism, the forty million dead in two world wars.

Mark shows me photographs of his family, and I reciprocate. Black and white scratched photographs, anonymous and questioning faces. In my mind I see the photographer's studio with a rug on the concrete floor and bamboo draperies as background. The pictures are taken at exams, a new job, a win on the national lottery. The relations are all given copies. The photograph corresponds to the gilt-framed painted portrait in middle-class European homes in the past. It confirms that the subject has a certain social position, a rôle he or she is proud to support.

I remember all the white homes in Africa in which I have leafed through albums, those confused and treacherous documents, while the servant served tea and scones, and soon I didn't know whether I were inside or outside the covers. Photography makes the world manageable and episodic, the opposite of understanding it. It freezes a moment in the swift race to oblivion. In that lies its beauty and unreliability.

The girl on the photograph, that vet's wife, is a black American, also a vet, and they met at a conference in the USA. They have one child now. She has a job at the Department of Agriculture, but is not a Zambian citizen. She doesn't like Africa and wants their child to go to school in America, which he has nothing against. He is worried that she is moving away from him, and he sees no solution. There is no place between Zambia and Pennsylvania where they could start a new life together. He is a victim of a collision of cultures, one of the most usual and painful.

'I can't see ahead,' says Mark. 'I suppose that's why I'm not a politician. I don't know what to advise her – or myself.'

His voice sounds hopeless and surprised. He has a gold ring on his finger. His ears are large, almost without folds. They look innocent, like the ears of cattle before they are branded with their owner's name. Perhaps he is so open-hearted because we are the only educated and travelled people this night in the Western Province. He has also spent some years at the university in Salisbury, and we know the same teachers, most of them exiled, or moved away.

A fan hangs still in the ceiling, and in the kitchen the powdered coffee is also locked up. When I have gone to bed under the mosquito net, I see a vampire bat hanging with folded wings where a beam protrudes from the gable. Suddenly the creature comes alive in the light of the single bulb. A claw scratches a stomach, and from nowhere a slim limb appears and stiffens, its tip shaped like a small flower, then runs like a sensory antenna back and forth over the bat's mouth and head. The limb is almost as long as its body – perhaps it is catching a signal from the world about it, for all of a sudden, the bat launches out on to the runways of the night. I fumble for Henry James.

3.

In the morning, I accompany Mark to the nearest village. We meet a responsible person who is dealing with vaccination and slaughter-control, and who knows a lot about soil erosion and distribution of grazing. Each man here farms the land he has inherited from his father, but new ground is ploughed co-operatively, the harvest shared according to work done and the size of the family.

The village is in my eyes like thousands of others, and it is easy to forget that we are in an exciting field of world politics. The cattle-pens are surrounded by thorny fences against hyenas and other intruders. The women work in the maize fields with the youngest children bound to their backs. Small children with protruding stomachs stand quietly in the shade of the fig tree: pregnant gnomes with large eyes. A girl milling butter-nuts, some older boys fencing with sticks, an old man with a clay pipe hunched under his ragged monkey-skin cloak. Sitting inside a hut on a goatskin is an emaciated old grandmother, a beer jar in a corner – a lovely red colour made by boiling bark.

A man with a pock-marked nose and clay-coloured eyes wishes to start a conversation with me, but is turned away by the others. He points at his hut, where he clearly keeps a fermenting brew. I am told he is an ex-Catholic priest who started tasting the communion wine and then became skilled at distilling the juice of tamarind fruit. He soon sank into sin and his excommunication came as no surprise.

The headman of the village has a table outside his hut, his bicycle and a hoe beside it. He has a carved stick in his hand and is bidding a hunting patrol farewell as they set off to find wild pig and guinea-fowl. He offers us a piece of cooked chicken with groundnut sauce. A woman brings it on a tin plate, then later a mug of weak tea.

We sit on stools and chairs under a tree, more and more men appearing and sitting down, turning it into a palaver, a bilingual dialogue with stories from deeper and deeper layers of memory. A world standing still – crisscrossed with human voices, laughter, touches. The words stream in all directions and are drawn again to each other like scattered blobs of quicksilver being reunited.

The apparently endless chat is a form of fellowship. It goes on as if there were a *Scheherazade* hidden inside each of them – someone who wants to continue until dawn but is unwilling to get on with silent work, with toil, planning and activity-bearing results. I have often experienced this, in Ghana and Senegal, with the MPLA guerillas in Cabinda – the concept of 'wasting time' does not exist. Talking to each other is to use the time well.

But the women do not take part. They have their own palavers. When I visit African villages – with the exception of Ghana and Nigeria – I usually find it difficult to get to talk to the women, the old, too. Silently, the women serve the food and retreat to eat the leftovers with the children. They giggle with embarrassment and think I'm joking or flirting. Many women have a freedom of their own in that they are paid money for their own work. But in the rural villages, although she may dominate in other fields, the woman is not allowed to speak for herself or the family.

I see Africa's women burdened with household chores, five or six hours a day grinding corn and fetching water and wood for meals. That time and energy could be used so much more sensibly. Far too little thought is given to how simple machines, maize-grinders, for instance, would help the women, so that they could learn to read and write and grasp the connection between intestinal worms and privies. If the Third World's food problems are to be solved, the women must be made more productive. If the soaring birth rate is to be reduced, women's dependence on children must also be. So long as motherhood is considered woman's most important task, she has good reason to go on having large families.

I look at the old grandmother preparing a piece of meat. She puts it in a hole where the fire has burnt down to embers. She fills the hole and lights another fire above it. That will burn until evening. Then she digs up the meat. She is bent and wrinkled, her skin lighter in the folds. Behind her and the huts are huge grey rocks, worn by centuries of erosion, their tops like ruined fragments of bombarded mediaeval fortresses.

A young man shows Mark and me his essays that have been returned corrected from a correspondence institution in London, a greeting from a distant fairy-tale world. The others flock admiringly round him. He is what they want to be. He has already ceased being one of them. For them, the distance to Lusaka, Ndola and Kitwe is also long. His course is on bookkeeping and administration of a small company, a co-operative dairy, for instance, or an abbatoir. His father, a primary school teacher, a party member and brother to the man with the most cows, has been able to afford to give his eldest son a chance. But will he stay in the village? Wouldn't it have been better for the village if he had failed his course?

More often than with us, progress in underdeveloped countries is the result of favourable circumstances rather than personal ability. Most people exhaust themselves and get little for it. Another inexpensive person can always be found. Machines are dearer to mend, so they have to be looked after. For work which in Sweden provides a holiday-home, a car, schooling for the children and social guarantees that we shall receive health care and various kinds of security, most people in the underdeveloped countries receive nothing at all, perhaps one child of six at school, perhaps one child fairly well fed and the others exhausted from deficiency diseases.

Mark brings democracy into the conversation, and someone asks me to define the word. Not forcing your opinion on anyone else, but making sure other people's opinions are heard. The majority not deciding on a matter until extensive discussion has given everyone a chance of putting forward their view – that's democracy, I say.

No one thinks that worth talking about. That form of agreement through conversation has existed since time immemorial in this society. They remember nothing of dictatorship, only that the opinions of elders carry more weight than those of younger people – roughly as our members of parliament are considered to express public opinion better than those who hold it.

Another side of democracy arouses less response. This is respect for the independence of the individual, the freedom to be your own master as long as justified interests of others are not affected. The Africans' struggle against a harsh countryside, a sometimes overwhelming environment, offers little room for individual thought and taste. When a solution is found after a great deal of testing, a formula, they stick to it. Experiments that might lead to an improvement in life are too daring.

With us in Sweden, the protective social net appears to be so closely woven that some people find it the opposite of freedom. In Africa, on the other hand, life is precarious and guarantees are few. To survive at all, the family, the age-group, the clan, must all stick together – at the cost of individualism being obliterated, both ambition and aggression are subdued. Within any ethnic group, security is great, responsibility mutual. Ill-treated children, women beaten by their husbands, abandoned widows, old people and orphans, are all unknown phenomena in traditional communities. But so as not to be marked out as deviant and thus losing your power, the innovator must disguise himself as a medicine-man, the poet as a bard and seer. In a monotonous existence, common experience means more than new discoveries and ideas which might break the monotony. Death becomes an entry into the past of ancestors, a moment when one's own life is added to the store of wisdom of the tribe.

When Mark has finished his inspections and notes, he drives me back to the Government Rest House. He has a microscope, tablets and large blue exercise books in his briefcase. I have a feeling the villagers regard him with respect and some distrust, but I never got around to asking him about that.

We are two people in authority, in whom ignorance and wisdom have combined in a different way from that of the villagers, and we don't know if they can use what we have said. If that happens, it will perhaps be only because our form of knowledge has a gloss and prestige rather like that of the English correspondence course. We are Henry James' ambassadors.

4.

Our rest-house is silent, the manager invisible. A liana has grown through the window, and the frogs are singing dismally and piously. We stay another night.

That evening I talk about what it was like the first time I visited Africa. Churchill had stated that he refused to preside over the dissolution of the British Empire. But Harold Macmillan, Prime Minister in 1960, did so without raising his hooded eyelids. He undertook a journey to Africa and when he spoke in Cape Town parliament on 'the wind of change', people realised, especially in England, that the Empire was coming to an end. A few formal burial rituals, lowering of flags, memorial plaques, medals for patriotic societies – then it would all be over. No one was prepared for Macmillan's speech. In South Africa the day before, he had made the usual propaganda tour of a Bantu village, a model township for African workers, and had had a leopard skin draped round him. According to one journalist, Prime Minister Verwoerd led him round like a stuffed bear on wheels and spoke of England's responsibility to the Empire. Macmillan, resembling more than anything else an actor on his last ever tour of draughty village halls, appeared to embody a world which had no sense of change. He was a member of all the clubs, the Carlton, the Turf, the Athenaeum and the Beefsteak. He seemed to have stepped out of one of Trollope's novels. He shot grouse and went to Ascot, and when he spoke he was seldom understood, so skilfully did he conceal himself behind drivel that said nothing. What he said at the time was that the British Empire had existed a long time – and few heard how the sentence ended – 'long enough.'

According to Churchill, the main purpose of the Empire was to bring peace to warring tribes, to create justice where all was violence, to loosen the chains of slaves, to extract riches from the soil, to sow the first seeds of trade and wisdom, to increase all men's capacity for enjoyment and reduce their chances of suffering. As he claimed, what more splendid ideals and what more valuable reward could inspire the toils of mankind?

Those great aims were seldom fulfilled. Though Frenchmen,

Portuguese, Germans and Belgians should have more on their consciences than the British. André Gide travelled to the Congo and Chad in 1926, and gives examples of the eradication of local villages. Villages refusing to put bearers at their disposal – fifty pounds to carry for a twelve-hour march in untrodden forest – were burnt down and the women and children shot. The population of French Equatorial Africa fell between 1900 and 1920 by approximately ten million. When the bearers arrived at their goal, they were weak, exhausted and undernourished. To get back to their villages, they had to do the return journey, carrying similar loads, only to find their land sold and their grainstores plundered.

To put an end to African opposition to wage-earning, the French thought up a number of new methods to force them to earn money. With punitive taxation on local salt production, the government forced Africans to buy imported French salt from the company stores. An 'entertainment' tax was put on drums and other instruments, so Africans could not even console themselves with their own music at the end of the working day. A personal tax to be paid in cash was levied several times a year. Soldiers took wives as hostages and raped them until the tax was paid.

The Germans lost their colonies in 1918 – after they had done their best to wipe out whole tribes. Forced labour continued in the Portuguese colonies. In French areas, conditions improved in the Thirties. The English were the mildest, but they also put great weight on what Churchill called the fourth aim of the Empire – to extract riches from the soil. Echoes of Churchill's words on the Empire can be heard in many speeches on the aims of African independence and unity made by Zambia's president.

'I worry about Kaunda,' says Mark. 'Will he survive? South Africa, Smith, the Soviet Union, and some of the men in the liberation movement – none of them likes him. The multinational companies want a dictator friendly to the West – like Banda or Mobutu. Kaunda is the pacifist driven to buying modern arms to protect us from the threat from the south, and he will have to take to force against tribal hostilities, if he wants to keep the country united. Many people are after him.'

'The outlook may seem gloomy,' I say. 'Over the last fifteen years, there have been thirty-seven coups in black Africa. In only one country, Somalia, has the government fallen as a result of an election defeat. Three states, Botswana, Gambia and Mauritius, allow an official opposition. Eighteen states are under direct military rule. Three have military leaders in civilian clothes. Two others are absolute monarchies. The remaining twenty are one-party states.'

'I'm not pessimistic about development in general,' says Mark. 'White idealists seek in vain for miracles. But the people are now slightly healthier and live longer. We've learnt that poverty can be overcome, and that doesn't happen by hanging around city street corners. There are more lamps, buses, pumps and tractors than ten or twenty years ago – in relation to the population, too. That's always something.'

The following day our destinies part. I turn off at a small place in the upper Zambezi. The river flows along in uneasy curves. When I catch glimpses of it from my road, branches of trees polished by the rapids and as smooth as ivory are floating slowly past. Soon they will be smashed to pieces by the Victoria Falls. I have seen its façade of apparently immobile pillars of foam, and inside it the roaring mill grinding water and earth together, while yellow and white butterflies flutter above the cataracts and are again sucked into the clouds of vapour.

A few months later, I have reason to contact Mark, and he tells me in a letter that his family has gone back to the USA, and it is the beginning of a reluctant separation. The political and military threat from the south has increased, he writes, and their lack of coastline seems more troublesome than ever to the economy. He is tormented by claustrophobia and impotence. Freedom of movement for foreigners has been restricted.

But perhaps we shall meet once again at the Government Rest House, he adds. He knows that whenever that happens he will recognise me from an unread novel I am faithfully holding in my hand – like someone who is lost and has brought the wrong map with him.

The example of Mozambique

A journey in 1974 and a Postscript in 1976

1. Frelimo and the Historical Moment

After half a century, Mozambique turned a page in her history. From July 1975, she became independent, and the year up to then, she was governed by a transitional government in which the liberation movement, Frelimo, held the majority of posts and Portugal the remainder.

It was a time of upheaval and a remarkable year in the decolonisation of Africa. Africans had re-conquered their country. They had made Portugal change her state of mind. During the April revolution, everyone could see the liberation movement's ideas being transferred from the Africans over to the Portuguese. It is very rare for Africa to have influenced Europe in a similar way.

These movements offered the world a spectacle of political and military brilliance. They opened a way out of the cul-de-sac the neo-colonial system had inherited from Europe. The negotiations which led to the Lusaka Agreement in September 1974 showed that Frelimo was never prepared to accept compromises, but preferred to continue the struggle.

Decay, ignorance and poverty were so great that nothing less than a transformation of an entire society was acceptable. Everywhere – in schools, health care, industry, a new organisation had to be set up.

The liberation movements were forced to take up arms and fight with great sacrifices for over ten years. This struggle has given them the experience which is lacking in what are called the free African states. It has taught them to fear neo-colonial solutions which look good on paper: huge increases in production such as in the Ivory Coast and Liberia, where very little goes to the people or to goods the workers and farmers need. Such countries – and they are the majority in Africa – are élite states; although they achieve individual social improvements, they do not even succeed in creating indigenous capitalism. The surplus they produce goes abroad.

It is not known how Frelimo will carry out its socialist decentralisation programme in a country so strongly marked with its one-sided economy of exports of raw materials. But what is most important perhaps is that people can start coming forward with suggestions and ideas. Those who took part in the war have experienced liberation from traditions, home villages, the limitations of the tribe, and they have learnt to work together with people from other places. This has widened their outlook on the world. The ideas that made them endure and hope, while outside observers often gave up hope of their struggle, will now be tested on a different and more peaceful reality.

National re-education has to occur if it is not all to have been in vain. Northern Mozambique – the liberated areas – has for ten years been part of a different way of life, economy and fellowship. In the towns and on the plantations in the south, the picture is different, luxury and poverty, class-differences, a war that never came physically close.

The sensational thing about Mozambique – as I experienced in 1975 – is not the drama, but the calm determination and co-operation, despite everything. Frelimo is being put to tests which cannot be judged for a long time. It must maintain unity in the country through tolerance and education. At the same time, it must fulfil the resolution and not stop at half-measures. For the Portuguese system – which even Captain Henrique Galvao pointed out in 1961 – produced nothing and delivered nothing that was not directly or indirectly dependent on African forced labour. Now the workers know their rights. They can leave their jobs and look for new ones where there are any. And the previous maximum wages have become minimal wages, twelve pounds a month in the cities.

There is an undertone of realistic optimism, an enduring determination in Frelimo people. They have had to act for so many years, not sit passively and lethargically in refugee camps. They have escaped the usual route from idealism to cynicism. They are partisans. From the start, they preferred a dying death to a living death in exile or forced labour. Now they are in the capital, in the centre of a new administration. There is no way back from the task they have undertaken.

Marcelino dos Santos, Vice-President of Frelimo, has written a marching song:

The effort we make
is neither small nor great
It is what it must be
The March goes on
Three or six hours or more
until we reach our goal
with rest or no rest
a stream of six or ten comrades
or a whole river
sweat washing away fourteen days' a fortnight's or a
 month's
flowing and drying
endlessly silvering our bodies and clothes
The effort we make
is neither small nor great
It is what it must be.

'After five hundred years . . .' say Frelimo people, for they are also brought up with the Portuguese view of history. 'After five hundred years, we stand here as our own masters and are trying to find out whether we can be ourselves beneath the pressure of hostile neighbours, foreign capital and strategic interests. After all that long time, we have managed to come of age.'

That is what is strange – these countries in particular, suddenly free, the most backward and undeveloped. Here, where the Portuguese constantly spoke of Henry the Seafarer, Vasco de Gama and the Lusitanian tradition across the oceans of the world. Here, where practically no one lifted a finger to feel the wind of change. Here, where the whites laughed at the troubles with world opinion their friends in Rhodesia and South Africa were having. There were so few people abroad who knew Portuguese, and illiteracy put great obstacles in the way for black protests to get through, and anyhow, there was always the mixing of races as evidence of tolerance.

The colonial dream was to graft holy Portuguese civilisation on to Africa's coarse stem, then dark flowers would blossom forth. But then no one was to disturb it. The outside world's only rôle was to help finance it.

Frelimo tore away this veil of illusions, living lies, and self-satisfaction. Mozambique was a white country with clubs, a lively social life, a good standard of living for European immigrants, who complained about being ruled from afar by Lisbon. No one mentioned the blacks while handing out orders. Everything seemed to be functioning well. There was money to spare, a rare situation in Portugal. They had cars, houses and schools for their children. No one took religion quite so seriously as in Portugal, for far fewer were so poor that they needed God. The world was theirs, the whites', not the black children's. That's what it was like, and that was as it should be. But it wasn't so.

Frelimo arose in 1960, when the leaders of three groups in exile in Malawi, Rhodesia and Tanzania-Kenya decided to unite. Tanzania had become independent the year before, and Nyerere opened the country to the liberation movement. The 1961 rebellion in Angola had made the world press take note of Portugal's colonial oppression. Eduardo Mondlane, independent of all previous groups, became the leader of Frelimo.

He had seen a great deal all over Africa of what Nyerere called 'flag-independence' – national leaders like Nkrumah in Ghana becoming more and more remote and expecting little more of the people than that they should follow. Mondlane had seen national parties led by a minority of educated men, most of whom had lived in exile in Europe or America for a long time, and they only carried the workers and small farmers along with them because they symbolised freedom and progress. 'The greatest danger threatening Africa is the absence of ideology', Frantz Fanon writes.

Frelimo's leaders are aware of the need for an ideology, but also of the danger of a mechanically applied system. Revolutions can learn from each other, but should not imitate each other and force through structures and methods without regard to the culture and special conditions of the people of that country. In Mozambique, the change had to be based on the small farmers, and also owner-occupiers, and the women. Every detour that by-passes them leads to a new élite. No way round is too long, no victory too distant, if it creates mutual responsibility and participation enjoyed by all.

I remember an early breakfast with Eduardo Mondlane one summer's day at my home in Stockholm. He said that in a few months' time something surprising would happen, and on a table-napkin he wrote a date he favoured highly, 25th September, 1964. That day, Frelimo forces crossed the river boundary and broadcast a formal declaration of war. 'In the name of us all, Frelimo today formally declares total armed rising of the people against Portuguese colonialism to achieve complete self-government for Mozambique. Our struggle will not cease until Portuguese colonialism is completely eliminated.'

But the point of the war, Mondlane said, was not to drive out the Portuguese, but create a new awareness and a more just way of living, a Mozambique without hunger and with men and women equal and free. He warned against all kinds of dictatorship, both party and the movement's, which might stifle initiative and any sense of personal responsibility.

No one in Frelimo was allowed to fight against Portugal for purposes of revenge or racial hatred – he was stopped and sent away for rehabilitation. Education was social and political, intended to break the isolation of villages and achieve national unity round collective aims. As soon as a section of the country was liberated, that nearest the borders of Tanzania, the villages elected committees and councils, and from then on every decision had to be democratic. Even if military actions were thus delayed, Mondlane said people had to spend time teaching, distributing power, allowing generations and tribes to meet and talk, and defining problems and making them understandable to everyone. Military victories could wait. Ignorance was in the long run a much worse enemy than the Portuguese.

When the fighting started, Frelimo mixed people from different parts of the country, so that every army consisted of men and women from different ethnic and social backgrounds. In this way, tribal and local loyalties were transformed into a national and revolutionary awareness.

In the liberated areas, the people avoided direct confrontation with the Portuguese, and this was decisive for Frelimo's progress. The new nation was formed in mobile schools and field hospitals, in maize and millet fields where there was no need to hand over the crops to the whites. 'It is important for us to create human relations reflecting what we want Mozambique society to be', Marcelino dos Santos said in 1970. 'Shaping reality is in itself a conquest.'

The murder of Eduardo Mondlane in February, 1969, was a desperate attempt to splinter the liberation movement and stop the birth of a nation, and for a while it apppeared successful. The military offensive slowed down, the people's militia stopped cultivation and the transport of goods ceased. Many thought a whole heritage of possibilities had been lost.

The Makonde chieftain, Kavandame, one of the Frelimo leaders, went over to the Portuguese and advised his people to cease resistance. He suggested to the whites that they leave his province, Cabo Delgado, and hand power over to him. He did not wish to change the structure of exploitation. He has been pointed out in a secret Interpol report as a participator in the murder. The bomb was Japanese, bought in a shop in Lourenço Marques.

Uria Simango, one of the troika to replace Mondlane, soon went over to Coremo, a movement which gradually ceased to function. He demanded black power instead of white; Frelimo's colour-blind ideology of equality was too much for him.

Behind were left Samora Machel and Marcelino dos Santos. They were successful. Mondlane became a living legend in whose name the war intensified. Frelimo crossed the Zambezi river, the fighting spread from the provinces of Cabo Delgado and Niassa in the north to Tete, Zambezia and Manica y Sofala. Shortly before his death, Mondlane rejected a Portuguese offer of independence for northern Mozambique, economically the least wealthy part of the country. They will kill me for this, he said, for they don't understand that Frelimo has a collective leadership.

Caetano's Minister of the Colonies, J.M. Da Silva Cunha, said in one of his endless rhetorical statements: 'Providence has proclaimed that Portugal was to be given the task of bringing peoples from other parts of the world into contact with Europe. With European civilisation, we offer them the light of the Christian message. Our task has made us active and has demanded sacrifices of us for five centuries, and the result has become a country spread over several continents and composed of many races.'

Over five hundred years this civilising mission by the Portuguese resulted in one black lawyer and three black doctors, while about ninety per cent of the population remained illiterate. Within a decade, Frelimo had achieved far more in the fields of health care, schools, new production methods and economic co-operatives. By the April revolution of 1974, in the liberated areas there were about one hundred and seventy primary schools with about three hundred teachers and twenty-five thousand pupils. Primary education is for seven years, with an average of thirty-six hours a week for six days. Mathematics, history, geography, natural science, physics, politics and administration, drawing and practical work are the subjects, Portuguese the basic language.

This education programme – planned at the Mozambique Institute in Dar es Salaam, led by Janet Mondlane and particularly supported by Sweden – does not only teach people to read and write, but in this way also makes them acquainted with their own situation. Amilcar Cabral, the leader of Guinea-Bissau, said:

'The Portuguese made sure we abandoned our own history in order to continue as the last carriage in their train. We were driven further and further out into cultural exile. We were forced to deny our own thought-patterns.

'Now it is a matter of Africans managing to distinguish what is fertile in their traditions and replace the rest with a view of society capable of using the techniques and knowledge of our day. It is simple to get people used to factories, schools and new products. It is much more difficult to rid ourselves of witchcraft, magic and a religion presumed to be able to explain what happens in the world.'

It was Cabral's strength that he saw that political transformation remained a superficial phenomenon if it did not involve people in thinking out new methods of dealing with their environment. The liberation leaders in Portugal's ex-colonies, some of them poets, have more than any others emphasised the importance of cultural re-orientation.

A few years before he was murdered, I asked Cabral the usual question: how do you get villagers to listen and give shelter and support to the guerillas? How do you overcome their distrust?

'Not by talking about large issues such as independence and freedom,' he replied. 'That'll have to come later. When I give instruction on solidarity and trust, they ask: Have you any rice? Have you any cloth? What is important are local complaints, taxes, yesterday's wretchedness and today's injustice. A struggle for freedom which has nothing to offer except ideas or just goods is not worth the trouble. People don't risk their lives for ideas in someone else's head. They fight for material advantages, for a better life, for a future for their children.'

How will Africa achieve true independence? Development has failed in many ways, although a number of countries have become formally independent with remarkably little bloodshed compared with Europe. Africa has no severe population problem if the cultivatable land is taken into account, rather than available resources; there are no slums that can be measured against the worst of Latin America, and big landowners are relatively few. Yet Africa's assets are not mobilised. The few rule, the many are passive – except in a handful of states such as Tanzania, Botswana, the People's Republics of Congo and Somalia.

In this situation, unexpected hope comes from a small underdeveloped country such as Guinea-Bissau. Using PAIGC and its methods as a lever, a few hundred thousand people have heaved themselves out of apathy and anonymity, showing the way for many other underdeveloped countries and not demanding immediate succour.

'Quite simply,' said Amilcar Cabral shortly before his death, 'we expect everyone who has understood what we are striving for to give whatever help he or she is capable of to our people.'

Mondlane and Cabral were very close to each other. Their aims were the same. They give us hope for the future of Mozambique.

2. Transition

Only those who are free in some way can afford to worry over the meaning of freedom. To the enslaved, the meaning is perfectly clear.

For many people in Mozambique, freedom came as a surprise. Frelimo's message did not penetrate everywhere, yet it is amazing how swiftly people grasped the content of events and how much they knew about Frelimo.

The old Mozambique was a hothouse, its glass opaque with bird excrement, airless, suffocating and hot, and nothing could grow as it wished to. Now the glass has been shattered and people have been given the space to grow.

What is impressive about Frelimo is that the movement is based on responsibility, discipline at work and good sense. Nothing is mysteriously decreed from above. Every obligation has a clearly defined meaning. People know what minutes and account books are. There is no place for what Jan Myrdal calls 'operetta-revolutionaries' and 'baton-romantics'. They are out for results.

'A mango tree does not become a large tree on its very first day, but like a growing mango tree, we are deeply rooted in the soil that is our people, and the masses are now tasting the first fruits,' said Samora Machel, six years to the day after the beginning of the war.

Frelimo's war has been fought during endless discussion, simultaneously a war of ideas against fear, ignorance, superstition and sex-discrimination. Constructive criticism and self-criticism are part of everyday life, part of this new form of life called participatory democracy. Traditional customs, songs, dances and folk-tales are used as a binding force, contributing to the feeling of solidarity and continuity.

'It's tempting,' a leading Frelimo man said to me, 'to believe that you have solved a problem as long as you have defined it, and that you have carried out a plan just because you have sketched out the aim of it. It's easy to be too theoretical. We prefer to experience things and learn from those experiences. We know a great deal about how colonialism works. But there are people who don't want to start up a fertiliser factory or search for minerals just because we would have to use private enterprises. Then nothing happens. We can't afford that.'

The realism of the leaders of Mozambique makes a strong impression. It never allows the revolutionary goal out of sight. On the contrary, society is being changed at a pace which would be inconceivable in more industrialised countries. But they are not tempted by reveries, whims and fancies, by ephemeral fantasies or trendy prophets.

Frelimo's leaders are not fanatical utopians prepared to slaughter the present and read future happiness in its entrails. They are not seized with panic when the inevitable compromises arise, silent and grey like the caretaker in the Ministry of Economic Planning.

'The people who shout loudest about freedom are often the least concerned about it,' Locke the philosopher said long ago. In Mozambique, there is less talk of freedom than of unity, work and vigilance, but these lead to greater freedom, and that freedom is to be found in the very air, even if it is not compared with the previous oppression.

People with no freedom cannot take responsibility, but now the people have the freedom to acquire knowledge, to choose their work according to their circumstances, to stay in one place and not be deported to another.

Freedom concerns fulfilment of duty and solidarity. If you live in a country you like, among people you respect, you can work for them of your own free will and thus for yourself.

The risks, however, are great. In the Third World, it often seems that the actual absence of foreign rulers is sufficient freedom. The exodus of oppressors is celebrated years after they have departed, perhaps because there is no other freedom in sight. Freedom is then interpreted as a right due to people, a nation, not to individual citizens. But national freedom of that kind is also denied many people today. Estonians, Lithuanians, Czechs, Basques and Kurds are in a worse position than Guyanese, Congolese and Indians, because in their countries neither the individual *nor* the nation possesses anything worthy of the word freedom.

The danger for Mozambique is that freedom – especially after a period of consolidation – is interpreted as the freedom to do what Frelimo considers right. That is what it was once like in America. People who protested against puritanical rules of behaviour were told that they were free of the Anglican orthodoxy of England.

But so far, Frelimo is a decentralised popular movement with a broad-based anchorage. The revolution is no élitist achievement, but has come from below. This means the boy who used to wash cars and steal in between is now trained as a mechanic, a vaccinator or a plumber. Thieves build dams or join an agricultural collective. The unemployed are educated. In some important areas of principle, more compulsion than flexibility is used. The drift to the towns is being halted, the unemployed sent back to agriculture. For there is plenty of land, uncultivated or abandoned. Up to 1974, one per cent of the country's farmers, all white, cultivated half the land, while ninety-nine per cent of farmers, all black, cultivated the other half.

Frelimo says the task of creating a Mozambique for the people and not for a privileged group is easier when you start from the bottom and avoid aiming at an established system. During their thirteen-year struggle, Frelimo has managed to become a people's army and to integrate the army into civilian life. In an Africa plagued by military coups, it is an advantage to have come to power so slowly.

When I went to Mozambique for the first time, in 1959, the greatest impression on me was one of apathy and desolation. Prisoners were being shuttled between work in the fields and prison. The rattle of their shackles could be heard as they stumbled along in the heat. Women and ten-year-old children were working on the roads and I saw them hacking away and filling holes with gravel from the roadsides. Up to the 1970s, the railways were built by forceably recruited men who did nine months in exchange for wretched quarters and food, and then had to return home for six months at a time. I remember all those bowing Africans along the edges of the roads. As soon as they saw a white man, myself, tearing past, they had to bow, or expect a beating from their local *chef do posto*.

Human beings have lived at the very bottom here, enslaved and exploited. They have not been allowed to keep their traditions, nor take part in any new ones. Thanks to their own efforts and sacrifices, they are at last faced with the possibility of running their own country, their traditions and future. They are very poor and can usually neither read nor write, but they can learn. They have confidence in themselves and each other. Until now, they have had no need for drugs, but they have acquired songs, speech, legends and adages.

So many more than in Europe have died of hunger, war and slave labour, and yet here is this irrepressibility. It is infectious with its rebellious music. It is easy to say it is based on unpretentiousness, on low expectations, on a lack of awareness of the dangers of technology and the lust for power in larger countries. And yet this confidence exists, arching like a rainbow over the country.

Pessimism and a sense of doom are common in the West. I have met young people in the USA who cannot imagine living beyond thirty-five – the average life-span of anyone from Mozambique – and who cannot imagine having any children. They are friends of the earth, but without hope. When a school class in Sweden writes a composition on life in the year 2000, when they will be forty, their vision is entirely black. The Baltic is a garbage tip and they are sheltering from radiation in filthy cellars. That is what the future looks like to the generation which, more than anyone else in the history of the world, has been protected by guarantees of social security.

In the Soviet Union, I have come across another kind of dejection. Some of my intellectual friends, engineers, doctors and teachers, have taken to drinking heavily, some have taken their own lives, all because within the framework of the Soviet Union, they have not been able to see any meaning in their lives. They are not allowed to travel freely, research freely or mix with people they would like to. They have not even old-fashioned Stalinism to rebel against.

Some seek back into religion, fewer into literature and art related to a more symbolic, less personal immortality – the continuity and solidarity of human beings over the centuries. Many people go in for experiencing immortality here and now, an experience which also makes contact with a form of transcendental reality. Through drugs, they achieve stages in which time and death are obliterated.

What was shattered at Hiroshima was man's sense of the connection between the past and the future, cultural traditions and the historical process. If the future doesn't exist, then what is the significance of history?

Living on in his descendants . . . in his works . . . in God's paradise . . . in the permanent revolution. A constant search for some kind of immortality.

It is easy to generalise. There are exhausted people in Mozambique, worn out by their labours or from disease. There are the mentally disturbed and the backward. Children die. On the other hand, Sweden and the West do not only consist of the querulous and ungrateful, the narrow and the decrepit. Far from it. Internationalism has become a fact. Schoolchildren work for Indo-China and southern Africa and popular movements have arisen like a protective wall round Vietnam.

Development has progressed very quickly. The Sweden of the 1890s was an unknown country. Hazelius was compared with Stanley. It was not possible to go by train to the nation's borders until the beginning of the century, when Sweden became something more than a native heath or childhood plot. The Tourist Association was founded, cycling started and writers about the countryside had access to new material. Our traditional seaside holiday places moved to Majorca and Tenerife. We learn about underdeveloped countries at school and the curriculum no longer includes such information as 'the Turks cannot measure up to the Greeks in untrustworthiness'.

'You people in wealthy Europe are sensitive about political oppression,' Joaquin Chissano, Prime Minister when I was there, tells me. 'You have been through Nazism and other dictatorships, sometimes as racist as colonialism. It's an experience you have in common with us. We have been without freedom of expression, consultation on wages and labour, choice of education and discussion of the future. You find it more difficult to imagine economic violence. Why should children starve, adults die at fifty, and most people be afflicted by diseases you yourselves are soon cured of? You seem to look on it as a natural necessity. You don't notice that we live in a hierarchy in which the actual word equality is a bomb – until now. The rich are rich because the others are poor. Perhaps they could be even richer if some of the poor were healthy, long-lived and literate. But if everyone were – then society would look different.'

So I found it remarkable and encouraging to observe Frelimo's form of community in places where there had been time for it to strike root. No one earns money and no one starves. The unemployed are given work, the illiterate taught, and the children usually manage to survive. They make use of the land and each other's labour and knowledge. Little is taken from outside, so expectations are very modest. Nothing is added to the gross national product, but there is an increase in self-reliance, in spiritual and physical health, for they are creating their own destinies and deciding on their own lives within self-imposed frameworks.

Perhaps one should have seen the country under Portuguese rule to notice the revolution and be pleased to see it. Perhaps this society will last for only one generation before it is inevitably invaded by foreign temptations, advertisements, violent films and superfluous consumer goods. Few countries seem able to isolate themselves – with the best of intentions. Let us hope that experience and education can give Frelimo's people a certain immunity to the abundance with which an envious world will want to bribe them.

3. Writers

Dawn in Lourenço Marques in 1975. Outside the large office block in the town centre, nightwatchmen are making tea and preparing to leave. The sun rises before six, high summer south of the Equator. Indian families living near the ocean are bathing, going down to the water with towels over their shoulders, then returning at dusk, when they park their cars in long lines and sit and talk to each other as they watch the sun setting.

Dockers are on their way to the harbour. Occasional policemen are on patrol. Some people are waiting for the first bus of the day. The market is not yet open in Chipamanine. At a quarter past six, the town is suddenly awake, the shops on the outskirts selling food, tea brewing, and at half past six everyone seems to be up and about, servants, street-sweepers, workers and cyclists.

At half past seven in the morning, I go to see José Craveirinha, fifty-four, a mulatto, librarian in the Department of Trade. The country's leading poet is sitting in the dim light between old-fashioned bookcases and shelves full of enormous reference books and dictionaries of trade terms and international statesmen of the 1950s.

He is a gentle, melancholy man.

'Why take a photograph of me when we're so near to the zoo? You must be disappointed to see me. Maybe you'd thought you'd see a poet?'

He has spent four years in prison, the same time it takes to take a degree, he tells me. He wrote all the time, sometimes with a pin on toilet paper. If writing is one of the conditions of life, you create the conditions. An acajou tree bears fruit, a writer writes.

Now inflation has hit writers. The doors have opened, but there is a shortage of paper, and newspapers have little space for poems. There is no literary magazine. Neither do people always understand what you mean. When in an ironically sympathetic poem Craveirinha used the word whore instead of prostitute, he was made to remove it, just as under the old regime, he says, leafing through a fifteen-year-old *Who's Who in World Trade*.

'Have you any reactionaries in Sweden?' he asks. 'It's good to have a few. One should make the most of them.'

From the poet to the leading prose writer, Luis Bernado Honwana, born in 1940, with several short stories in Swedish and a collection which has been translated into English: *Who Killed the Mangy Dog?* I didn't know where to find him, so I asked the Prime Minister's secretary.

'That's me,' he said.

He was sitting in the Governor-General's old house on a cool hill with the sea outside. He is very tall. He, too, has been in prison. In 1970, he went to Lisbon to study law. But that was camouflage. He had been assigned by Frelimo to contact socialists and communists. When he realised he was going to be arrested, he made his way to Tanzania. That was during the weeks just before the coup.

Now he is helping the Prime Minister with his speeches, taking part in state visits and sifting through interviewers and supplicants. On the table in front of him he has a list of Frelimo *noms de guerre* and their real names, which few know. The guerillas used invented names to protect their families. I see a letter with a Swedish stamp on it, addressed to Lorenco Mutaca. What happened to this Frelimo representative who was tempted away by Swedish welfare and refused to return to do his military service? Well, he's doing it now, together with his wife and children in school in Tunduru. Honwana praises him for his devotion. (The following year, I find Mutaca as an official in the Ministry of Economic Planning.)

Practically no one writes prose in Mozambique. It takes too long and seems to be a detour, Honwana says. He is just putting together texts suitable for teaching. Portuguese textbooks are on their way out. But some of the material Frelimo used earlier is no longer suitable, too much about war, rifles and sacrifices in it. The new school book must deal with peaceful, industrious daily life, and folk-tales and oral tradition can play an important part in that field.

'One out of ten at the most can just comprehend what I write. It's a sad thought. It is tempting to write for Lisbon, London and Paris. But in the long term, the prospects are brilliant and challenging here. If I call my collection of short stories a psychology manual, people would leap on it.'

I ask to be allowed to take a photograph of him in his capacity as author. A woman secretary comes into the room and says sternly:

'Don't let him. You're a Frelimo man.'

'But in my capacity as an author . . .'

'No!'

Yet he does so, adding that the Frelimo leaders wish to remain anonymous. No biographical information on cabinet ministers is published. In interviews, questions on what made them join Frelimo and take up the struggle are dismissed. They are too personal.

The camera registers Luis Bernado Honwana, individual author. But no one knows when he will appear in that rôle

again. From the hill where we are standing, he points at the shorelines to the north and the town's red-tiled roofs and says in a tone of voice I cannot fathom:
'In the course of a few weeks, you'll see the country we'll live in all our lives.'

4. The Sugar-Factory Manager's Wife

Near Moamba, one of the larger stations along the railway between Lourenço Marques and Johannesburg, is a gloomy great sugar factory. It has been nationalised, but Frelimo has asked the white manager to stay on, and he is proud of that. He is paid his old salary and the workers have been given increases.

'Clever people, the Frelimo,' he says in a tone of voice as if he meant himself. 'And adaptable' – like himself. 'Others flee – and God help them in their foolishness. They're going to need it.'

Until recently they were favoured, these white men, who considered they had become rich from sheer energy and moral example. Now they are lost, and it is no longer their fault, but the fault of communists, liberal priests, crazy captains in Lisbon, perhaps Swedes and Chinese. The blacks they have employed and trained in the name of development were nothing but a pain in the neck.

'I've worked my way up from nothing,' is one of the most common colonialist remarks. Then it is a question of landing on your feet with your hands full of rewards seized for your labours. That usually works, too.

The manager's wife, Estrela, offers me tea and a small glass of madeira. She tells me a Frelimo officer in camouflage uniform had one day called and asked for their assistance. What a well brought-up young man! He had been given tea, too, but he drank neither wine nor spirits.

'Quince jam,' she complains, 'loses its taste as soon as you open the jar.'

Well, it was like old wine, unable to tolerate the fresh air, and things were no better with her other preserves, apple-jelly spiced with orange peel, the guava that was a beautiful red cream full of pips that got stuck in your teeth.

Keeping open house out in this empty crude countryside was not easy.

'Try making a layer-cake yourself at eighty-five in the shade,' she says. 'The cream melts. It gets sticky.'

The shutters are closed to prevent the sun fading the furnishing fabrics and wallpaper. So beautifully laid out, so beautifully arranged! Neatness creates a front against chaos out here.

Mrs Estrela is wearing a dark-blue starched cotton dress with a white collar. She has used her eyebrow-pencil, but no other make-up, yet I still see her as more camouflaged than the Frelimo officer, who would anyhow have been shot if he had appeared for afternoon tea a few months earlier.

I would hazard that she bears a grudge against life, an unsatisfied hunger. People have to give her more, appreciate her more, take more notice of her. Perhaps what's wrong, and she doesn't realise it, is that she has never had a chance to sacrifice herself for anyone or anything.

The people who make sacrifices are the men and women of the guerillas. They are considered by their distant adherents to be unimaginably brave. I don't know. People do what they find meaningful. The guerillas in Rhodesia and Mozambique have no difficulty finding recruits, but they find it much harder to train them, to eliminate their desire for revenge and get them to see the contours of a new society clearly.

People, most of all young people, living under constant harassment and violence, are prepared to risk their lives for the chance of improving matters, if they survive. I can imagine those frighteningly innocent youths heading for suicide and death, but they do so with open eyes. It is the survivors who have the responsibility for making sure these people have not sacrificed their lives for a society that continues the old oppression in different forms.

The basket-chairs creak. A pile of picture postcards from Europe lie bundled up with an elastic band round it. They have stuck together in the heat. The manager of the sugar-factory tilts his glass of madeira as if he were trying to help a goldfish up to the surface.

'I admit the workers' wages here were wretched. But what

did we get? Lisbon took its share. I like this country. I have a bit of money and we could leave and live well elsewhere. But when you see other people packing up and selling out for nothing and leaving . . . for what?'

The servant comes in with the tea. Nothing has changed on that front. Everyone wants work. Mrs Estrela follows my gaze.

'Jorge has been with us for six years. I asked him a little while ago whether he thought Frelimo would win. Yes, he said. I've always believed that. But you never said anything to us, I said. You would have dismissed me, he said. And yet you haven't plundered us, now the country is yours, I said. No, he said. Frelimo forbids plundering. That worried me. Was it only Frelimo's orders keeping him in check? Had he no morality of his own?'

'I'm sure he has,' said her husband, 'but we don't know.'

Many white people believe they live in symbiosis with their servants, and they also think they know them better than they do themselves. White people are the huge tree. Black people are the creeper climbing up it, extracting nourishment from it and finally perhaps choking it.

'I can tell you one thing,' said the manager, 'on the plantations where there's no white boss, production is going down, straight to the bottom. The workers cut the tops off the sugar cane. They think freedom is not having to bend down. But the sugar collects at the bottom of the stalk. It turns sour later.'

He laughs, not in a worried way, but with irritating self-satisfaction over the fact that he knows what is happening in the country now, and that he himself knows all the tricks of living with his new rulers.

I would hazard that Frelimo won't want him to stay on his advantageous colonial terms. They will suggest a six month political rehabilitation course and then ask him to turn the sugar factory into a collective under African management. In his turn, he will resent being treated like a schoolboy, and shortly afterwards, the family will have gone to Lisbon, awaiting a sign from General Spinola.

But for a while longer, Frelimo and this family live in a state of mutual tolerance. The madeira will come to an end all over the country, and the servant will not appear, however much the wife rings her little hand-bell.

Over the years, I have got to know the houses of the whites in Africa. I am drawn to them in my memories – the mangle screeching in the wash-house, and the stairs creaking rather like those in houses in the country in Sweden. To a remarkable extent, some people and some conversations remind me of things I experienced in my childhood back home. Tunes one has once heard are easily recalled.

Visits to houses of the whites in Africa sometimes remind me of a sinister little poem by W.H. Auden. It is about cracks in the walls, death and the threat behind an apparently cosy and protected existence.

The glacier knocks in the cupboard,
The desert sighs in the bed,
And the crack in the tea-cup opens
A lane to the land of the dead.

5. People's Market

By eleven, the fish has all gone, both fresh fish from concrete benches beneath the shady canopy and the dried fish out in the sun. The market women in their colourful long skirts and head-scarves settle down on empty crates and start chatting, then soon start up a song. They egg each other on, laughing and gesturing, clapping their hands and dancing around, each on her own. The children make a circle round them, and farther away, self-conscious and amused, are a few men.

A fat woman is the leader, and when laughter triumphantly takes hold, they sing nothing but songs which would have landed them in prison in colonial times. Yes, that's what is already being said – colonial days, as if they were a century, not just a year ago. In the end, fifty market women are clapping in time to revolutionary songs, thinking up new ones in the meantime.

'Frelimo's rooster, it crowed cock-a-doodle-do, it is dawn

cock-a-doodle-do, Frelimo's rooster crowed right in the middle of the day . . .'

The rooster is Frelimo's rousing symbol in this country of illiterate people. Imitating animal sounds is an African song tradition. Then they sing roughly as follows:

*Now we'll begin to understand
though we've always understood.
And what have we understood?
That freedom is here
and more shall we have.
But not because of them
but because of us.
For we are Frelimo, Frelimo, that's us.*

The song has many variations, starting as a hymn and ending like a traveller's song. The women joyfully seize mangoes and pineapples and lift them up above their heads. A woman so old she can hardly walk is lifted up by strong arms. Viva Frelimo! the women cry to her. But she says nothing and is inscrutable. Perhaps she is thinking that youthful activities are fleeting and now they are once again doing something they will have to pay dearly for.

A boy onlooker is wearing a jersey with the Frelimo flag on the front. He has a madonna amulet round his neck, a US army badge on one shoulder and FBI on the other. He has covered himself in this way.

Apart from fish, trading of other kinds is going on. Parasols shade pineapples, paprikas, cabbages and sweet potatoes. Tomatoes are stacked in pyramids as when one plays marbles. Salt is heaped in various quantities. Dried tobacco leaves are being ground into snuff. A woman is suckling her child as she mixes a *caril de amendoim*, prawns, groundnuts and tomatoes.

A typical assortment arrayed on a trestle table is as follows: baby powder, enamelled plates, insulating tape, bottles of soft drinks, mirrors, a bunch of mlala twigs to be whittled into toothbrushes. Silver-framed portraits of Brigitte Bardot and Elvis Presley – remainders from some agency's wares for the young – and the first pictures of the President, Samora Machel. Cheap thermos flasks in which to keep water. Pants and bras from Macao, the Portuguese colony of fireworks and gambling in Asia.

A Frelimo soldier with a dried fish in his belt appeals to the women to keep their prices down and not speculate in the food-shortage. Children and vegetables are being washed under a pump covered with verdigris and with an iron lion spouting water. The soldier stops and drinks. I ask him what he is doing. Frelimo has ordered a freeze on wages in the towns so that the countryside can catch up, so it is important that the prices in the market don't rise.

'I was an errand-boy in the main office of the sugar-factory,' he tells me. 'The management said that if Frelimo attacks our plantations, we'll line you up in the corridor here and shoot you. I escaped and got a job as cook in Vila Pery. Frelimo attacked the area and I ran away and joined Frelimo at the new year in 1974.'

Water is cheaper than alcohol, says a notice on the public lavatory. Sales of beer in Lourenço Marques have broken all records since the revolution. Save, build houses, clean up at home, says Frelimo.

The flies swarm above sun-dried blackened meat that will keep for months as long as it isn't exposed to damp. The women's shoulders are bare. They wrap the cloth round their breasts and let it fall to their knees. Their plaited hair makes them look like pin-cushions. There is a liveliness about the trading of their grain and spices which is quite out of proportion to the income they receive for it. It is a question of spheres of power – they are defending their own products.

For the women, this era must be quite revolutionary. They see their own conditions being changed alongside those of the children, much faster than the men's. They look you straight in the eye and are no longer timid exotic creatures. They are prepared to go into offices, and next year, they will be found as bus-drivers and builders. The barriers are being torn down. Owing to ingrained habit, the last profession that will be open to them is probably fishing.

I remember the Governor in Beira, Comrade Mendonca, sighing as I came in.

'I've got a problem. I don't really know what to do.'

A woman Frelimo leader had made a speech on women's

rights. As it was the women who brought up the children, they had to study, and the men ought to learn to wash clothes, cook food and till the fields. The man reporting this in *Noticias de Beira* had gratuitously commented on this, saying that despite the revolution, we have not yet changed the planetary system, and her demands were beyond all boundaries of good sense. Should he call on Comrade reporter and ask him to be more objective in his news? Should he have someone write a counter-article?

In a shady corner of the market, I read one of Samora Machel's many speeches on women, one he wrote before the revolution:

'Women are the most oppressed, humiliated and exploited people in society. A woman is also exploited by the man who is himself used. She is beaten by the man who is himself beaten by the Palmatorian, degraded by the man who is crushed beneath the boot of the boss and the colonialist. How can the revolution succeed without the women being liberated? How do we abolish exploitation if one section of society continues to be oppressed? You cannot pull up half the weeds without even stronger weeds spreading from the half that has survived . . .

'How can we guarantee a revolutionary upbringing of the generation who are to continue our work, if the mothers, the first educators, are left on the edge of revolutionary development . . . Women are aware of their subjection and need to change their situation. Society's dominance can crush their initiative and prevent them from thinking about how to start their struggle. . . . The idea of waiting until later to liberate women is wrong, entailing reactionary concepts getting a foothold, and we don't start opposing them until they have become strong. It is like not fighting the crocodile on the shore, but preferring instead to attack it in midstream . . .

'Knowledge has always been regarded as the monopoly and exclusive domain of men, in civilisations of the past, just as in today's capitalist societies. Keeping knowledge from women is to prevent them discovering that society is created to function in the service of certain interests, and it is impossible therefore to change society. . . . We have to realise that centuries of subjection have to a great extent reduced them to a state of

passivity and even blinded them to their own predicament . . .
'For us, love can only exist between free and equal people sharing the same ideals and involvement . . . The moral and emotional empathy that love entails is based on that foundation. We need to discover this new dimension, hitherto unknown in this country.'

I wander around the townships in Lourenço Marques, Silex, Zilhatha, Chipamanine. Nowadays, a main asphalted road runs through them all. It was put down so that the Portuguese police had free access. The houses are numbered. That was also done during the war, for the police to find their way.

It is strange walking here. During the Portuguese occupation, everything was different. I remember a white man pointing at the slums and saying, 'A few whites live there, too. Side by side with Africans.' As if this made the slums excusable. South Africans tell you they have crushing racial problems and the world misunderstands the solutions they have chosen. The Portuguese tell you they have no race problem, so the world should not chase after a solution of a non-existent problem.

Now the atmosphere is happier and lighter. No one appears to be afraid. The hippo-whip glimpsed behind the door of white houses has been put away. No one curtseys or bows, and neither is there any fear of strangers. That is unusual in Africa. The blacks in Lourenço Marques were for a long time forced to live on the wrong side in the war. Their morale was low and led to lying, opportunism and revenge. But Frelimo's mental decolonisation seems already to be successful.

The long road to independence has also been of some psychological advantage to the whites. Salazar and Caetano clung to colonialism for so long that its rottenness was revealed to large numbers of Portuguese. Portugal took raw materials, manufactured them into goods, then sold them back to Mozambique at high prices. Many people became embittered and Frelimo acquired secret adherents, especially among the soldiers and younger members of the middle class.

To hear leading Portuguese today talking about the colonialism they obviously detested all their lives does appear a trifle unreal. They say things that a few years earlier would have been high treason.

'It's strange,' says Vitor Crespo, the last Governor-General, 'that we, a poor country and a suffering and oppressed people, have been forced to copy the other imperialists to satisfy the pride and selfishness of a powerful ruling minority.'

On my way through the slums, I am joined by Josefata Machel, brother of the President and his double – many people greet the wrong person. He is philosophically calm and friendly – although he is a busy co-ordinator of Frelimo's activities in Lourenço Marques. After eight years in prison, he was released a few months before the coup. People constantly come up to us to exchange a few words, mostly older men. They are members of commissions or councils Frelimo started up in every township. They are responsible for the water supply, cleansing, re-painting, literacy and public order. It has become meaningful to work. Their will to resist has turned into a sense of themselves. Perhaps only during this transitory stage between two systems do the problems appear so simple, as if the whole of Mozambique were willingly and enthusiastically spelling its way word by word through a huge open primary school reader.

'When we sow cassava, cassava grows. When we sow nothing, weeds grow,' Machel says.

That's right, they say, nodding and studying the posters in the slums. The United Nations declaration of human rights is there. So is advice against accepting bribes and accumulating possessions, and exhortations to get rid of class barriers, to live modestly in harmony with neighbours, to think about the sacrifices liberation has entailed, to bear in mind that every action may have a political content.

Students write and stencil easily understood posters. Be on your guard against rumours, don't spread rumours, they say. Don't become victims of confusion and fear. When a patrolling Portuguese soldier dropped a grenade by mistake and some people were injured, the radio at once broadcast that this was not provocation.

Vigilance, one of the three Frelimo key words, does not mean another political police force, says one poster. It means being on guard against racism and tribalism: the enemy within putting the interests of the group before those of the people.

The sand moves when it rains in the slums and the drains don't function. At the moment, it is dry, the sun shining clearly, the garbage trucks driving at night. There are pumps at frequent intervals. I see hens and pigeons, but hardly any dogs and cats. Everywhere, people are making chairs, building walls, putting on roofs.

'Hullo, baas,' African boys say, cheekily ironic. They think I'm from South Africa.

The people make the slums human. Their lives appear to be more dignified and natural than life in the high-rise blocks in the centre of Lourenço Marques, where a number of Africans also live. I remember the children at a boarding-school who couldn't be persuaded to sleep in bunk-beds – they have to have contact with the ground to be able to sleep. It is also easy to talk to teenagers here. They lack the usual sullenness and aggression of adults.

The main problems in the shanty-towns are water and ignorance. Radio Mozambique patiently gives instruction in hygiene and the care of children. But public order is good in this apparently disorderly world of thousands of tin shacks. People are visible, busy doing something, and social control must be almost complete, the opposite of Soweto outside Johannesburg, where a million blacks are shut in at night, white police and black gangsters making the nights lawless.

Here and there, a smart car stands outside a shack. There are coloured prints of saints and political leaders on the walls, but no furniture. The corrugated iron roof is anchored down with stones, the floor earth or concrete. Hollow-cheeked old people sit in the shade of a fig-tree – they have seen everything. The church is empty. Catholic missionaries, probably often instruments of dictatorship, have fled from the suburbs. Neither does religion play nearly the same rôle as it does in Latin America.

Two children are sitting doing their homework underneath a table laden with pineapples, lemons and mangoes for sale. Other children are playing ball in the sandy street. A boy is bowling a car-wheel along with sticks. Football Club 007 is training on a field. The undertaker is doing no trade – the white lily is of plastic, as is the armchair set out for the mourner. The proprietor is sitting on it now, the radio instructing him on what is wrong with private enterprise as he eats his maize porridge and fried fish. His firm will shortly be taken over by the community.

The photographer's studio consists of a room with chequered linoleum on the floor and a jar of plastic flowers recommended as background to group photographs. A watchmaker, bald and stripped to the waist, takes the magnifying-glass out of his eye and asks me to take his six boys to a Swedish school – all honour to Frelimo, but the classes are too large.

The children go to their classes at the school in the morning, adult women in the afternoon. The teachers are students of every colour working for nothing in their free time. Illiteracy among the women is ninety-nine per cent and the highest in Africa. Schools for whites and blacks were not integrated until the Sixties, officially, though not in practice. The government then also took over the responsibility from the church, although most of the teachers of black children continued to be appointed and paid for by the Catholic Church.

The number of black children in school doubled during the Sixties. An educated labour force was needed and it was important to show the liberation movement that Portugal stood for a better alternative. Of the 350,000 children the Portuguese stated were pupils in primary schools in 1965, only 230,000 went to the preparatory year. In 1968, there were eight Africans at university.

A teacher in the slums tells me about the new school. Anyone who had just left the final year is not to be in any way superior to anyone who had to leave in the middle. One can be productive in all fields. Everyone is to be able to read and write, but most things can be learnt outside school, at home, from the old, in agriculture. Who says illiterates are ignorant? On the other hand, parents are not to make the children stay at home because they are useful at harvest time and for household chores.

'Studying for a career is alien to us. It's easy to think yourself stupider than others, just because you've gone to school late in life, or because there's little space at home to sit and work. Differences in privilege are often taken for differences in talent.'

In every district, in the wealthy residential areas as well, Frelimo followers have formed Grupos Dimanizadores. A number of younger whites do so in secret, because their friends call them traitors. Others have been shocked by the contempt of their friends and have broken with them and found new friends. A girl tells me that her boy-friend tried to stop her teaching in the evenings and said: 'What do you think savages will do with the alphabet? Forge certificates and cook the accounts. And classrooms are disguised brothels.' So she had said goodbye to him for ever.

The first lesson for the women in Chipamanine is syllables associated with Frelimo. Fru fra fri lu la lo mu mi ma. Frelimo appears gradually out of obscurity. Then they move on to the colours in the flag and important words such as water, fresh, sun, work, health. They sing songs about united Mozambique and the liberation which started in the north and moved southwards. Singing, they learn the names of the provinces by counting out the places they will defend.

A similar lesson is going on outside the classroom at the same time, in the shade of a tree. The younger girls are also learning to spell and read according to the famous method of the Brazilian Paolo Freire. In two months, they will have learnt to read and write sufficiently for ordinary everyday purposes. It goes more quickly if 'Mother washes' is replaced with 'work for all, compulsion for none.'

I see a people's army in the service of knowledge, an educationalist's dream. Classrooms in the open air, no walls and everyone wanting to join in. I think about the marching sons of the workers in 1890s Sweden:

Are you with us on the road to the mind
through the dark morass of prejudice blind?
Are you with us ploughing knowledge's field
as the gold from the rock is revealed?

After the lesson, I go home with one of the girls. Her father died in the war, her mother and twenty year-old sister work in a textile factory, and her seventeen year-old brother is a carpenter. They are middle-class Africans with a fine corrugated iron house, a well-swept floor, paraffin lamps and a radiogram run off a car-battery. A jar of plastic flowers stands on a red crocheted cloth, a shell on the sideboard, a painted biscuit tin lid is used as wall decoration and there is also a newspaper photograph of the football team the son plays in. Above the mother's bed is a photograph of her dead husband in a raincoat. Wearing a lot of clothes is a sign of wealth and esteem.

The family pays about fourteen pounds a month in rent. Monthly wages at the factory have just been raised to sixty-five pounds.

The yard has been tidily raked. Beneath a shady canopy roofed with grass is the kitchen – a beaten earth hearth and a few stones. The girl sizzles some fish in the frying-pan and comes back in. A blindingly white bra is hanging on the line, a store of fuel stands in the corner. The toilet is a hole in the sand inside a special enclosure of reeds. The neighbouring woman is sitting on her porch selling nuts. She is a dressmaker, her husband a long-distance truck driver.

Nearby, there are some barracks in a square round a yard, two large trees and a few maize plants. Single people live there, or people whose families are elsewhere. They have a room each, so small the bed and mattress are propped up during the day. A shelf above the bed with mosquito-powder and tea on it. The walls bulge.

Chores are being done in the yard at a calm pace. One man is polishing chairs, another mending a motor-bike. A woman is washing, another filling an iron with glowing charcoal. Two women are lazing on a raffia mat, indicating that they are resting after a hard night. Frelimo is struggling against prostitution. They get up, pour paraffin out of the lamp on to the charcoal hearth, then light it and put maize-cobs on to roast.

Someone is cooking groundnuts and prawns in a pan. Oilcloth is hanging out to dry. The hens fall silent, the rooks quieten into black spheres in the dusk. I am offered small green bananas, steamed and wrapped in leaves. I am told you can kill chameleons by pouring snuff into their mouths. A boy is playing the flute on a bicycle-pump with holes on it. Another has fastened a shank and a few strings on to an oil-can and the sound of this guitar is not the same as it would be if it were a Texaco can with its special soldering.

There is an inescapable beauty in these African townships. It comes from the people, their warmth and capacity for endurance – until now, when their hopes for the future have been given firmer ground. But the beauty also lies in every single thing being used, as vessels, pails, toys or shelves. Anyone who wishes to study how to preserve what exists, with cunning and without purchasing anything new, should go into African homes.

A hundred thousand people live here, in tin shacks built on shifting sands which the heavy rainfall moves. All round them is the white city of skyscrapers, dazzling and apparently inaccessible. But on the Ginger Ale bottle painted upon the wall, the top is in Frelimo colours these days. Things fizz below.

6. The Last Garrison

From Vila Cabral, four thousand, two hundred feet above sea level, on the fertile plateau of Mozambique east of Lake Nyasa, I manage to get a seat in a Fokker Friendship chartered by the Portuguese army command. The plane is full of returning twenty year-olds in camouflage uniforms. We fly low through heavy thunder-clouds, lightning dancing on the wing. Down there on the ground, land-mines are still exploding, killing someone every day, although it will soon be a year since the revolt in Lisbon.

The African plateau is splattered with huge blocks of granite, Stonehenge and the menhirs of Brittany in different form, and there, too, yellow thorn grows at their feet. But no one maintains they are pillars of unknown temples or sightlines of a prehistoric observatory. In the trembling heat, they resemble sunken cathedrals in an ocean of air, or underwater reefs piling up for invisible ships.

The world's most ancient primaeval mountain – the central African plateau – has crumbled away and become earth, but here and there these enormous blocks remain standing. They have escaped erosion, just as a huge vertebra is sometimes all that remains of an elephant. Sometimes there are clefts at their very tops and seeds of trees land in them, strike root, and soon green foliage is waving in the wind, a plume in a primaeval hat.

Then we land outside Nampula and the pilot drives me to

the town's hotel. From this place – a small town – General Kaulza de Arriaga directed the Portuguese anti-guerilla operations. This is where the napalm bombs against villages and crops were stored and where prisoners were brought for questioning, torture and execution.

The jukebox is in action in the hotel bar. A couple of air-taxi pilots complain about no longer being able to fly either officers or tourists. But they are going to stay. Things are worse in Portugal. Marcello Caetano's portrait has been replaced by Samora Machel's. But the frame is the same and fills the same square on the dirty wall.

New posters have been pasted on the façades of houses, on top of colonial appeals. They proclaim 'One Single Aim – Independence. One Single Force – the People. One Single Guide – Frelimo' 'Down With Racism – we are Mozambiquans, black, white, mestitsa and others. We are part of international society.'

One of Frelimo's most famous guerilla leaders, Comrade Panguene, has moved into the Governor's villa. He says with a laugh that his predecessor put a price of thousands of pounds on his head. That same man was now in Portugal, though just where is not clear. Panguene offers me orange juice at his headquarters. Not a single piece of furniture or picture has been moved. Governors stare down from the walls. But in the guest cloakroom, children's toothbrushes stand in a row, and now and again a soldier steps in onto the wall-to-wall carpeting, is given an order and vanishes, apparently unmoved by the splendour.

In the Governor's decrepit car with its pennant on its radiator, the journey goes on through the night to the island of Mozambique. The windows are down, the road full of potholes and we are flung hither and thither, although our speed is not great. Wild pigs, their back hairs on end, rush ahead of us. A galago or a bushbaby flings itself between the trees, an uneasy glowing satellite in lower space.

Ten minutes of rain. The thunderous noise as if we had lost our silencer. Afterwards, the stars re-appear, newly washed.

Another shower at dawn. Breakfast is served on the dot of six at the hotel facing the sea, black clouds on the eastern horizon, hooked to each other like goods wagons. They are slowly moving sideways, sending up spirals of paler vapour. I am told it is a female cyclone having a rest out in the Mozambique channel. In the evening, she will perform for the Cormores, whose shaken audience will not forget her in a hurry. (But in Australia, the government of the day decides that from then on, cyclones can have male names.)

In the fortress of San Sebastian, the oldest and largest on the east coast of Africa, guns point in towards the mainland as well as out to sea. On every corner of the huge walls is a whitewashed Christian cross. The guns and the church presuppose each other. The building of the fortress began in 1508 and this is where the first Christian church south of the equator was built – in 1503.

In 1498, Vasco da Gama sailed into the town of Mozambique, long since inhabited by Arabs and Persians. He captured a canoe, and according to the logbook found in it 'fine cotton cloth, baskets plaited from palm leaves, a glazed butter jar, small bottles of perfume, some Mohammedan prayer books, a box of cotton thread, baskets of millet grain, a fishnet of cotton'. Judging from the description, material standards here were as high as in Portugal of the day.

This is where the white man had his first permanent residence south of the equator. Mozambique Island remained the country's capital for four hundred years.

During the seventeenth century, the Portuguese vainly tried to exploit the country's legendary wealth of gold and silver. Merchants competed with each other and worked together with Arabs. Malaria and yellow fever raged. No authority could count on total obedience, for people lived too far away from each other. Tete in upper Zambezi had twenty men in its fort, and a few Jesuits and soldiers lived on the borders of what is Rhodesia today. The King in Portugal sent impractical instructions to them on how to work mines which even today have not been found worth exploiting.

With the help of sailing-ships, Portugal wanted to conquer half the world and create an ocean empire mightier than that of Alexander. But there were not enough people to administer such a scattered realm. The beginning of the eighteenth century was a period of decay which lasted for two hundred years. Contact with India virtually ceased and missions became rarer.

In the places where they were not abandoned, in the interior of Mozambique, in Tete, for instance, some whites stayed on and created a multi-racial community with its own laws and few communications with the outside world.

A large part of the interior would almost certainly have reverted to the Africans if the Hindus and Catholic Goanese from India had not emigrated there at the beginning of the nineteenth century. They established trading-posts in the Zambezi valley. They are still there today. The Portuguese and others regarded them as unwarranted rivals, calling them the Jews of Africa and refusing to admit to their great civilising influence.

Despite the talk of five hundred years of her presence in Africa, Portugal first started colonising Mozambique in the 1900s. The Africans resisted and were crushed in about 1920, and not until the second world war did the colony have its own administration. In the middle of the 1940s, the Portuguese in Mozambique amounted to only about three thousand people. White immigration occurred during the two decades before the 1974 revolt, and the whites by then amounted to 180,000, almost as many as the whites in Rhodesia.

Over half of these left the country again in 1975, among them almost all the doctors. For Frelimo, this entailed getting rid of their opponents, but also losing necessary specialists. The starting point of the new Mozambique is harsh: there are fewer educated Africans than in any other country of equivalent size.

In the San Sebastian fortress, I find the remnants of a Portuguese garrison. Boys of nineteen are washing their clothes and packing. They are half-naked and unarmed, sleeping below cool vaulted roofs in the cellars, as they would have done two hundred years before. They are pale, despite the sun, with black moustaches, and they look more like decadent poets from the turn of the century than modern warriors.

The garrison is departing. In a few days, Frelimo will take over the fort – an action of weighty symbolism, as it was here Vasco da Gama declared all visible land to be the property of the King of Portugal and placed it under the protection of the Christian god.

The statue of Vasco da Gama, wearing some kind of suit with shoulder-pads of grey stone, stands on a plinth on which there is the inscription 'Discoverer of Mozambique'. He is gazing over towards the mainland of Africa, insatiable, yet majestic. Sailing boats cross the sound with their cargoes. The air is still, though the sea shifts as always. The mainland is a green belt fringed at the bottom, and in amongst the green can be seen a few white marks, a church, a mission or a fortress.

No music comes from the pavilion by the statue, the Chinese grids are shabby, the yellow paint worn away by monsoons. The lamps are green, Victorian, but broken. A god and a goddess – demi-gods of Antiquity, half-good savages – lift the light up to non-existent musicians.

A long-legged brown girl in a very short dress walks into a pale green house in Travessa das Floras. She has stepped out of a Tauber song, but she lives here with her aunt in the school holidays only. Otherwise she is in the top class of a secondary school in Lourenço Marques. The town is small, and I find all this out before the end of the day.

The black women in the town whiten their faces in the daytime to keep their skin damp and protected from the sun. In the evenings, they take the pancake off again and drape themselves in colourful materials, while the men are usually dressed in what the white man has discarded from his wardrobe. No national costumes as in Nigeria, or religious gowns as in the Islamic countries, but shorts and shirts, uniforms and overalls.

The Governor, Estrela Baptista, sends a message that he is in the bath. While I wait in his old palace with its red wooden beams and white walls, I see sweating men unloading sacks of maize-flour from barges lying in the ebb-tide mud beside a warehouse owned by the Ferreira dos Santos trading company. One man goes halfway and when he meets another, the sack is slung from one head to another.

The Governor resembles a genial business man I meet every day on the Vaxholm ferry boat at home and who was living on Resar Island, which is slightly larger than Mozambique Island. The Governor leafs through the latest annual reports from Lourenço Zoo. He is on the board of the Zoological Society. He has sent a primate into captivity in the capital, but it has not reproduced itself.

'And the political prisoners here on the island,' I try, 'are they all free?'

'Long ago,' he replies lightly. 'No one knows where they've gone. Clever people, Frelimo. You could say we have made them what they are.'

He talks about anything and everything but goes no deeper. I have missed a huge wedding. I ought to try some mango chutney made by his friend from Goa, a merchant called Ginwala.

'Sweden must be a peculiar country,' he says. 'No wine, but the water is said to be good. How is it you ended up so far north?'

He is just about departing. Mozambique Island will cease to be the Governor's province, and will be united with Nampula. I imagine he's managed to salt away quite a bit of money, or so his optimism implies. He has a past in Timor and Macao. The man who has never travelled always praises his mother's cooking, he quotes from an African saying.

He returns to zoology. Have I really missed the red admiral, the butterfly, not Rosa Coutinho, Angola's president for the moment? From his headquarters we had just heard the brown-breasted cuckoo call in a fig tree. He knows no other person who has heard it. With that experience in his luggage, he will leave Africa.

If Mozambique Island were slightly cooler, it could be a place of retreat for retired people who like strolling about, taking tea and green wine at a pavement café or picking over materials in a Goanese shop. All those people who have been shot or hanged throughout the centuries can no longer be heard, the blood on the walls disappearing beneath the constantly renewed plastering the damp makes necessary.

White school children from Beira are celebrating the weekend at the only hotel, dancing the shakes throughout the night. It is a rare occurrence. At breakfast, the girls are asleep at the table, the mild January wind forming skin on their *café-au-lait*. A metallic shimmering weaver-bird in a plaited reed cage has lost its gloss and died.

On dim mosquito-netted verandas in the town, lemonade is served to Portuguese children. The owners are waiting, unable to decide whether to leave or see things out; the annual 'spring-cleaning' is postponed, dust settles on the bust of a Lusitanian poet, and wallpaper loosens, its heart-shaped green leaves melancholy and withering.

This is the end of a widespread coastal empire. On the island, nothing but the connection with the past is felt, and now the threads have been cut. The soldiers leave their fortress with their rusting double bunks, saucepans, water-bottles and souvenirs. They add to several centuries of graffiti with their own names, imagining their initials will speak of their time in Africa. The merchant ship *Marcello Caetano*, not yet renamed, is anchored out on the coral reef, where the water is as clear as a childhood aquarium of zebra fish, neon fish and Black Mollys.

7. Cabora Bassa – end of an empire

Tete in north-east Mozambique, by the Zambezi river, is one of the hottest places on earth. You think you're at the end of the world, although it is only two hundred and forty miles from Salisbury, the capital of Rhodesia. But no one ever dares travel that way. In actual fact, you find yourself where this five hundred-year old empire came to an end. For when Frelimo advanced into Tete province, the whole basis of Portuguese government crumbled. This was where the cruellest massacres took place, reported by missionaries who were then imprisoned or deported. Their testimonies made the whole world realise that the civilian population was being ruthlessly exterminated in Portugal's colonies.

Here in Tete province, the Cabora Bassa dam became a symbol of inhuman technical civilisation, which without any consultation with Africans moved them in their thousands from their homes, to build a dam that was to provide electricity not to African villages, but to South Africa's gold mines.

It was also here in Tete that the establishment of good relations between the warring factions – after the April coup in Lisbon – was at its best. Portuguese boys with no particular love for fascism were sent here. At the beginning of 1974, the Frelimo were only about twelve miles away from Tete.

Three hundred years before, six hundred emigrants had

settled round the fort in Tete, and women with no parents were promised dowries by the government if they married white men. On his journey across the continent of Africa, Livingstone arrived there, sick and exhausted. He thought he was dying, but he recovered when he saw Tete.

For other people it was probably the opposite; the sight of these ten dusty streets in a cauldron by a sluggish brown river, the air boiling and the temperature forty-three Celsius in the shade, made them reluctant to stay. But if you are looking for a timetable, there is nothing that fits at the travel agency, posters of long-since cancelled tours of Lake Nyasa (Lake Malawi in English today) on the walls, or maybe a military plane will tomorrow, or the next day . . .

When I come to places like this, I feel it is important where one dies. Look thy last on all things lovely – but they are not here, at least not to the untrained eye. Everything depends on your starting-point. Livingstone was pleased, because he came from Zambia's marshlands and thought the sea was within reach.

War made Tete flourish. The main garrison defending Cabora Bassa was here, which meant a few apartment blocks along the asphalt road, dusty streets down by the river, plus a petrol station, a café, a stationer's and a cloth-dyers. Wind and cars swirled the sand high up on to windowsills, ventilators and lamp-posts.

The moneyed – the soldiers – gather on the Zambezi Hotel's roof-terrace in the evening. They are quiet, have a steak and drink beer and Coca-Cola. Not a single woman, except a gruff old lady in reception. The bar with its padded seats and high stools is an imitation of the great world, and outside, the cold arc-lights glare above the bridge across the river.

The white-clad waiters earn about fifteen pounds a month. Unemployment is high and hotel servants sleep ten to a washroom. Not that the guest rooms are much better. An old-fashioned shower shakes its head when you turn on the tap and not until you have forgotten it exists does it produce a spurt of rusty water which soon runs out. Then the cockroaches rush out, lured by the damp, and you are forced to leap onto the iron bedstead, which squeals all night like some tormented creature.

A game of football is played at midnight on an illuminated pitch to a huge audience. People are asleep along the walls of houses. The temperature has fallen to twenty-eight Celsius. Players and audience are silent. Once every half-hour, a car crosses the Zambezi. A placard outside the stationer's urges all those who can read to volunteer for the literacy campaign.

A fire is smoking outside a house which reminds me of old bathing-huts by the sea in Nynäs Harbour in Sweden. There are still glimmers of light behind the shutters. A hibiscus tree glows in the darkness and Orion is immediately above, upside-down. A radio mast winks on a distant mountain, the only communications here being signals from mast to mast.

In the morning, the Frelimo comrades arrive, full of goodwill and anxieties. They want to do everything for me, but they can't. The roads are either flooded or mined. The Portuguese have taken every single helicopter. The car-rental firm has not rented out a car for several years.

In the end, Comrade Neves finds a jeep that works, and we drive over seventy-five miles through numerous road-blocks to Cabora Bassa. Neves comes from a village near Beira and has had six years schooling. The priest signed the application form stating that he wanted to go on, but he was not allowed to. He made his way north and joined Frelimo. His father and brother worked on a cotton plantation, seven days a week for tenpence a day plus food and a pair of trousers per year.

Eventually, Neves was sent as commander-in-chief of Tete province. He points at rolling undergrowth along the road.

'We ambushed military transports from there. The Portuguese responded by bombing and shooting. Every field here has its dead. The Portuguese were easily deceived and cowardly. We attacked, then the whole unit came, and we attacked in another direction, the unit was scattered, and we went through the lines in a third place. In March 1974, we were within two and half hours' marching distance of Cabora Bassa. But we didn't want to destroy it.'

A white observation plane now flies peacefully over the area. A baboon family flees and birds flash like emeralds through the air. The grass in the rainy season is soft and brittle as in Sweden, not the coarse kind used for covering roofs. Africans move over the fields with buckets on their heads and stakes in their hands. Soon the power cables from the dam start winking in the sun, double cables swooping across maize fields and green hills.

'The Portuguese took hostages, attacking the innocent,' Neves tells me. 'As soon as the Portuguese walked into a land-mine, they would destroy the nearest village. The murdered people were counted in the statistics as Frelimo soldiers. Frelimo got a great many new recruits. If the village had really laid the mines, it would have moved. The Portuguese took Africans directly from the missions, led them out into the sea, told them to clap their hands, and then they shot them. They dressed their own black soldiers in Frelimo uniforms, forced them to plunder and rape in a village and filmed it all for their own propaganda purposes. They bought poisonous defoliants, napalm and monitoring apparatus with American money. But they were not skilful with them. There was always something that did not function. Mozambique is not like Vietnam. It is almost impossible to telephone anyone in this country. Now we can re-build and forget.'

Joao Neves has his machine-gun with him in the jeep. You get used to armed idyll that quickly, because you consider machine-guns serve a good purpose. Neves' task is to keep himself informed about the needs of Frelimo posts for arms and supplies.

We visit the Chamba *aldeamento*, a strategic village the Portuguese had constructed. Over a million Africans were taken during the war to similar fenced village camps, where many died of starvation or while 'attempting to escape'. Neves gets the inhabitants together and explains that they are free to live where they like, but Frelimo would prefer them to stay. A school has just been started and a soldier will help them with cultivation and looking after the goats.

The huts are of grass and mud, the old people look weary, the children undernourished and with ruptured navels. Women naked to the waist pound away at the maize with long poles. A boy is shooting with a catapult, some black pigs are rushing about. Up until about a month or so ago, the inhabitants thought the Portuguese ruled the province. They had been forcibly moved from the dam, where the waters rose over their homes and the graves of their ancestors. They would have preferred to have been drowned, but that was not allowed, some were shot, so they moved.

The Frelimo soldier helped them tell us that by moving, they seem to have lost contact with the land. They can hardly summon up the energy to keep alive. Yet the area is fertile, the maize green and straight, and there is no reason for them to starve.

Frelimo want to transform the *aldeamonto*, a concept similar to a concentration camp, into something positive, a core of civilisation in the low forest, a production centre with a collectively run mill, a veterinary station, a store, a school, a district nurse, and a citizen's committee for the welfare of the area. And round the village, the maize will stand as tall as a man, the papaya trees laden with fruit, the bananas turning from green to yellow, both small sweet bananas and coarse apple-bananas. Porcupines and mongoose will rustle about and the old will soon rest in the earth and become the forefathers of the coming generation, thus blessing this ground, too, the ground to which they once were moved in despair and under useless resistance.

We come to Songo, a town constructed for workers and technicians at the Cabora Bassa dam. It reminds me of Lamcos Yekepa in Liberia, but it is simpler. At the army-post we are met by the Frelimo commander, Thai, and a Portuguese lieutenant-colonel. They joke and thump each other's backs.

'We're friends,' says the Portuguese. 'The victory is ours and theirs, the defeat fascism's. And our commandant is in prison.'

Comrade Neves catches sight of a white sergeant and exclaims: 'I've seen you through my binoculars several times. Lucky I never shot you!'

They thump each other. The war seems a distant nightmare, a disastrous misunderstanding.

'Didn't you understand what was going on?' I ask a young lieutenant.

'Well, I did,' he says. 'But I came here four months before the April coup. I was a militant communist in Lisbon.'

He is doing his national service and is going to return to his studies. One of his friends says: 'We were told nothing. We had blinders on. Now we can see and listen quite freely and suddenly you understand a whole lot of things. But we

respected the Frelimo. We noticed they didn't want to kill us.'
White soldiers set off with some Frelimo men to detonate mines laid by both sides.

The Portuguese death patrols, the famous commando units, have been imprisoned or sent home. The soldiers left behind are young national servicemen, some of them unable to read, and a Frelimo comrade is helping them make out their letters from home. We see a white hand and a black hand on an African boy's teeshirt – unity. We find ourselves a mile or so from villages where bestial massacres took place a few years earlier. This idyll is one of the most remarkable I have ever come across.

'There was a rumour that the water was bad here,' a Portuguese corporal says. 'So we went in for drinking wine and beer and whisky. We weren't good at fighting.'

We go on to the Zambezi and the dam. The sun has heated the rock so that it burns through your sandals. It is difficult to stand still. Below, the water-level is slowly rising, drowning abandoned dwellings. Along the edges of the ravine, tall tree tops protrude for the last time. Rotting underwater forests sway about in the depths.

The Zambezi, the fourth largest river in Africa, has a lonely, apparently prehistoric course, and it flows for sixteen hundred miles from the highlands of Angola through Zambia and Rhodesia and out into the Indian Ocean in Mozambique. It passes no large towns, and no civilisation has arisen around its banks. Not until the Sixties and Seventies did it meet its fate. The two deep ravines where the river hurtles down from the central plateau of Africa – Kariba and Cabora Bassa – have been closed off by dams.

Cabora Bassa was said by Livingstone to be 'the place where the hard work stops'. The river below the falls was navigable, then a hundred and fifty miles to the coast. The main fall is three hundred feet. The dam is 564 feet high. Its base 240 feet, the highest width 900 feet, the depth of water about 420 feet.' The dam will be 155 miles long with an area of water of 560 square miles, the largest artificial lake in the world.

The generating hall is a temple 180 feet high and 660 feet long. One and a quarter million tons of mountain have been blasted out and transported away to make room for underground chambers. Two parallel power cables, nearly a mile apart, run from here to Irene, near Pretoria. The current from Cabora Bassa will probably be twice as cheap as the coal-fired electricity of South Africa.

They are starting producing eighteen thousand million kilowatt hours per annum, rising to forty-five. The Aswan dam produces ten. The dam-building project has been financed through export credits from France; in round figures, forty million pounds, from Germany sixty-five million, from South Africa thirty million. Siemens built the power-station, AEG Telefunken the transformer-station, the Italians the power cables when Swedish ASEA were forced to back out so as not to break the boycott of Rhodesia.

Since 1969, the technicians in Songo have lived under siege, behind innumerable barbed wire fences, security guards and road checks. Songo had ten thousand inhabitants, though now many have left, but a line of thirty-five ton trucks still streams up and down between the high plateau and the lower part of the ravine.

For Mozambique, Cabora Bassa, over and above the income from South Africa, means it will be possible to drain the marshlands, make dry fields flourish, cultivate two and half million acres in the Zambezi valley and, with cheap electricity, exploit Tete province's iron, copper, manganese, uranium and coal.

The power-cables are now protected by Frelimo, who say the dam belongs to the people and is to benefit everyone. Comrade Neves speaks with enthusiasm for this country which is now his; sawmills and pulp factories in the north, iron mines in Tete, tourists on the endless white sandy beaches. The Portuguese listen benignly.

For me, it is exceptional to be in this secretive corner of Africa. For years it was kept hermetically sealed from the outside world; Cabora Bassa, heat of forty degrees Celsius and more inaccessible than the south pole. Long before the dam was thought of, this roadless province was as good as barricaded off to tourists. Only those on their way from Rhodesia to Malawi could stop overnight in the town of Tete, but there were few who indulged in that experience.

In 1959, I was living east of Salisbury in Rhodesia, near the main road to Umtali along the border and on into Mozambique.

'Portuguese East Africa' it said on the notices. The white families I knew went there once a year to breathe the lowland air. They went swimming in Beira over Christmas or at Easter flew to the Paradise Islands outside the town of Vilanculos. There were also islands without restaurants, where you lived in huts, swam with harpoons in the coral reefs and came home with a swordfish. Hunting licences were expensive, because there were animals which would never dare stick their noses inside Rhodesia. People were hunted freely. Animals belonged to a more exclusive species.

My visit to Mozambique that time was brief. I was given a visa in my capacity as a wild-life poet and butterfly-collector living in Salisbury. But when the poem appeared in article form, I was deported 'for life'. That life lasted sixteen years.

Afterwards I remembered best the small guest house and cafés, where hefty Portuguese women stood by the stove grilling thin slices of meat in olive oil, which were served on rickety rusty tables together with wine from Dao and Estramadura that had gone sour on the journey. Alcoholism was noticeable. Some of the plantation managers paid their contract workers in wine and spirits, a way of getting them to stay for life and compliantly accept their conditions. The Africans made their own spirits by distilling the kidney-shaped cashew-nut, Mozambique's chief export.

I remember the subtle notices by two separate hatches at the post office: 'For telegrams handed in by the sender', and 'For telegrams handed in by messengers'. An African who could afford to send a telegram was not part of the equation. Apartheid – an inconceivable word – was economic: zone laws, rents and high prices at cinemas and restaurants were in practice enough to create a segregated way of life.

I remember the letter-boxes and their labels: Local – Portugal – Overseas. They are still there, but certainly not for much longer.

Begging was forbidden then, as now. In this Catholic subject state you were not allowed to save your soul by giving alms to the poor. A Portuguese told me the motive behind this. 'As all savages are born without possessions, it is only compared with us that the word poor can be applied to them. And that would be meaningless.' So the problem was evaded. People without possessions are not poor, but simply have another background.

Now it is sixteen years later, and I am travelling with Comrade Neves along the unmined road from Cabora Bassa to Tete. We stop by a river, its bed as good as dried up, but a thin rivulet runs here and there and then disappears. The women dig for water, scooping away the first dirty layer, then filling buckets and jars they carry on their heads. Where the rivulet is deepest, a group of women are washing, pounding and rinsing. They finish by undressing and pouring water over each other, old women, mothers with taut breasts, girls with strings of pearls round their waists. The young ones leap about laughing. Their customs and gestures are primaeval. At the same time, a long-distance truck thunders across the bridge, loaded with empty Manica beer bottles from the thirsty soldiers at Cabora Bassa.

'The war improved the road network,' says Neves. 'Asphalt roads are difficult to mine.'

But how were they built and how many hours of work for forced labourers, who did their military service for Portugal in this way? They worked almost naked, slept in tents by the roadside, fell ill from infected drinking water, and crept into the bush to die. There were others to replace them. Twenty barefooted men pushed the heavy roller over burning tar, the white foreman standing on the grass verge, irritated by the heat, and also harassed by the military commander who had to get his troops and supplies through.

There are other roads, the road which runs from Lourenço Marques north along the coast, for instance. It is stone-laid with small cubes of granite, and even today you can still pass small groups of Africans sitting hacking out stones. Their hammer-blows sound like an S.O.S. in morse, while vehicles stream past, night falls, and even the frogs start hooting like car horns.

So far, Frelimo has been mild to white landowners. Yet they are the people who recruited forced labour, took the best land, and had Africans cultivate it without giving them any part of the harvest. Where an African had one and half acres of land to support his family, a white man had an average of 570 for his, roughly the same proportion as in Rhodesia.

'We must show forbearing,' says Comrade Neves slowly, as

if he were reading out his homework or deep down doubting his own words.

'How can you?'

'We've waited for so many generations, we mustn't get carried away now. We have to show people who thought they were our enemies that we were fighting against a system which also kept them prisoners. We have liberated them as well. It'll take time for them to understand that. But if they try to take away from us what we've gained, then we'll hit back, then there'll be no forbearance, for we can fight for ten more years, yes, hundreds.'

'The Portuguese will probably try to,' I say. 'And when they don't succeed, they'll go. Then you'll have a vacuum to fill.'

'We'll fill that with ourselves, not with others. Outside, you'll all say Mozambique is sinking back to the Stone Age. But that's where we've been all the time, most of us.'

Then we're back again at the Frelimo party office in Tete, in the boiling cauldron of the Zambezi, and brown kites soar above us like a screen. When you kick out at the dense darkness, there's the clatter of empties and the buckle of Orion's belt.

8. Diary from Mozambique

Samora Machel's picture has been put up in the tea lounge of the Polana Hotel in Lourenço Marques; a jungle warrior, born in 1933, now in this Edwardian atmosphere, where over the years some millions of gallons of gin-and-tonic have gone through the human body.

I find a copy of *Traveller's Guide to Southern Africa* published in 1973. 'Mozambique is southern Africa's undiscovered paradise . . . Lourenço Marques is a miraculous synthesis of European sophistication and African drama . . . The Portuguese temperament, always sensitive to the environment, warmed in the European south, is naturally suited to Africa.'

The guerilla warfare of the time is indicated in one sentence:

'The province of Cabo Delgado has little to offer the tourist at the moment.'

The churchyard in Marracuene is a field run wild, an African herb garden, the white crosses sinking into the foliage, graves a flat piece of red earth, where the plants have been kept at bay. They are marked with a number plate. Some have faded roses or plastic lilies in a plastic bag on them, double protection from the fierce elements.

One grave is just being dug, two men hacking away at the soil, a third with a framework of coarse branches to measure the width of the grave. When they have finished, they sit down on the edge, mumbling and laughing. Death is familiar, regrets well known. Most people die in their villages, among people they are related to, swiftly committed to the soil because of the heat. They go to death in full view of many eyes, but some die far away from home, on contract work, on alien plantations. They can seldom be traced, for statistics and church records are not that good. They remind me of lonely people who die at home in Sweden and the social services put an announcement in the paper, signed Friends.

Friends – they are old people's homes in Sweden where everyone should feel one of a family. In Mozambique there are no such friends.

Frelimo's man in Marracuene and his Portuguese equivalent arrive and ask what we are doing among these decaying and overgrown graves. Do we wish to imply that Portugal also neglected her dead? In a quiet aside, the Frelimo man makes it clear he doesn't mind either way, but he has no wish to hurt the Portuguese unnecessarily.

Later, I am present when the five year-old son of a leading African is buried. The mother wailed and screamed by the grave, speaking in the child's voice in between. She was two people, mother and child. She gave her grief form to rid herself of it. The men stood at a distance, laughing and talking; life has to go on.

African women have to mourn for every other, or every third child. Milk, eggs and chicken are often tabu for pregnant women; after it is weaned, the child dies of too coarse and one-sided a diet.

One day, the country's largest newspaper doesn't come out. *Noticias*. The reason is the shortage of paper. Its colleague in Beira has to give news on its eight pages. Of these, one is devoted to advertisements, one to sport, one to information about Cuba, one to African news, one the rest of the foreign news, three to their own country. There is a daily column about Frelimo's activities, mostly the literacy campaign. Various comrades preach about honesty and helpfulness, warning against bureaucracy and high living.

The newspaper has become a school textbook and reader. It produces useful information on health and agriculture, on solidarity and the meaning of work. Its previous readership was a white élite. Now it has to reach the mass. It is being turned into a people's university in summary.

Freedom of the press as we know it will no doubt remain unknown in Mozambique for a long time ahead. Portugal allowed none. As only one in ten people can read – and not that well either – Frelimo reckons the task of the newspaper is less that of free debate than of practical information useful to the community.

There is no pre-censorship. Journalists are voluntarily restrained. They may not print military secrets or things that might disturb relations between races or encourage tribalism. So almost nothing is written about Portuguese atrocities. White experts are needed, so there is no need to add to burdens. The silence on massacres and murders is almost oppressively great. The whites have learnt how generously Frelimo treated their prisoners, but not that the Portuguese of the day tortured theirs to death. The PIDE agents have gone. They were released from prison in October, 1974, by white sympathisers, and were taken to South Africa.

The newspapers on sale are often a month or so old, weeklies sometimes several years. In some kiosks, for a very small sum you can borrow a ten year old magazine for the night. So you unexpectedly come across people talking about Princess Grace's wedding, or Churchill's funeral, as if they had been in today's paper.

Home of the Sun is the name of an abandoned guest house in Lourenço Marques, a low colonial house with a shady veranda.

Between the pillars with their imaginative capitals are basket chairs and worn cushions. You can sit there and watch the traffic.

The guest house is not locked when I try the door. It seems to have a nightwatchman. Someone has left a stick on a chair. Reception is a desk on which are a few brochures for those who want a quiet life in the city by the sea, close to the Tropic of Capricorn . . . but also for those who want to take some friends, a friend, to an intimate cocktail party in a garden which is not overlooked.

Quiet it certainly is. There seems to be no one either inside or out. A cat scratches soil over its excrement in the sand, lizards sleep in the cracks in the wall and the handsome trees in the English Consul-General's park can be seen in the distance. Buses pass on their way from MacMahon Place to Chipamanine, Africans hanging halfway out of them.

The guest house had once been secluded, but is now quite central – and empty. The hotel register is still there, the guest-list largely Portuguese; Rosaline Celeste Abalada, Aletta Villiers (South African), Adam Ibrahim Ismail. Names, identities . . . they have slept, showered, gone. Or moved to a better guest house: Pensao Princesa Patrica or the Aristocrata in Avenue 24 Julio.

'The owner? Dead, Señor, I mean Comrade.'

'His wife . . .'

'Ran it for a long time. But has fled, that is, moved. To South Africa probably. Her plan was to open a guest house in Swaziland, in the mountains, more tourists. If only she could sell . . .'

'Is it for sale?'

'Yes, but she doesn't advertise it. That would attract unauthorised people, thieves, robbers . . .'

He speaks uncertainly, briefly, the man I finally get hold of. He came in when he saw the door was open, an uneasy expression on his face, expecting anything.

I think I have been here before. There are other guest houses, on the border between Uganda and Zaire, also suddenly abandoned. Frightened whites, who paid their servants badly, simply left. They must have had money elsewhere. A desolation like that found in holiday houses locked up for the winter, familiar smells gradually becoming alien, and lonely, non-human objects and materials taking over, linoleum, curtains, mosquito nets, the air-conditioning apparatus choking with dust.

I remember a small inn outside Ndola in Zambia, what was then Northern Rhodesia. Belgian refugees were pouring in from Katanga and the landlady served lemon biscuits and ginger wine on a silver tray, reproducing French phrases, *quelque chose de terrible*, as if they transmitted the actual horror of being uprooted from the familiar. The glasses trembled on the tray and her chestnut hair flopped over her forehead as if it had come loose.

Leonel Wilson, twenty-four, a mulatto from two generations back, is with me as interpreter on certain assignments. He is a teacher and attending the top class of secondary school at the same time. He has been to Swaziland and South Africa as a small boy, but never to Europe. He was discharged from the army in September, 1974. He had fought with the Portuguese in Vila Cabral and in Tete. That was natural then. His father is a mechanic and has a garage. One brother manages a factory making tackle, fittings and other articles for ships. His cousins are doctors, musicians, football-trainers. He belongs to the middle classes.

'Was there any criticism in your circles before the coup?' I ask.

'My father wished Portugal in hell. He loathed the spying, the racism and the bureaucracy. We talked about it at home, or whispered in restaurants.'

'But nothing more?'

'It's impossible to be a conscientious objector. We heard about Frelimo atrocities when doing our military service. But in the evenings we listened to Frelimo radio. We realised they dared think freely, and we saw there was no need to be frightened. If we were taken prisoner, Frelimo wouldn't kill us. Luis Bernado Honwana's banned stories circulated secretly round national servicemen. We knew practically nothing about the rest of Africa.'

Leonel also tells me:

'Our sergeant took us to a ravine and told us that was where

Frelimo were. They could kill us all if they wanted to. But they didn't. We learnt to respect Frelimo. They were fewer than we were, but they had an aim. We didn't believe in what we were doing. A friend of mine came face to face with a Frelimo soldier. He expected to be shot. But the soldier turned away.'

'I can think with my eyes and ears now,' Leonel says. 'I don't believe propaganda any longer. I can start studying seriously and teach whatever I know. Life's beginning to have some point.'

The misanthropic young men and girls with bleached blond hair don't know what to do on the beach where Mozambique's whites gather on Saturdays. They wander about under the eucalyptus trees swaying in the wind before the monsoon, and the sand-banks in front of them stretch for miles and miles to the north.

A spaniel is scratching in the bushes, panting in heat he cannot have been created for, another sign of the unnecessary luxury of colonial life. People gather round bright parasols, tents, sports cars and station-wagons. They grill meat and swim. Some try to play poker, but the wind takes the cards, so they turn to dice. They appear untroubled, but are probably thinking they're being raised and lowered on waves of foreboding and expectation.

Far away, they can see African families in tight bunches, and Indians in the same direction. They don't mix. When the sun sets, lanterns light up announcing miniature golf and dancing. A jukebox starts up, but fades in the wind.

In the Seventh of March park in town, a small orchestra is playing in a rusty pavilion, hibiscus heads fall, and smart teenagers of all colours show off the latest fashions, smoking and leaning against each other.

It is a calm town in the evenings. Cicadas sing in flowering avenues, families sit at pavement cafés, drinking beer, orange juice and green wine. A lone Frelimo soldier is on patrol. The stars shine, competing with the merchant ships lying at anchor.

'The Portuguese did nothing,' says my friend Mario Mendoza. 'Just drank beer and ate sea-food.'

They still do – those not packing to return to the Portugal which has so suddenly shattered their pattern of life. The cafés are full, conversations in low voices and conspiratorial, but it is too late for a Portuguese Ian Smith, too late for white rebels. Frelimo is united, where Angola is divided. Mozambique is poor, whereas Angola is one of the richest countries, potentially at least. The great international companies know this. Mozambique is left more or less alone, while bribery and intrigues, tribal rivalries and super-power games attempt to hinder Angola's only liberation movement, MPLA.

9. After a Year of Freedom

Mozambique became independent on 25th July, 1975, thirteen years to the day after the founding of Frelimo in Dar es Salaam. It is a young country, poorer and more at risk than most. In area and population, it is about the size of Sweden, but there are only forty highly educated Africans in the administration. Thirty doctors and three hundred nurses live there. The rest have left. Trade is minimal since the border to Rhodesia was closed, mineral resources are unexploited, the electricity from Cabora Bassa to South Africa not yet switched on. Swedish aid in 1976 was fifty-three million kroner, over five million pounds. President Machel likes mentioning in his speeches about how Swedish schoolchildren worked for distant Frelimo. Help from other countries has hardly begun.

When Mozambique was ruled by a provisional government, I was taken everywhere and could speak to whoever I wished. It was easy to be seized with admiration. I saw enthusiasm and discipline, but no brutality. I had never experienced people united in a common purpose in a way so free of coercion. The decay, ignorance and poverty were so great that only a revolution of the whole of society was acceptable, and national education had to be undertaken if it were not all to be in vain.

Mozambique is prepared to do this according to largely the same principles of self-sufficiency as in China. It is being governed by people aware of their responsibilities. Most African countries are stamped with élitism, corruption and foreign economic dominance. In Mozambique I don't question their desire for justice and equality.

But Frelimo is carrying out its radical programme so quickly, it is both impressive and terrifying. When it comes to collective villages and nationalisation of medical and legal practices, housing, funeral parlours, and more, Mozambique has in one single year surpassed Tanzania. Though not everyone wants to move to communal villages. What was easy to do in wartime is now not so urgent. Opposition is growing to increasingly centralised policies formed by a *politbureau* which is on principle anonymous.

Most modern revolutions end in austerity and bureaucracy. At first the war is fought against a flesh and blood enemy, then the struggle is against underdevelopment which is harder to conquer, and does not arouse the same fighting spirit. After the revolution, increasing distrust also arises between those who fought openly and those who were promised forgiveness, but consider themselves disregarded. They thought they should also have a part to play, but easily become passive, frightened and discontented. New class differences cut the old.

The happy atmosphere, the lack of fear of strangers and the openness I met a year ago – where have they gone? The sudden collapse of the Portuguese has worsened race relations. Foreigners may be *agents provocateurs*. Journalists and diplomats have been given limited freedom of movement and have to report to the authorities. There is no Western news agency. Frelimo finds it hard to understand why communiques from the Minister of Information are not always considered the last word.

But often enough there isn't even a last word. When the President's wife, who is also the Minister of Education, has a daughter, this is not officially confirmed – with the result that rumours start spreading about an illegitimate relationship. Portuguese refugees spread bitter distortions of reality. South African newspapers talk about underground presses and resistance movements. If you ask a Minister whether there is any truth in this, the question is considered to be bordering on treason. President Machel is indignant that I even mention the rumours – whether they are about rehabilitation camps or non-existent Cubans. This unwillingness to give information freely means that bizarre and obviously false political information is not even denied.

So Mozambique has become a more closed society within a year. Does it have to screen itself off so as not to be invaded by neocolonialism in various forms? Does it have to relinquish some freedom so as not to be deceived into 'the same easy pleasant route as capitalistic Kenya' – as Luis Bernado Honwana said to me. Perhaps President Nyerere is the only person whose advice really penetrates. With his self-criticism and fearless clarity of mind, he has much to teach his neighbour, who is free thanks in part to Tanzania's generous help.

It is difficult to take the pulse of Mozambique, difficult to find things out. Most people pretend to know nothing, only ministers uttering their unassailable opinions, and those extremely capable people appear to be worn out by all the information they have to spread, all the decisions they have to make and all the work they have taken upon themselves. They travel round holding meetings to inculcate the value of physical labour and to promote national unity. The people in the shanty town slums are jubilant, for cleansing is functioning, preparations against floods are great and maize is flourishing.

'You must understand us,' says a minister. 'It's not easy to clear up the estate of colonialism. Judge us by results in a few years' time. Think what we're fighting against – immense ignorance and poverty, the after-effects of economic plundering. And there's the help we're giving to Zimbabwe's liberation movement.'

It is true. I am tempted to suppress my criticism, partly because it may reduce people's willingness to give aid, partly because it is preposterous – you don't ask a two year-old to work out an algebraic equation.

Eduardo Mondlane issued a warning about dictatorship by the party and the movement, which reduces initiative and any feeling of personal responsibility. Today that warning seems justified. Decisions according to the principles of democratic centralism are now absent. Every question is being considered by internal consultation at a high level. Not until then is any announcement made by the president or vice-president, who is also the party chairman and vice-chairman. But about a great deal nothing is said at all.

One reason for this silence could be that national unity is so important and vulnerable that internal discipline has to be kept and opposing views solved by silence. For the country is still spiritually divided into two halves. The north took part in Frelimo's toil of building the nation and sees a new society being realised with its common efforts. The south was never part of the liberation movement. To it, Frelimo was a distant saviour who was going to give better wages and less work.

One result of centralised power is the President's own security police, SNASP, which is anonymous and watches out for slander and rumours. According to information, it prevented the army revolt in December, 1975. It has wide powers to arrest suspects without taking them to court and without having to account for the reasons for the arrest – this gives rise to the temptation of personal vendettas, as in the days of PIDE. The armed forces, on the other hand, have been deprived of their right to arrest people, and the ordinary police must first have the authority of the court or the criminal police. But there are no limitations for SNASP.

Only in Maputo central prison, in the Summershield district of the town, named after a doctor from a Swedish family – are there a hundred or so political prisoners. They can have visitors three times per fortnight. Apart from the local paper, they have nothing to read and no work. Their food is maize porridge. No one has testified to ill-treatment or torture – which in Africa is unusual. But the risk is that the prisoner is forgotten – because an uneducated official has not learnt to deal with the paperwork. Frelimo points out that they have had to take over Portuguese prisons with no toilets. They have not built any new ones, and neither do they intend to.

Machel harbours a distrust of missionaries – as opposed to Nyerere, who is said to have warned him against being too hard on them. Frelimo thinks the prosperity of the Catholic church is partly due to child-labour.

But individual Catholic priests and many Protestant missionaries have heroically resisted Portugal and made considerable social contributions. Some have now been imprisoned, and the remainder have to sign two-year contracts and agree to work anywhere for what are indeed good state salaries. As a result, man and wife have often been assigned to work in different places. Most of them consider they are most useful if they are together within their old field of activities, so have no choice but to leave Mozambique. Frelimo's lack of flexibility stands out in contrast to the Prime Minister's positive attitude when I spoke to him a year ago.

'We never expected any thanks,' a black priest I meet tells me. 'But nor that we would be regarded as enemies of the state. We were loyal to Frelimo all through the struggle for independence and several of our people died in Portuguese prisons.'

Frelimo fears the church may offer a different radical vision. On paper, there is religious freedom, but the church 'may not mobilise the people'.

'Frelimo people out in the countryside ask me to preach the gospel in their churchless villages,' another priest tells me. 'I go there. I baptise their children and instruct them in the spiritual world – but only if they ask. The church no longer takes the initiative. Sunday mornings are now devoted to Frelimo's political exercises, and then the church must not divide the people. Children belonging to Christian youth movements instead of Frelimo's may have to leave school.'

'I want to work with Frelimo for justice and equality,' a black Anglican says. 'But there is a spiritual dimension which cannot be administered from Maputo. People are prepared to die for it and go underground. But Frelimo does not want to understand that, although they themselves did something similar in the struggle against Portuguese oppression and Portugal's strange concept of God.'

My criticism is not concerned with Frelimo's revolutionary rehabilitation programme, which I find worth supporting, but the brusqueness with which they are moving, so that 'the innate dynamic of the revolution' shall not cease. It is uncertain whether the villagers are allowed to talk through problems as they were able to before in the liberated areas. There has not been time to apply the much-discussed democracy which was Frelimo's pride, however convincing the motivation for the missing decision is.

Finally – when, without permission, I go out to villages and suburbs, I am once again filled with joy. The people cultivating the fields and feeding themselves are there. The women who crept across the lines with food for the guerillas are there. The schools teaching the children to sing and spell out the new

Mozambique are there. All the people who unhesitatingly and repeatedly risked their own lives for a life free of foreign oppression – they are there.

In the dawn of Maputo, women in flowery skirts sweep away feathers from run-over chickens and pamphlets from demonstrations against Ian Smith. The schools start their shifts with filled classrooms, young people in the mornings, women mostly in the daytime, factory workers in the evenings. University students throw their sleeping-bags on to the backs of lorries and set off for a month in the villages to build health centres and clean out wells. Orphan children, often left behind by Portuguese soldiers and prostitutes, sleep under the Maputo night sky, then find their way to the bowls of rice and maize porridge put out by workers' families. There is also fellowship and helpfulness between the almost destitute.

10. Diary from Mozambique, 1976

An anonymous grave in the middle of a yard between the huts in the border village of Pafuri, a low fence protecting it against the goats. Two white-painted overlapping boards cover it to keep the spirits in check and to indicate two dead.

Here lie Albertina Judicibo and her six year-old daughter Laurentina. They had hidden in the hills outside the village during a Rhodesian air raid on 24th February, but lost their lives all the same. A sister of the mother points silently at the clouds. Six other people died that day.

The Frelimo commandant in the village, Francisco Muchanga, is twenty.

'They came at five o'clock,' he says. 'They were white but their faces were painted black. They said they were nationalists from Zimbabwe. Yet they wanted to know where the guerillas crossed the border. We said we knew nothing, there is Rhodesia, go that way! A six month old baby was lying on the ground. What's that? said the soldier. My child, said the mother. They stamped on the child's head, crushing it. The mother attacked them. The soldiers struck her unconscious. Then the Frelimo crossed the river. Over the radio, the

Rhodesians called in five helicopters with forty-six soldiers in each one. They killed only civilians. We've come back to punish you, they said. For what?'

I looked at the bombed village café. Glasses scattered about, the refrigerator smashed. The poster declaring Freedom for the Oppressed is charred.

For safety's sake, we, a handful of foreign journalists, have landed in Mapai, fifty miles or so from the border, by the Limpopo river. There are about ten concrete houses there. The children and citizens have dug air-raid trenches round the school. (Three months later they were needed when Rhodesian bombers attacked Mapai.)

We were taken by truck on the last stretch to Pafuri and the border to South Africa. This border was also closed at the same time as Mozambique closed the border to Rhodesia. South Africa had put up a fifteen foot fence and shone searchlights over onto Mozambique at night. I spoke through a grid to the South African border guard, who thought it was stupid to stop the Mozambiquans going to the mines in Johannesburg.

Borders are fascinating – these artificial lines through Africa appeal to man's sense of territory and desire for drama and confrontations. Lines drawn between life and death, between the everyday life of work and the nightmare of torture – but which side stands for consideration and which for outrage rarely depends on international conventions.

Here is a three-country meeting-point of unimaginable importance to Africa – it is a mile or so to the Rhodesian border. But there was no way across.

We cross the Limpopo, the river boundary, by outboard motor-boat. The boat ran aground, so we waded through muddy water and walked a mile or so through fields of maize six foot high, meadows of tall grass, wild tomatoes and blue trumpet-flowers. We could see no more than two feet in front of us and were ourselves invisible.

Suddenly we were faced with a fence that might have enclosed a Swedish paddock.

'This is Rhodesia,' said the Frelimo commander formally. 'Speak quietly, so no snipers hear us. They often shoot at our posts.'

Together with a young Frelimo soldier armed with an

automatic pistol, we stared into the inpenetrable foliage. Rhodesians might have appeared just as unexpectedly. But there was no one to be seen – except the daily observation plane flying along the border and vanishing over South Africa.

Anyone who is not afraid of the dark and knows the terrain can go in either direction at night. Frelimo is worried about all the children between five and fifteen who cross the border and demand to be trained as soldiers. They are put into school instead. Rhodesia tries to stop this mass flight by penning the people into the eastern part of the land in strategic villages and camps.

We made our way back to Mapai. The sun went down. The wind got up, and rain threatened. Lightning drew statistical graphs on the black sky. The plane could not take off. We stayed in Mapai.

A meal was conjured up in the bus company building. Beds were made up in various directions. An American woman, who had been a teacher for many years in Frelimo's only secondary school, and I had to share a bedroom in the house of a landowner and business man who had left. The Frelimo commander flung out his hands:

'The Portuguese just go. Either they're too demanding, or too frightened. They can't be used to justice and equality, either.'

At ten o'clock the only light bulb above the bus terminal in Mapai goes out, the electricity is shut off and the water stops flowing. The full moon is reflected in the vanished landowner's picture of the Virgin Mary and of a windmill in Portugal. The mild night wind brings the scent of bog-myrtle through the mosquito net, and then a faint tinkle is heard from all the crystal glasses in the finest house in Mapai, both the purple ones for Rhine wine and green for Moselle.

The few ships at anchor in Maputo harbour mostly take on South African iron ore which is still sent out by rail from Johannesburg. Mozambique has little to export. The young priest at the Flying Angel seaman's mission in the capital is from South Africa, but he married a Japanese woman and had to leave the country. At most, he can arrange a football match for the crews, or change their paperbacks. He goes out and asks them what their problems are and they reply wine and girls.

But such frivolity has been banished from the Frelimo mainland. Wine is abhorred because in the intoxication of freedom many people say self-sufficiency means not paying for your drink and everything belongs to the people and I am the people. And girls, who previously gave Lourenço Marques a reputation along the whole coast of Africa, have been sent to the interior to grow maize and beans and teach the children sums.

In 1976, the government decided every person was entitled to own only one house and a holiday home, but not rent them out. That put an end to profiteering on a huge scale, among Africans as well. Housing is a right, not a field for speculation, Frelimo says. Though crafts, industry or anything else you carry out in the house is still private. Compensation for nationalised housing is paid for in the country's own currency.

'They used to take their money out with them,' said Luis Bernado Honwana, the writer who has become the President's secretary. 'They bought bombs and set up hostile organisations in South Africa and Rhodesia – with our money!'

At the Portuguese Consulate in Maputo, the queue goes right round the block. Departure fever has seized the whites and they are leaving at a moment's notice for anywhere. Huge crates stand on the pavements outside their houses. (A few months later, only a few thousand remained. Forty-five thousand went to South Africa, Rhodesia and Brazil, and most of the others back to Portugal. Only a small percentage had lived in Mozambique for more than two generations. The majority had been there at the most thirty years.)

The waiting people express themselves freely.

'It's the end for the Portuguese. This is the *third* world! Two hundred years backwards in one year,' shouts the owner of a haulage firm.

'Bloody monkeys out of the bushes,' mutters a red-faced insurance agent. 'They'll soon be nationalising the teeth in your head.'

'Think of the capital damage! Anaesthetic apparatus and building cranes, they're all rusting up. Look at the natives' houses. The blacks can't even learn to build an ordinary simple house.'

None of these whites had been threatened with clearing up war damage in the countryside, or the rehabilitation of those who had atrophied mentally and physically in the prisons. They had only heard rumours of such punitive exercises.

The hysterics of the Portuguese petty-bourgeoisie was obvious. They thought it was enough to swear loyalty to a new master and then Mozambique would go the same way as Kenya. Then the whites would continue with their favourite occupation, real estate. When that didn't work out, many of them revoked their Mozambique citizenship. This selfish attitude revolts the Frelimo.

Now a rumour is going round that on a certain day Frelimo will take all the children to state homes to make them into socialists, and the parents will be allowed to see them every other week. Frelimo denies it to no avail. One Portuguese gives me a typical opinion:

'First they nationalise our houses so we lose the rents. Then they take our cars and children, and it'll be the women next.'

They are the property of life. That Frelimo could nationalise the masters of the world, the men, does not occur to him. Man is the only thing that cannot be owned.

But the indignant mood of the Portuguese is not entirely incomprehensible. The President himself had warned against inverted racism which is the consequence of propaganda against exploiters and colonialists, i.e. the whites. This finds expression at places of work, and women and children especially are confronted with it in shops, on buses and in everyday life.

Another phenomenon is that while African traditions and cultural forms are brought back to give people an identity, everything Portuguese is scorned as decadent and sterile. So as far as the capital is concerned, violent crime and theft follow in the tracks of unemployment.

When friends and useful acquaintances such as doctors, lawyers, teachers, grocers, or chauffeurs leave, the habitual network of contacts is cut to shreds. The social vacuum is terrifying, and Africans are not very welcoming. So the circle of cause and effect closes, and one departure is added to another, until there are only a few Portuguese left – just as it has always been over all the Lusitanian centuries until the Second World War.

The Assignment

*These are days
when beetles hurry through dry grass
hiding pieces of light they have stolen*
W.S. Merwin

1. The Road to South Africa

Dr N., an Indian doctor who has fled from South Africa, is sitting in a Dar es Salaam room into which light seldom penetrates, for the view is hidden by the lighting ramps and iron fixtures of a Pepsi-cola advertisement taking up most of the building's façade. He is a doctor but not a medical doctor. He has studied the unpleasantest species of ant, the insane Anoplolepsis longpipes, which is small and red.
These ants don't bite, but they swarm over anything alive and persist without ceasing in all possible directions up and down the body and along all the limbs. Damp is what attracts them. They seek out the damp areas of the body and accumulate round eyes and ears. Children have died of shock when they have been covered by these small insects. They move quickly like the flickering of a television screen, lay their eggs invisibly among dead leaves and do not build ant-hills. They are impossible to get at. One day, Dr N. came here for research purposes – because of the colour of his skin he had found it increasingly difficult to carry out research in South Africa. He came to the reserve or Bantustan of Ciskei. He was looking for

these destructive and almost imperceptible ants, but what he found was a human garbage tip.

Old people and children, pregnant women, the unemployed and sick, all black, had been transported there in trucks or had walked from the nearest bus-station with a sack or a bundle containing all their possessions. There they starved and there they died, the crosses in rows looking like newly planted forest. Names and ages of children were on most of the crosses, their only toy lying beside it.

The physically strong among the children grew up in desperate and ruthless demoralisation, their fathers in distant factories in the white areas, their mothers often having to look for work across the Bantustan border as washerwomen, textile workers or servants.

All social rules collapsed, Dr N. tells me, young people robbing the old, knocking down pregnant women, eating what they can find to survive. They see people dying of hunger, apathy and meaninglessness all round them. So a generation grows up with no sense of any value of human life.

White South Africa is deliberately creating within its borders the suicide-pilots and terrorists of the future, ice-cold people who have never come across the slightest glimpse of love, understanding, or consideration, so they do not even know what those are.

It could be said that a regime of this kind is digging its own grave, but at whose expense? Dr N., a scientist who had placed himself outside politics, saw the exhausted mothers in Ciskei, the wild homeless children imprisoned in a reserve where they had been left to destroy each other in the hope that they would thus not have the opportunity to injure whites.

Dr N. decided to leave the country and was given an exit permit which banned him from returning. Whenever he has time over from his evil spiders, which seek out every earthly cranny, he works for the change of the South Africa regime. For it speaks for itself that racism, apartheid, also has the capacity to penetrate into every cranny of life in Africa.

In Ciskei – and not only there – year after year, this cold-blooded destruction of human beings who happen to have black skins is being carried out.

Dr N. is one of many I meet during the fulfilment of my assignment.

Another is L., who holds a senior administrative post at the university in Nairobi. The amazing thing is that when I first contacted him, I discovered we knew each other, but had not met for over twenty years. He was one of the first two Africans in my life. He was from Kenya – this was before Mau-mau, in Africa's colonial past – and the other was a student from Nigeria.

We were five to a room in a student house in Primrose Hill in London. We lived for a pittance a day in a basement with apertures up by the ceiling facing a tangle of rhododendron bushes which plunged the room into permanent twilight. I remember a student from Iran who read *The Blind Owl*, a Persian classic, out aloud as a bedtime story for those of us not out on the spree.

The two Africans were neater than the rest of us. They seemed to us to live way above their incomes or beneath their dignity. They wore dark suits and white shirts and club ties they had bought at Harrods. Their faces shone with shaving tonic, their nails were polished and they leafed cautiously through the compendium of the summer course.

They were not really at home in this adapted private house, which a retired country vicar and his wife ran between them. The tea was tepid and as black as coffee, the milk-bottles stood in a row on the steps and soot accumulated round the ventilators below the window-sills. The red stair-carpeting was worn and the linoleum on the floor was covered with damp rings and marks from dropped cigarette ends. The chairs were covered with cracked vinyl.

In the mornings, we sat in the bacon fumes and worked out from gloomy closed faces who had been out too long the night before. I was nineteen, and with considerable difficulty had acquired a reader's ticket for the British Museum library. I had given my research subject as architecture, and on my rickety table in the typing-room, mainly inhabited by ladies smoking and typing out a new edition of the *Encyclopaedia Britannica* that was coming out, I placed two stalwart volumes on Inigo Jones.

Angus Wilson was the senior librarian in the Reading Room

at the time, and I soon found I could request fiction of no great nutritive value for my research. I remember reading everything by Denton Welch, Forrest Reid and Rosamund Lehmann. I failed to get through Dorothy Richardson's suite of novels, but slowly, and for life, acclimatised myself to Ivy Compton-Burnett's strange and inimitable artistry.

I used to walk through the late summer mists from the Museum to the Cameo in Charing Cross Road – a pornographic cinema today — and watch another episode of Jules Verne's *The Secret Island*, and then I took a bus back to the basement room and the greenery of Primrose Hill. I told the Africans about what I was reading, and L. from Kenya lent me Jomo Kenyatta's *Facing Mount Kenya*, saying I probably wouldn't like Kenyatta's defence of female circumcision, a subject on which I had up to then not held any views.

Kenyatta never saw a white until he was ten. Africa's white history is short and disturbing. The whites rushed quickly on ahead, seldom seen. Lightning that smells bad – as an African said to me long afterwards.

L. knew Karen Blixen, but there were no books by black writers and neither did he think that necessary. He regarded literature as thin decor on the surface of life, a frivolity and a luxury for idle train passengers. I held the opposite opinion and this led to conversation. The Nigerian commented in between with schoolboy quotes from Shakespeare or Byron.

Both of them seemed to be far too suave for the lecture rooms where they listened to expositions on economics and statistics. The Nigerian also seemed to be richer that the rest of us. He had a gold signet ring and a gilt cigarette-holder with his initials on it. He received letters with windows in them, which we presumed contained cheques from some feudal Hausa father.

One evening, L. picked up an Agatha Christie and buried himself in it when he noticed the Persian expectantly fumbling for *The Blind Owl*. Some kinds of literature could clearly be useful – in self-defence.

That is a long time ago now, and although I think I am largely much the same, L. is a different person, with a senior, though hardly guaranteed, position in the élite Kikuyu-dominated Kenyan society. He is just as neatly dressed and just as surprised as I am to meet again. Neither of us connected the other's name with that student room in Primrose Hill. But he has aged and grown fat. The years go by, I think. He says the same, as he stirs his cup of coffee on his desk and gives me a look.

'I see them ageing round me. They find it difficult to keep up.'

On the wall of his office, below the air-conditioning apparatus, is a list of Gandhi's seven deadly sins:

Politics without principles
Health without work
Pleasure without conscience
Knowledge without character
Commerce without morality
Science without humanity
Worship without sacrifice

We talk about night-schools, adult education, extra-mural activities. The thirst for knowledge and hunger for education among Africans is always encouraging. Books go from hand to hand. People chase scholarships. They teach each other. If Scandinavia can be compared with an appendix in Europe's guts, then you have to know something about geography and the human body. Learning is intensive – as when fallow fields are at last ploughed. It is easy to lament over Swedish bingo culture – despite all that teaching on the radio and television. Education – for many people it has become managing the Saturday crossword and watching George Sand make Chopin cough blood on the colour television.

In Africa, the mysteries of knowledge and language are alive, the sounds drumming through the mists and new children knocking on the door.

Can one talk about threadbare stones?

I tell him a little about my assignment, cautiously, risking no delicate connections. I dare to do this because I have been given indirect information about him, I know a little about his position in the bureaucracy, the pressures that can be brought to bear on him, and the political and economic context he is involved in.

'Africa's countries are like European small towns,' L. says. 'You'd better reckon with everyone knowing what you're up to, especially if it's something secret.'

'That's just what mustn't happen.'

'Someone might get on the tracks of what you've come for.'

I reply that the day that happens, my secret and I will have gone our separate ways.

2. Librarian in Tabora

Graham, librarian in Tabora, also lecturer at the girls' training college, cultivates a moustache for four months of the year and shaves it off for the next four. It is a form of variety. Otherwise Tabora is a quiet place. He doesn't like the Indian who sits on a sugar box outside his shop early in the morning, cleans his teeth, gargles with an inhuman sound and wakes the librarian.

The library gets supplies from UNESCO and voluntary organisations. Worn, dog-eared and spotted editions come from British public libraries, clearly indicating the reader has mixed the volume with their breakfast. The climate is fairly dry on this plateau in Tanzania, so the glue doesn't dissolve. Graham has plans to let the inmates of Tabora prison take up the universal therapy of binding books – if the authorities allow it. At the moment they sew mail-bags, make rope and tack shoes. The dividing line between them and the outside world is a six foot palisade. They receive numerous visits and do not run away; unemployment awaits them outside.

Young people borrow D.H.Lawrence's *Women in Love*, missionaries take *The Forsyte Saga* or Churchill's *History of England*, Graham tells me. There is a great deal on God and Nyerere and Chinese agriculture, and a special notice urges everyone to study women's rights, the UN report on women and advice on family planning. Worn issues of the *National Geographic Magazine* report that the world neither ends nor begins with Tabora, but abounds with strange items, dramas and remarkable customs. But perhaps Tabora is the hub of the universe, the stillness in the eye of the storm.

So as not to be tempted by long drawn out whiskies more

often than alternate evenings, Graham has started a night-school on the other evenings – reading and writing, mostly for women whose education has been left out.

An atmosphere of loneliness, lemon tea and rum surrounds him. I remember him from the university in Rhodesia. He was active against the kind of apartheid which was there euphemistically called partnership. He lectured in English Literature and organised the library. He was beaten up by a white racist in the street, then deported. Now he was in Tanzania as a result of some agreement between the government and the British Council, one of thousands of Englishmen who preferred the ex-Empire to his homeland's Marks and Spencers, tube trains and long woollen underpants.

He takes me to watch a dance in a village outside town. They are celebrating a good harvest. Some kind of excuse is necessary. Several of his adult students live in the village. They greet us good-naturedly, and inquisitively examine his springless 1960 Morris Oxford. Someone gives us a raffia mat to sit on if we get tired.

While we're watching the dancing, Graham tells me about his wife, whom I have never met. She became peculiar, spiteful and dissatisfied. In the end, she didn't even want to see him. He moved from Zambia to Tabora. But no divorce. She returned to Ireland, to Dublin, where she had come from, where she was taken to hospital. She had an incurable brain-tumour. She had died a couple of months earlier. The end of her life was peaceful, and before then she had raged against everything and everyone she came close to in life, friendly only towards doctors and other people she had never seen before. She thought she had navigated wrongly everywhere, almost as if the tumour had heightened a craving in her, although it had always been there and no earthly power could satisfy it.

Graham was shaken by the fact that the person who had loved and hated him most was his wife. He is dissatisfied with the medical explanation. Was it perhaps another disease which made her love him from the start? So easy to see the body as a laboratory in which chemical fluids are mixed and make pronouncements like a barometer: stormy or fine weather.

However she has behaved, I am innocent, he says. So I can't be pleased I ever made her happy.

The dancing moves into another phase. All this time, an elderly woman with a blue cloth round her head has been sitting tramping on a sewing-machine, viewing the entertainment, but never leaving her work, a lantern glowing from a mango branch above her outspread material. Who will write an ode to Singer sewing machines, tramped everywhere along all the roads of Africa?

Graham talks while the two of us stand watching the spectacle. Our eyes don't meet and I have little to say. His new moustache is half-grown. He seems as exhausted as the landscape around us.

The loneliness of the white tribes often seems crushing to me.

The village is African, a community, if on definite conditions. The town of Tabora is a German creation, a railway station on the stretch between Ujiji by Lake Tanganyika and the sea, a place you go through, a temporary abode. It means a hotel with Irish stew that seems to have been simmering on an Aga stove since the Germans left and the famous East African Mint was swallowed up by bracken and lianas. It means old films in flickering scratched copies: *The Prisoner of Zenda*, *On the Waterfront*. Though for those who go it is nevertheless a premiere.

The water flows out of cisterns on tall straddled legs, tastes of rust and gives you gastric 'flu the first week. Then you're immune. Immune to water and impressions, deaf to the screeches of the green woodpecker and blind to the shrew swinging on a dry leaf.

'The beautiful thing about Africa,' Graham says, 'is that there are so few monuments here, no churches or ancient royal tombs. Farming country and towns, a few bars. But no theatres or concert halls, no one making you go out to things. Some people hire a car to look at bits of granite they call Stone Age tombs or a fortress – as if that were something remarkable. The remarkable thing is that there's so little. A wasp's nest under a fallen arch – you can't expect much more.'

There are still remains of German colonial architecture in Tabora, Bavarian half-timbering with projecting roofs which were originally intended to protect the house against avalanches. Insects burrow into the tarred beams, and there is a rustling like dead palm leaves when the plastering decomposes. Fantasies and memories were taken to the equator, built up and cemented, glimpses of home, the railway line to the coast a hope of returning.

In the museum in Dar are menus left by the German headquarters in Tabora, pork chops with *sauerkraut*, potato *au gratin*, fat pork strips and *Frankfurter* sausages. Fruit cake is still garnished with truffles at Christmas at the hotel, and in the evenings faint clicks from the billiard room can still be heard. They sound like someone knocking on the shell of the empire.

Graham's office at the library is cramped. An unshaded bulb he has painted yellow to make the light cosier hangs from the ceiling. His upper lip is beaded with sweat and he says apologetically:

'I've only myself to blame. I chose to come here. I rest in peace.'

Outside is a churchyard with wild creepers covering the low wall and continuing over on to the gravestones. A very fat black woman is moving slowly, hunched like a rabbit, between the dead.

John Shaw died here in Tabora, Stanley's companion and friend on the expedition to find Livingstone. He fell ill, fell off his donkey and asked to be left behind, but Stanley made him go on. One evening, Shaw was sitting in Stanley's tent playing the mouth-organ Stanley had given him in Zanzibar. The notes sounded celestial, and when Shaw had played *Home Sweet Home* for the last time, they were both feeling very upset. Stanley wanted to put his arm round him and weep on his shoulder, but his masculine control prevented him. The next morning, Shaw was taken away on a stretcher by three men. He had bread with him, a can of cold tea and a fried chicken leg. That was in September, 1871. No European was ever to see him again and he was the first white man to die in Tabora.

In the morning, I see some children making kites out of light branches, some kind of bamboo, then fixing between them newspaper or coloured thin wrapping paper they have been given in the Indian *duka*. Some kites start up at the same time and become entangled in each other. One lands on a treetop and sits there like a light-buoy for the birds.

The plateau is everywhere, yellowish-grey as an old sail, the wind whistling through ragged rents, the sail shuddering, the huge craft straining but not moving. Gradually the end of the day comes with the swift dusk, the tree roots creaking as when a rope is caught by a seaman and the boat is made fast.

I stay for a few days in Graham's three-roomed low concrete house, with diagonal slats instead of windows, glazed tiles on the floors, running water and an elderly servant called Bismarck, who looks after the house in the morning and then disappears to a shift job on the railway. I strew ant-powder in the cracks between wall and floor. Graham has an enlarged photograph of a seashore above his bed, and a yellow jar of coarse-stemmed flowers which are Africa's nearest equivalent of daisies.

We lunch off grapefruit and porridge and wonder who in Tanzania might like to read Anthony Powell's *Dance to the Music of Time*, the well known series of novels now also arrived in Tabora. Better to bind up a few years' issues of *Punch*, Graham thinks, more fun and more easily understood. I notice a cuttings book of causeries Graham has written for a Kenyan hunting and wildlife magazine.

'I'm supposed to be publishing them,' he says. 'I would have called it *Ninety Degrees in the Shade*, a title a European reader would understand. But then there was this hellish business with my wife and now I think I'll burn the whole lot when I can be bothered.'

I go down to the railway to see if anything is happening. Some women are sitting cross-legged on the platform in front of sacks of cassava- and maize-flour and papaya fruit they are to sell to the restaurant-car or to hungry passengers in the third and fourth class. They sit as if their bodies were a decorated waiting-room to stay in for the hours before the train roars in from Kigoma.

The only thing that happens on the platform is that I meet a spider, a kind of daddy-long-legs, and farther away I can see a rapacious scorpion that has stepped out of some cranny. I bend down and change the direction of the spider's route. It is the middle of the day and hot. The sun has turned the air into jelly. The workers shifting sacks of coal move in slow motion, the air shimmering round them as they stretch their necks to peer.

I fetch Graham, who is cataloguing anthropological theses,

and we have a gin and tonic at the railway hotel. The salty biscuits have gone soft. Thin squares of butter swim round in salted water. The fans in the ceiling flap like vultures rooted to the spot. The high white-plastered dining room reminds me of Eastern Europe. But here there is sun and movement outside, and *there* usually nothing but solitary people stirring their coffee, no newspapers, and no one speaks to anyone so as not to disturb the programmed fellowship.

'The termites ate up my first salary,' Graham tells me humbly.

I am here to talk to him about the assignment. I have had it on the tip of my tongue for a long time, but again and again stop myself. There are other things to talk about during the short spell when dusk falls, that half-hour between dog and wolf, when white people are visited by anxiety.

Graham tells me that some Italian cultural institute has sent the library yet another translated novel with a penis as the main character, Luigi Malerba's *The Protagonist*. This penis is fastened to a radio reporter and directs its lust at a stuffed whale, an Egyptian mummy and a statue of Garibaldi's horse. His woman waits naked on the bed in vain. Not until in her grief she has taken her own life is her patience rewarded.

'Who reads a novel like that in Tanzania? Who has the slightest interest in that?' Graham says dejectedly. 'Maybe one of the Swedish craft teachers and well-seekers passing by occasionally?'

We go back to his place, fry lamb kidneys and boil rice. The Tanzanian wine tastes of burnt nuts. It's a patriotic sacrifice to drink it. The thorn trees are black against the sun, which soon rolls down below the skyline, then the moon comes up and hangs like a lantern in the acacia trees.

'I admire this country,' says Graham, 'but I've lost my grip. People like me aren't counted in development. Most of the other whites out here, the ones who've lived here all the time and not come for various kinds of aid, they're bourgeois.'

'What do you mean?'

'One of the essences of the bourgeoisie is a refusal to think about how the world can be changed. They complain without imagination. They are intolerant in an evasive manner. An artist is something deviant to them, so he must be made to stop his activities, or be given a medal to make him respectable. Culture is considered something subversive, the newspapers a correspondence page for a paid mafia and intellectuals a loud-mouthed clique ruined in their youth by academic grants.'

The pioneer spirit has gone from the whites and has been taken over by the blacks or at least by Nyerere and the best in TANU, Graham says. The whites are more numerous than ever in West Africa and Kenya, but they are in Africa on contracts and will eventually return home.

Graham pulls at his moustache and ironically recites William Hamilton's classic poem on the pioneer's longing for the immense and apparently unpopulated empire:

I pine for the roar of the lion on the edge of the clearing
For the rustle of the grass-snake; the bird's flashing wing in
the heath;
For the sun-shrivelled peaks of the mountains to blue
heavens rearing;
The limitless outlook, the space, and the freedom beneath.

We soon move on to another common subject in Africa, Albert Schweitzer, post-war secular saint, worshipped by statesmen and philosophers all over the world. He faced increasingly sharp criticism from visiting journalists whom he had never invited. He was vain, but not so vain that he wanted unnecessary visitors. He spent half a century in Lambarene without learning the two local languages or taking any interest in folklore. He had gone to Africa, driven by great compassion for the sick, the forgotten and the suffering, but he did not really like them.

In Europe he was praised as a Goethe of our time, but in Africa he was liked for different reasons. He lived a simple life, his hospital – described by many as a danger to health rather than a cure for diseases – was adapted to huts in the villages. Relatives were able to share the patients' lives, cook their food, clean, fetch water and work in the common kitchen-garden. The patients were immune, while magazine journalists contracted dysentery, and the hospital had none of the in-house infections with which modern hospitals are afflicted.

Those who dislike Schweitzer are largely African intellectuals who, not without reason, accuse him of arrogance towards the blacks. He was never known to invite an African to share a meal with him or even sit in his presence. He called them by their first names, but did not reciprocate. He trained African teachers. He was a patriarch, a great family father, a farmer from Alsace.

'My general rule is never trust a black man,' he once said. He tried to explain this by saying it would be unjust to burden an African with trust, rather like Jan Smuts in South Africa, who said that 'the Negro is the most patient of all animals with the exception of the donkey' and when reproached for this statement, maintained it was a eulogy to the Negro.

Schweitzer was not changed, but Africa was changing all round him, and there he met resistance. On the other hand, his other teachings found favour with the post-war young and their distrust of technology, the philosophy of growth and the exploitation of the environment.

'Poor man,' said Graham. 'His piano went out of tune after a few days in the damp. A man who would have preferred to sit down by the river and play Wagner so that the crocodiles gasped.'

The next morning, the acacias spread their dark green lacy cloths over the plateau and the larks are singing as if spring had just arrived.

At tea, I mention my assignment. I feel very sure of Graham. And indeed – it's O.K. For a moment, I think his dejection lifts, the depression which afflicted him at his wife's death: nothing that happened was his fault nor did he deserve it, so he was therefore outside and not responsible. I think he will once again be drawn into a circle in which he moved before and he can again feel he is involved.

3. Colonial Officer

Harold is an Englishman of fifty-seven. He started early in a career in the colonial service and has been in Singapore and British Guyana, but otherwise in Africa. His son is an engineer in Leyland Motors, his daughters have completed their education and married. Only he and his wife Pamela have still not returned 'home'. Like most of his colleagues he has had to work his way out of his profession, abolishing himself from post to post.

The Union Jack has been hauled down one midnight all over the Empire, the lights extinguished for a minute or so, then the flag of the new country knotted to the line, the lights put on again, so the spectators witness a new flag hoisted for the first time in Africa's night darkness. The United Nations acquires a new member, the world another name to keep track of. Politicians, the military and businessmen exchange suspicious handshakes. A few bars from a Beethoven symphony wins the competition for a national anthem, and the composer receives his prize without giving a thought to Beethoven's heirs.

Harold is one of my previous contacts, absorbed in his job, eloquent, his heart with the blacks even when carrying out differing orders from Conservative and Labour governments at Westminster. Instead of becoming an insurance inspector or an official of the local Coal Board back at home, he stayed in Tanzania when the country became independent in 1961. He is now consultant to a black Provincial Commissioner, a man younger than himself, but who has been given a higher office than he ever had.

He likes the work and will receive a double pension, one British, the other Tanzanian, and when he is sixty-two he is thinking of retiring to a cottage in Swanage in Dorset, going bird-watching, buying a flock of sheep and a sheepdog, and possibly writing his memoirs to be serialized in the *Dorset Courier & Gazette*. And he hopes to see more of the children, for that happens seldom at the moment. Linda, who works voluntarily for organisations and societies, misses them very much.

Their home is near Moshi in northern Tanzania, not far from the green slopes of Kilimanjaro. The dining-room walls are two shades of blue, and when I am offered apples and pineapple and drinks, I seem to be floating in an obscure space lined with yellow and white rays from the incoming sunlight. The floors are covered with thin worn Persian rugs, no parquet flooring under them, for the termites would have consumed that, but instead a concrete floor painted white. The living-room has meadow-green brick walls decorated with cowslips and daffodils and yellow tulips – yellow and green, the Anglo-Saxon spring.

As far as possible, the house tries to be an English limestone country house, with Virginia creepers and leaded windows, but it is different from the originals in that it has no tall chimneys protruding from the roof. Africa needs no chimneys.

'A number of white colonialists still live here,' says Harold. 'Though a lot of them have sold up and gone. They're scared, but they earn money. They're too lonely here. They transmit their fear of African culture, which they accuse of superstition and sexual extremes. It's a way of drawing a boundary, so that they themselves can distinguish their threatened identity. They don't choose Tanzanian citizenship. They don't register in Africa. They are a nomansland. They get the *Illustrated London News* by air. That's as expensive as all the papers put together here.'

Africans seldom move outside their own circle. Lone whites are not remarkable in African eyes, because white people have a great many inexplicable habits. A white hermit is not regarded as anything odder than a white bibliophile. To be an unmarried younger man must be much more difficult in the USA, where it is considered shameful to be alone, and the nuclear family is regarded as the essence of life. Television bombards you with advertisements saying you ought to have a baby, a little boy to take to the park on Saturdays, a dog to feed on Fuddy-Duddy meat extract, a wife with a never-deviating interest in the caprices of the family's digestive system. With no dog or membership of the local parents' association, with bad breath and wearing the wrong kind of pullover, the lone television watcher is made to regard himself as an abnormality, a side-step in nature.

I have never felt the cold draught of poverty, loneliness and privation in Africa as in the Irish part of Boston, or London's Notting Hill, children playing under sooty viaducts carrying roaring traffic, helpless elderly people wandering about with staring eyes as if they were already dead, the whole city apparently as mute and inhospitable as a crater on the moon.

But I have experienced the isolation and lack of imagination in the upper classes, the loneliness between the two tropics, Cancer and Capricorn. Subjects of conversation as stringy as asparagus. Your hostess's slow gaze over the white tablecloth, as if examining insects in a field, and a vague nostalgia of the kind that once made Jan Smuts, Prime Minister of South Africa, exclaim that for the Englishman in Africa, the centre of the world still lay somewhere on the railway line between London and Cambridge.

For Harold and Pamela, Africa is the centre, even if they are going to retire back across the English Channel. He talks about the lack of economic maps, about roadless and waterless areas that have only been sighted from the air. No houses, no ruins, only rocks some comical force has stacked up. Neither did Stanley and Speke dare step off already-made paths. They had guides who took them from village to village; otherwise they would have died. A few butterfly- and plant-collectors struggle their way into the terrain for a few hundred yards, the guerillas are forced to live there, but otherwise huge areas of Africa still lie untouched.

Harold talks about the colonial service, the structure of which has to a great extent been taken over by the free nations.

'Some people think we went round with whips, ready to radio back for tanks and troops as soon as trouble starts brewing. I felt more like a pupil in the fifteenth century sent out as a locum priest, or like a country judge and village schoolmaster rolled into one. You lived close to the inhabitants. You handed out knowledge or pointed out ways of acquiring knowledge. You kept the peace and you learnt a lot yourself, for instance that their form of administration of justice often coincided with ours.

'To have spent your life in the Colonial Service is not to have been a colonialist. The resident white farmers were colonialists, and most of all the companies that stayed in Europe and invested so little of their profits in Africa. I was District Commissioner first in Ghana, then in Sierra Leone, the best time of my life. My best photographs come from that time, memories, too. We hoisted the flag and hauled it down outside the District Commissioner's building, sometimes I handed over an award for faithful service or some particular contribution to the benefit of the district and the Empire. The fact that this way of administering countries in Africa would lead to independence was obvious. The difference of opinion was all about the timing.'

Pamela is fair, slim, the same age as Harold, but looks younger. He has very blue eyes, a wide mouth with large front teeth and a narrow lined face. I seem to have seen them both before, in other places, in other contexts. It's some years since we last met, but I at once feel at home with them.

I also find I'm here for too short a time, although I go to Africa every year, or every other, and so I never get to know them any better. We remain on a superficial level, which we constantly broaden without penetrating below it. We will link and re-link and dig into what is common to us.

But perhaps I am wrong. The more we talk about what touches our external life and experiences, the more openings we make to the levels below. Anyhow, it is poor symbolism to see your life on several levels – it would be better to see it as a landscape of hills and dales, where on clear days you have an overall view.

I ask about Harold's childhood on a small estate in Gloucestershire. It is the evening after his return from Moshi in his old Rover, the sun still visible behind the slender papyrus trees. I can see a couple of workmen hacking into a termite stack with sharp spades. They are mending holes in the road after the rains. They fill them in with this soil, which a fluid in the termites turns as hard as concrete.

There's a honey-coloured glow over the fields, the road red from laterite, and in the distance I can just see green coffee hills. Kilimanjaro is shadowy in the north, a single dark cloud emerging from the mountain like steam from a volcano.

'My father hunted and went round pointing with a stick,' said Harold. 'He thought that was farming. To the hurried visitor, it probably looks as if I do the same here. But that's an illusion. Here it's a question of good organisation if it's not all to fall to pieces.

'Father didn't like me going to university,' he went on. 'He gave me money for hunting but not for studies. I had to borrow that. He thought cricket was good if you went in for it, but studies were useless. And also there were niggers at the university and then you knew what standards applied. If he'd seen me here in East Africa among so many black people . . . the only time I ever heard him say anything positive in connection with Africa was when he praised someone who came here in a hot-air balloon. He liked balloons. He had a fantasy about being imprisoned by a Labour government. Then his friends would land in a balloon in the prison yard, hypnotise the prison guards, and they would slowly rise up into the sky. A celestial sign of victory for the individual.

'So much buttoned-up loneliness,' he said. 'Then sudden bursts of temper, like fits of coughing. He had obsessions about certain things, folding bamboo chairs for instance, and impregnated raincoats. He had several, which he shook the water off. Isn't it time to wax them? he used to shout to my mother.'

He smiled slightly with embarrassment, as if he had said too much, with no claims to be told anything in exchange, as if he had established an unexpected link backwards – as when Proust felt the uneven paving stones of Guermantes' yard beneath his feet and in ecstasy was taken back to St Mark's in Venice where there were similar knobbly stones.

'We don't know what the children think of us,' said Pamela. 'Crazy, probably. They haven't been smitten with Africa. They have only one home, England, with its Scottish and Welsh national movements and three unions for every occupation.'

Stars long ago extinguished and those still bright shine down on us with a clarity never seen on a Swedish January night. The evening has been transformed into one huge frog-stomach of noise, croaking and death-throes. A night-monkey lets out its hungry mating calls and flees. The servant cries out in his sleep in the garden hut, as if he were being thrown down a precipice.

The bats start hunting insects. It is the hour of the vampire. We move indoors.

There is an African saying which runs: Distrust a man with snuff under his nails. He doesn't put his hands on the table. Harold seems to me to be a man who always has his hands visible and does not play games in secret. So I take the risk, and talk to him about my assignment, though I need not have done. If he understands what it's about, it will depend just as much on his trust in me as mine in him, on the feeling that we have a common base, fairly similar views on the value of human beings, racism and injustice, on the realisation that neither of us, under any condition or persuasion, would be prepared to lure the other into a trap.

I just call it the assignment, my main occupation on various African trips. Although it doesn't always take up most of my time, everything actually turns on it. Through it all, I listen to chat about servants and quince jam, hear the hum of generals' limousines and the rustle of official forms.

It started long ago. I met someone in a Greek restaurant in Amsterdam, someone else in an Indian restaurant in London, and they didn't know about one another, and all the time I knew more than they did. It all had a purpose which seemed good to me, and more so; about the most important thing one could devote oneself to.

But you couldn't talk about it, and that was strange for someone used to writing and talking and not having secrets. It would have suited a lawyer or a doctor better. But I was involved once and for all, neutral, gradually becoming well-known, in many people's eyes inspiring confidence. I could have been a swindler. All I can do is to show in a general way that my aims are supported by some governments that can be regarded as respectable, and that they may not ask inquisitive questions, either.

Every time I have gone back to Africa, the assignment has gone with me in some form. It gives me insight into different milieux. It allows me to meet the upper classes, business-men, well-disposed liberals, junior officials, union officials, and resistance men with no permanent abode.

Sometimes it is trivial and time-wasting and in between it pursues me and gets the better of me. It also lives with me when it doesn't take up my time, something that has to be done, although I want to do something else, but when I do something else, I at once start thinking about the assignment.

It can happen that the assignment takes up all my time and nothing much gets seen or experienced in a country. Everything is reflected against the background of southern Africa, and only what happens there is truly real. What I am doing may entail life or death for some. First and foremost, it may mean five years in prison instead of ten, a year instead of four. The source must be protected, channels concealed. No easing-off policies make the assignment any less necessary, on the contrary, for detente is based on a mutual show of strength, a calculation of the power of the other party.

There are many people I never have time to meet, much I never have time to see, and I can leave a country no wiser than when I arrived. It is much the same with conferences in Africa, or about Africa, I have attended. You get caught in the corridors, and what is whispered and plotted seems more important than everything that might possibly happen in the rest of the world. You come into a closed existence in which you exchange wordings like currency between countries, sidestepping, taking it back, dodging aside, taking a step forward, making conditions, dividing yourself and uniting yourself.

When it is all over, as a delegate, I mostly have the impression that at least some good has been achieved – you can't expect much more. But out in the daylight, free of the buzz of interpreters in headphones, I wonder what I have really been doing. All those days, all that time gone, all those bars and committee rooms and papers, all those tense decisions, all those corridor conversations and whisperings in rooms – where are they, what did they lead to? The years, the years – I could perhaps, perhaps not, have written novels and poems, but it became mostly papers, recommendations and semi-secret thoughts on how one might be able to carry out something for someone.

My assignment is nothing remarkable, only secret, which is not the same as mysterious, vague or misleading. It is secret because such strong forces in the world want South Africa, Namibia and Rhodesia to have governments based on the wishes of the people who live in them.

I am trying to do something practical of which the liberation movements approve and encourage. I am not out to discuss and reason, even if I have to do so when trying to contact people for the sake of the assignment and not until after long conversations can I decide whether it is worth producing what I have come for.

But talking to people is nearly always pleasant. What doesn't suit me is making the transition from one aim to another, so that what we have just talked about appears to be an excuse for something quite different. And I must try to do it in such a way that a negative reaction does not entail any risk to the assignment.

I sit talking to Harold and Pamela for a long time. It grows late. She takes out some home-made digestive biscuits of pleasing dryness. The cut-glass bowl of raspberry jam contains a multitude of pips. She sees me looking.

'Surprisingly enough raspberries grow and ripen several times a year here, but the starlings are after them, just like in England . . .'

Before we go to bed, Harold tells me an African myth about how in the beginning God was resting in his heaven, which was a thin hide just above the earth. He put down his hand and gave man and woman maize to grind. But the woman with her long pounding stick soon struck the heavens and it split. God swiftly retreated so as not to fall to earth and has never worried since about the fate of human beings. Humanity has been left alone with its pain and death and attempts to find food and shelter.

4. A Hotel in Swaziland

For my assignment, Swaziland is dangerous but necessary terrain.

Otherwise it is an idyll, an old-fashioned kingdom, fertile and peaceful in every way, with a conservative population which by African standards is well-off. It has never been under foreign supremacy, though the country was indeed called a protectorate for a brief colonial period, but it was Swazi who voluntarily asked for British protection from the roaming Boers.

Men with monkey-skins round their waists and cudgels in their hands are not on their way to tribal dances, but to the biscuit factory and asbestos mines. The iron ore goes to Japan, sugar and fruit out into the world. Sometimes, South Africa uses the word Swazi on their oranges in order to sell them more easily. Half of the total national income comes from their customs union with South Africa, but who pays whom is a matter of controversy. This mutual dependency is, however, a problem for the weaker partner.

King Sobhuza II has a hundred sons roaming around among black goats and cows, blackberries and clean mountain streams. Schools are numerous, and medicine men, medicinal herbs and traditional wisdom are highly valued. After much early devastation, Africa's largest forest plantation is growing, including hardwoods such as stinkwood, which are attacked from within and fall suddenly with a crash. If you go and look, you find no trunk, just a heap of splinters. Monarchies disappear in the same way.

I meet an ageing chieftain. His son owns four buses in the capital, Mbabane, and drives passengers, poultry and boxes of fruit from the highlands to the lowlands. The old man remembers the tall kings of the North. He has seen them in some Sunday supplement he has saved, Haakon of Norway, Christian of Denmark, Gustaf of Sweden, the tennis-player.

'Are they still there?' he says.

'They are dead.'

'Respectable, sensible men', is his comment. 'Tall and thin. Presumably owners of cattle.'

I spend a few days in Swaziland. The hills are green like onion domes, the skyline jagged with acacias, the crops on the mountains bathed in light, and every day is a summer's day. I see a girl put a ladder against a guava tree and climb up it, the sun glittering in her hair, the sinews tense at the back of her knees. As the huge clouds move like a lumbering herd of buffalo, her father stands on the roadside verge talking to a priest. Chicory glows blue and there is a smell of earth. It could be in Sweden to anyone who fails to see the mamba asleep under the gooseberry bush.

So as not to arouse any unnecessary attention, I book into a reputable country hotel just outside Mbabane, not so expensive or so modern as the Holiday Inn. The country's slightly strict atmosphere prevails there, expressed in the notices in the Royal Swazi Casino: 'Long trousers for gentlemen only' and 'Parents are requested to keep their children quiet after dinner'.

After registering, I fall into conversation with the landlord. I introduce myself as a biologist with private resources which enable me to roam about in various directions. He finds this quite acceptable and adds, slightly enigmatically, that he thinks he has met me before.

The hotel has good English standards, kippers for breakfast and proper Yorkshire pudding for lunch. I seem to hear the storm whistling over the heath of the Brontë sisters. Colonialists have always been good at conjuring away Africa, which then does not return until they are back on home ground, when it is used for writing their memoirs.

My landlord takes an active part in the management, either leaning over the roast lamb with a sabre-shaped knife, or rustling mysteriously in his safe. Does he hide pornographic films in it to show for a special fee to visiting South Africans? He has a bristling moustache, impossible to twirl, and his complexion is sunburnt to the colour of a business envelope.

His wife is seldom visible. She is mostly in the kitchen – I am soon told – in order to discreetly stop the servants from eating themselves to death at the expense of the guests. Swaziland has been free for ten years or so, and race discrimination is against the law. But servants are much the same as ever, especially if they are black, my host, who has seen most things, confides in me.

He was born a country squire, ex-Major in some regiment in Malaysia, and sorely tried by life. He bought the hotel through an advertisement in *Country Life*. Swaziland is a temperate realm, to which one can retreat when one's strength begins to fail. It is part of the world politicians have forgotten and God has remembered. He was quite convinced of this until recently.

However, no man is left in peace in this world. South Africa on the right, Mozambique on the left and Swaziland wedged in the chink in the door, squashed between conflicting forces.

'Will we be dragged into the conflict?' he says, giving me a gin and tonic.

No one knows. Both South Africa and Mozambique benefit from neutral Swaziland. The Portuguese refugees have gone, most of them to Europe. There is no work for them here. No one drinks madeira and *vinho verde* on highland farms. But one day there could be a stream of blacks and whites from South Africa who do not want to be forcibly ordered into racial warfare.

'I wanted the children to study music,' my host says, 'but they want to do other things. Music is the last redoubt when everything else has become politics.'

'Frightful,' his wife exclaims after afternoon tea. 'The servants seem nervous. It's all these upheavals. They hear about it on the jungle telegraph. Exaggerated, all of it, but it goes to their heads. Cream, sugar, anyone? Sorry he spilt on you. The tea's imported via England. Our own is too weak, as dry as grass. A hot table-napkin . . . here! It won't come out. Tea and blackcurrant juice are the worst. Turpentine is the only thing . . .'

'Please don't bother!'

'He's not really a bad servant,' she says, in his presence.

'One day we'll wish there wasn't a single servant in the whole world,' hazards my host.

'Listen to that – you've become a communist,' says a man who appears to be in charge of the hotel's food supplies.

'I'd like good members of staff, not uneducated people who take no responsibility,' explains the sorely tried squire, turning to me. 'You gradually learn to distinguish the types. Suddenly, when you're thinking sadly how little you pay him, though deep down you know you're paying him far too much, your left shoe disappears, followed by one sock, a pyjama jacket, a cuff-link. All odd things that can be considered forgotten on some trip. After a while, your servant comes and suggests you give him these things – for a poor man, one shoe is better than none.'

The hotel landlord assumes my inexperience. But I once appointed a servant in Kenya. I remember his various testimonials from which, after some trouble, I managed to extract his previous employers' characteristics. 'This man says his name is Stanley and has been employed by me for two weeks.' Signed: L.T.Trevelyan, Provincial Officer. 'Stanley has served in our household for three months. I know nothing of his religion or his morals, although there has been reason to enquire.' Signed: Dr R.N.Pine, Medical Officer. 'Stanley has occasionally shown evidence of thoughtfulness, prudence and friendliness not confined to himself.' Signed: Mrs Anna S. Titmus.

It was perfectly clear no one was particularly keen to keep Stanley in service, and his qualifications, if he had any, were intended to surprise rather than be taken for granted. He turned out to be a pleasant man, with no penetrating intelligence, nor was he criminal. His industry was confined to tasks leading nowhere. He polished stainless steel and bone or plastic knife-handles with the same ardour as he would a brass door-handle. He polished tables rather than wiped them. He was a polisher. Everything round him was to glow like riches.

The teatime conversation goes on to the increase in thieving. The words 'oiled lightning' are used to describe the naked man who climbed into the vet's, took the cocktail-shaker and a pair of binoculars and – just as the vet was about to catch him – turned out to be greased with groundnut oil and as slippery as an eel.

Thieves are rare in the countryside. In huts with no locks, everyone goes in and out. Social control functions, and if a thief is caught, he is severely condemned. Breaking into a locked house is considered worthy of a lesser punishment. Anyone who locks his house has something to hide and cannot call on the social guarantees prevailing out in the villages.

It is not the first time my assignment has taken me to Swaziland.

The quickest way there is via Jan Smuts airport in Johannesburg. On my first transit passage, the passport police established that I was strictly forbidden entry into South Africa. Together with two supporting Swedish friends, I was locked in a room which appeared to be a store for useless life-vests. A silent Boer soldier stood on guard outside. When he was having a break, we managed with persuasion – the kind called political expenses on travel bills in underdeveloped countries – to suborn a frightened Indian into extracting a bottle of white wine from the airport staff kitchen. We were released sixteen hours later.

This time a number of comfortable but telephone-less rooms on the top floor of the airport building have been equipped for unwelcome transit passengers awaiting transport to Swaziland, Lesotho or Angola *Dracula's Guest* by Bram Stoker is the only interesting book I find in the newspaper kiosk. It is gothic, ghostly. A locked gate to a tomb, a mad wild cat with glowing eyes, a horse that shies at trees in the mist. Broken promises, curses never lifted ... At the spa hotel, the head waiter waits in vain for the guest to return in time for his *truite aux amandes*.

In the end he takes the dishes away and discreetly starts preparing for a new clientèle. A parable of South Africa – one of many.

The English-language newspapers from Johannesburg provide merciless examples daily of Dracula's world:

'The mother of eleven year-old Coloured boy, Godfrey Lambert, is trying to get her son psychiatric treatment at the Groote Schuur Hospital. Through the Coloured Persons Representative Council, she is also requesting an operation for Godfrey. Three white railway workers caught Godfrey taking lumps of coal from the railway yard. They beat him, undressed him, greased his body with engine oil and held him in front of the engine's firebox. He was treated for third degree burns. The men were given a suspended one year sentence. Mrs Lambert says she is requesting psychiatric treatment for her son, because 'I don't want him to grow up with a fear which will turn into hatred. It will destroy his whole life. He wakes up screaming in the night. He won't go with me into town to go to the doctor because he is too frightened. If he is not with someone he trusts, he refuses to go anywhere and won't speak. He cannot lie on his back or sit down.' Mrs Lambert was dismissed from her job after bringing a case against the three railway workers. As she has to look after Godfrey, she cannot look for other employment and is dependent on friends for her daily food.'

Another common report refers to one Sandfor Kapenga, an African in Johannesburg, who climbed into a bedroom, stole some clothes and a radio, kissed a white woman and left. He was give thirteen years imprisonment, of which, according to the judge, one was for the theft and twelve for the kiss. So highly can a light touch be valued. A deadly blow in the other direction would have passed unnoticed.

A third report in the *Sunday Times* concerns Jan Diedericks, a Coloured eighteen year-old, sentenced to six months solitary for stealing fruit worth two pounds from a shop. On appeal, the sentence was later reduced to six months' hard labour. Judge Diemont commented on this humane decision, saying the prison food would have consisted of '220 grams of rice boiled in two pints of unsalted water per day. This food weakens and breaks a young person down mentally. Solitary cells are built of concrete, with small grid openings, never any sun, the air unhealthy and stinking. Wild animals are given more humane treatment.'

This happens day after day, in one of the richest and most industrialised countries in the world. We know it, and yet it is hard to grasp. It may be easier to believe all that beautiful propaganda. At the airport is a poster from South Africa's tourist association. 'Do you remember the day you discovered champagne . . . that's South Africa. Suddenly you have found the good life your taste demands . . .'

I have not been in a position to scrutinize that good life for a long time, however much I might wish to. But in Swaziland, I can scrutinize the arrival of South African tourists at the border. Since Mozambique has become all too risky for holidaymakers, more than ever make their way to the casino in Mbabane. Swaziland – with no racial barriers and state roulette – means a few days in conditions many whites deep down admit is more normal than at home. Master-status they have anyhow, because of their money.

Some of the profits from the Casino go to social welfare and pensions for land-workers. Girls hang around the casino offering a trip across the race barrier. Sexual intercourse with a black girl in South Africa costs a white man – apart from his social reputation – something like three hundred pounds in fines and two years in prison. Sexual intercourse with a black man costs a white woman much less than the man, who usually gets seven years in prison, if he can't be got for rape, for which the death sentence is obligatory. Against that background, a Swazi girl can demand quite a lot for a night of the most illegal of sins, sometimes enough for a whole term's boarding school fees for her child.

At the same time, tragedies are played out in South Africa which in other countries at least don't take the following form: 'Lynette Wilson and Moegsien Solomon, both employed, have lived together for three years and have a seven month old baby. But Lynette is white, he Coloured. Lynette's mother reports them to the police, who come to their home at midnight and find them and the baby in a double bed. Six months imprisonment for both. The child is allocated according to the law to the darkest of the parents. Lynette wants to be classed as Coloured, but there is no possibility of that in law. In future, she may see the child only occasionally and only in the company of others.'

I have known Dr B. since South Africa. We meet in his garden. He has a melancholy, lined face – like Samuel Beckett's. He has vegetable seeds to sow and he prunes his plum trees himself, preaching at the adult educational association on the benefits of a more vegetarian way of life. He has also talked to the municipal council on the possibility of raising the price of meat and subsidising vegetable-growers.

He has an English passport, is South African of Scots origins, and has retired to Swaziland. His children went to Waterford boarding school together with the children of white liberals and the children of Nelson Mandela and Walter Sisulu.

'A pleasant country, but uneventful,' he says.

Two bright yellow orioles are sitting absolutely still in his magnolia tree, their beaks closed, as if painted on scenery. If Axel Eriksson, butcher's son from Vänersborg in Sweden, had been there, he would have caught them in his net, skinned them and sent them to the museum. I often think of that singular museum harbouring the Eriksson collection of African birds, one of the most magnificient in the world.

'I'd have had no objection to being a reformer within the medical world over there,' says Dr B. 'For the blacks, I mean. The whites can't go any further. I made a plan for dispensers all over the countryside with packaged equipment, all of the same standard. The Minister of Health was not amused. The obstacles were as bureaucratic as much as ideological.'

He smiles sorrowfully over his drink. A chained green parrot on the other side of the road shrieks: 'Shit on you!'

'The whites are utterly dependent on the blacks. Their whole economy would collapse without them. But they don't want to hear about that. Brooms and vacuum cleaners are kept in a shed far away. Tools and machines shall not be visible. Everything has to be hidden away beneath chrome and glitter and smooth surfaces – like a dishwasher in a kitchen. Away with them! But the fear and the shame and an indifference requiring stronger and stronger spices to break through it are still there.'

'It's strange,' I say. 'You've all been bathed, powdered and caressed by black women. And then you've learnt to despise them.'

'It has marked our relations with everyone, with women especially, perhaps.'

I notice a bitter note in Dr B., which no doubt he turns on himself in those moments when he can't escape from a lifelong experience of South Africa. He talks about the whites alternately as 'we' and 'they', each time hesitating slightly at the pronoun.

He is perhaps sixty years old. He has a boyish face, aged before its time. I suspect he was once full of confidence, perhaps arrogance. Then he was forced to retreat, become less noticeable, to avoid renunciation of honour and morality. He too became one of those who had to compromise to keep body and soul together and sorrowfully watch others doing the same.

'They have managed to legislate for every step the blacks take,' he says. 'May their adult children visit them in the evenings? The law knows. Everything is thought out so that life shall lose every scrap of meaningful content. What blind reckless lust for revenge must afflict those who have been robbed of everything in the middle of the abundance of others!'

The shops in Mbabane are also well stocked – electric guitars and Austin Reed tweed jackets, a vegetable market run by Indian traders. Everywhere in Africa, but most of all in South Africa, the contrast between what there is to buy and what most people can afford is striking. In Cuba and in China, perhaps only in those places, there are said to be shops in which nothing is sold which does not come within everyone's pocket.

South Africa casts its shadow over Swaziland, the same customs union. In South Africa are four million whites with their freezers, stereos, micro-ovens, swimming-pools and private planes. Not all of them, but more than anyone anywhere else. Those who are not white see how the whites live, and they know the privileges of the whites are so great that they cannot be overcome with reforms.

Increased equality would mean fewer swimming-pools, not more. The chasm between standards, class differences between black and white are far greater than a hundred years ago, when poverty-stricken Boers struggled through the country on their ox-wagons. In those days there was no technological abundance for anyone. Now the oxen and the hoes belong to the blacks, while the white farmer inspects his crops from a helicopter.

'Why did you give up your practice in Durban?' I ask.

'In the long run, I got fed up with the aches and pains of the rich. An Indian came into my waiting-room. I had given him a discreet time to come, but someone saw him. The rumour got around the very same day. Dr B. takes Coloured patients. Perhaps our urine samples stand alongside each other in the same cubby-hole! A dreadful, inconceivable thought! Some of my patients left. The Indian happened to have more money than most. He was furious and flew to London to consult a surgeon. My will to sacrifice did not extend to becoming doctor to the poor in the slums. I gave money to that sort of thing, a tenth of my white patients' fees. Perhaps I was prevented by pressure from my wife and her family. Things would be made difficult for them and there'd be whispering and sidelong looks.'

His wife is on a visit to her sister in Cape Town. We have another gin and tonic. The cockchafers whirl, the frogs croak. Light dew soon falls. The South African newspapers and the *Times of Swaziland* lie on the garden table, the latter published every other day and full of local gossip, a cyclone in Madagascar the main foreign news. But from the *Rand Daily Mail* it appears that South Africa's churches have ordered a day of prayer for all people held *incommunicado* and without trial in prison. The prayers are for 'our inability to understand the sufferings of others and our ability to live in comfort with injustice.'

The Star leader begins: 'Take a look at the ugly, evil and meaningless phenomenon of apartheid! See how it destroys human relationships, nourishes bitterness and even hatred. See how it degrades the nobler instincts of humanity.' The newspaper gives three topical examples. An oil tanker explodes off the coast of Natal. Black seamen save a white officer from dying in his cabin and they struggle ashore. But the blacks are at once told they may not eat at the same table, or even be in the same house as their white companions on board. The Indians in Pretoria lack leisure areas and are given a small lake outside town. But the Indians would have to travel through a white area, so the project is being opposed by the government party.

The black musical, *Meropa,* is given special permission to invite non-whites to two performances. Mixing them with whites is not possible, although the actors are black. And no more than two performances.

'Yet the press is surprisingly free!'

'Look at it the other way round,' says Dr B. 'When you know how much is forbidden to mention and how strong self-censorship is, then you have some idea what horrors are being concealed, for what we read is permitted everyday fodder.'

He finishes his drink and the lines deepen in his face. Clouds block a stretch of the horizon. Mbabane lies to the north, one of the smallest capitals in the world.

'What the hell can one do?' he says slowly. 'One grows old. Everything has an end.'

This brings me to my assignment, some of which he is in agreement with, while he has voluntarily foregone being told it all. To make sure we can talk undisturbed, we go out on to the roads round town in his Peugeot. Some men are preparing something over a fire outside the highway authority's tin shack. They have knives on the grass and a huge pile of thorn they have cut during the day. They are improving one of the approach roads into Mbabane.

At this time of the day, millions of fires are lit on the surface of the earth. In the slum areas and villages, in ravines and out on the fields, they glow like splashes from the wings of a phoenix. Electricity belongs to a limited area of the earth. But here and there a naked fifteen-watt bulb hanging from its flex does glimmer above a carpenter's bench or a couple of sacks of maize in a grocer's shop.

Dr B. still has good contacts both inside and outside South Africa. Individual patients still consult him, and he sometimes sees King Sobhuza's physician when it comes to assuring the old man a long life. At present the king is in full vigour, and his power and reputation will not lessen with increasing infirmity. In Africa, no one is placed under guardianship. But those who can correctly interpret his cough and glances will be met with increased respect. There are radical currents in the country, but they remain weak as long as the king himself is the foremost nationalist. He owns so much land and iron ore that he embodies the country itself, but he lives frugally and without luxury.

A great many people are sitting outside huts and along the roadside as we drive by. There is plenty of time and a shortage of work in Africa. But in Swaziland, the unemployed are not forced into camps. Some of them – few compared with Lesotho and Mozambique – go off on one-year contracts to the mines round Johannesburg. Most people try to manage in the homeland with cattle, agriculture and construction work.

The South Africans like calling Swaziland a Bantustan, an agricultural reserve. But in South African reserves, many people starve to death and are permitted to live there of their own free will. In the white areas, eighty-seven per cent of the country, unemployed blacks are arrested and sent to work-depôts, from where they are later sent to forced labour. Women, children and old people end up in the reserves. The men have to work for the whites for wages which are on average fifteen times lower than those of the whites. Work-permits are their passports, enabling them to stay in their own country.

We only have to drive for an hour or so to reach the borders of apartheid. According to the latest poster, that is where to find 'the westernmost country east of Greenwich for a peaceful relaxing holiday away from crowds and everyday life...' This is not necessarily untrue – for the crowds are imprisoned in well-guarded segregated townships out of sight and everyday life has been removed; half of all death-sentences outside the eastern states are carried out here, and 550,000 people in prison in any given year in the 1970s, most because of offences that are only crimes for Africans, never for whites.

When I return to my hotel later in the evening, there is a light on in the bar, though no one is awake. The light is probably to frighten off thieves. The breakfast table is laid with egg-cups and toast-racks, the hotplate ready for tea. The whole building is asleep, even its servants, who contribute to making the life of whites in Africa into a Victorian picture.

I try to look at this western life of rituals as seen from the road, through windows, my eyes on those walking silently past, cloth sacks on their heads. It is difficult, and I am too involved. I persuade myself that all peoples live by rituals, that is a presupposition to all social life, and for my part I live on a golden edge of the vast human slum, released from serfdom and bonded labour. I live among people who try to forget that all living things eat each other: the glasses are cut-glass, the cutlery gleams, and there appears to be light-years between the saddle of venison on the dish and the dimming eye of the dying deer.

From inside this hotel dining-room in Swaziland, where everything is waiting for Sunday morning and the gong to sound 'Breakfast is ready', this putative Swedish biologist looks out on to the people on the road, but soon stops actually seeing them.

5. Borders of Apartheid

We haven't met for several years, but I at once recognise Myrtle's oval ikon face, her smooth hair, now greying, the arched eyelids and narrow curved nose. She is beautifully Jewish-looking. Radicalism and Jewish origins have until recently been almost identical concepts in South Africa. Her dress is dark grey and red – like blankets in old Swedish peasant homes. The unusual stone in her ring makes me think of the eyes of the Finland-Swedish poet, Gunnar Björling, eyes which fascinated many people; strange yellow with a faint violet edge, and as penetrating as those of a lynx. She herself has a steady listening gaze which seems independent of her nervously lively hands.

Myrtle is temporarily in Swaziland, staying with an old friend who is a teacher. She has come in from Mozambique and is thinking of shortly returning to London. We have reason to believe that she is under some kind of surveillance.

Her husband was in prison for a couple of years after Sharpeville. She followed him, although she could have chosen permanent exile with her children. It was a difficult decision. She left the children with relatives and went to face the unknown. Indefinite confinement lasted five months, three of which were in solitary, forbidden to speak to anyone. She heard the African women on the other side of the exercise yard alternately wailing and singing hymns. As a white, she escaped maltreatment. A white prostitute gave birth in the prison hospital and screamed for a whole night when the child was immediately and permanently removed from her.

When Myrtle was released, her chief interrogator, a major, said to her:

'I'd like to have strangled you. No one cares about a communist like you.'

It is true she was a communist, which is a punishable offence in South Africa, but she survived because she had a British passport and was one of the master race. Today that would probably not have helped. When her husband was released, they emigrated to England.

Now, many years later, after we have talked for a long time, she says to me:

'I can't abandon communism. That would mean abandoning friends, ideas, memories, the whole framework of my life. I haven't the energy to take up anything else. Comradeship in the party can be wonderful, but it is never unconditional. I'd like to be free, because I've been betrayed and treated badly. But I'm caught. If I'm torn up by the roots, I'll die.'

She smiles slightly helplessly. She is an honest person. She has quite rightly found the communist party the only colour-blind movement in South Africa for a long period. She has been involved in arranging schooling for African children, correspondence courses for young people, legal aid for forced labour in the potato fields of Transvaal. She has known them all, Albert Lutuli, Nelson Mandela, Walter Sisulu, Oliver Tambo. She was there when the party changed name, some people went underground, others fled, and also when a breach arose between African nationalists and whites unable to yield an inch from Moscow's line, even when it was based on total ignorance of circumstances in Africa.

In the awfulness of exile, it is easier to sacrifice everyone who does not toe the line. There is nothing much else to do. CIA and Trotsky are watching in the abyss on both sides like ant-eaters over their prey. And there's no way out of the pit.

'I couldn't imagine living at other people's expense,' says Myrtle. 'So I became a communist. That's the simple reason.'

As long as she lived in South Africa, she preferred to dismiss the stories of oppression that continued long after Stalin. Czech uranium mines for political prisoners, Soviet mental hospitals for deviating writers, Polish anti-semitism – it was easier to pretend it was Western propaganda trying to turn her attention from what was essential, the revolutionary struggle against apartheid.

Now she knows better, and she admits it. But high aims are not necessarily the same in practice, and people are not necessarily the same as the ideologies they say they embrace. I think about what that liberal politician and writer, Alan Paton said: 'We should be grateful there are so many people prepared to sacrifice their personal freedom rather than their personal idea of political freedom.'

Myrtle plays a small but important part in my assignment. We hold the same views on apartheid, the aim and object of which is depersonalisation. For people to whom human life has a value, immeasurable and unique, apartheid is a form of the most extreme degradation and ugliness. White supremacy does not only oppress, it also finds it necessary first to distort. Before it can safely believe it is able to control people, it has to make them into objects.

Police hitting an African woman in a sudden explosion of hatred are at least acknowledging that she is human. For a moment, they *see* her. But for most of them, non-whites are impersonal tools lacking an existence outside the needs they incidentally satisfy.

When angry voices of Africa occasionally penetrate into South African living-rooms, the whites do not think about hungry and desperate men and women, but about hunger and anger, not about people in rebellion but about rebellion itself, an unwarrantable protest that must be put down by every means.

Back in Myrtle's temporary home, we start talking about rebellion as an element of the Western way of life. For the ancient Greeks, people were free because they lived under laws they had had a share in the making. For the Jews, people are free because they can choose or not choose to fulfil their God-given destiny. In both traditions, there are symbols of the curiosity and defiance of man: Prometheus stole the fire from the gods and Job dismissed all moralising consolation and challenged God to give meaning to his suffering.

Myrtle went to a Jewish school and reminds me that the Old

Testament breaks with the view of history as reiteration, nothing new under the sun. In the everyday world, practically everything is repetition, sleep and waking, hunger and satisfaction, growing and ageing. The boldest of imaginations is necessary to see history as a gradual manifestation of God's purpose with humanity.

Awareness of people's social existence here and now is also part of the Jewish vision. You work for a kingdom in which justice and equality will eventually reign. 'He has brought down rulers from their thrones and He has raised humble men', as St Luke says.

'Is that implication found in any other culture?' I ask. For poverty is an evil which many oriental religions accept as a cure for the illusion of life. For others it is the consequences of sins in a previous existence. But in Judaism, the poor and dispossessed are God's chosen people.

The Jewish prophetical tradition dismisses every compromise with existing society, with the wealth of the few and the misery of the many. In the Old Testament, a sympathy for justice and equality appears for the first time backed by the threat of punishment on Judgement Day. Ever since then that vision has been the dynamite of social change.

The West has exported the view of the right to rebellion all over the world. Anyone who hinders the revolution in underdeveloped countries is perpetuating poverty and corruption – that is Myrtle's conclusion. The poverty-stricken peoples hope for the possibility of at least being able to hope. Western colonialism bears some of the blame for their fate, but all the same, they are also basing their hopefulness on Western ideas.

Later that evening, Albert Dlomo arrives, as arranged. He is wearing a suit, white shirt and tie, and neither had I expected anything else. For a great many years, he had to make do with one pair of trousers only. He belongs to the African National Congress (ANC) and was released from Robben Island prison after ten years' hard labour. Several of us arranged for permission for him to leave the country and go to London. But he did not want to stay there in the long run. He wanted to be close to South Africa. As closed Lesotho proved impossible, he chose Swaziland.

He tells us about Robben Island, where so many – Africans

only – are serving life or twenty years. Several have died and not one of them has left that damp Atlantic island unmarked. Albert led a protest against the treatment of his cellmates. One was dying of cancer of the throat and had been vomiting for three months. Not until he could no longer swallow was he taken to hospital to die. Another contracted pneumonia breaking stones in the quarries but was not taken into medical care until the day he died.

As punishment for his protest, Albert had to forego visits and letters for two years. When one of his children died, he was not told until two years later.

Fruit and fresh vegetables are not part of the prisoners' diet, although the Red Cross donates money for fruit. What the prisoners buy is sold at five per cent higher prices than normal, the profit going to the officers' mess on the island.

Sixty men live in large cells. Albert Dlomo tells us about a comradeship in which every tube of toothpaste is shared, and every spoonful of food. They sing together in the evenings and are still part of a common struggle. They are frightened of being turned into the stones they hack year after year out of the quarries on the shore, but Albert says most of them manage to retain some sense that the future is after all theirs, perhaps not theirs personally, but the African people's.

Some cannot endure it. Donald Mathengala stopped eating the porridge they were given twice a day and started rummaging in the waste bins and stuffing himself with anything. Instead of taking him to a psychiatrist, twelve prison guards beat him for hours, and he was bitten by a dog. He was put into isolation, where he was overcome with self-pity and guilt feelings because his children had not been allowed to go to school because of him, and one of his cousins was under house arrest and no longer allowed to continue his correspondence course. He wept and demanded attention, but the guard's constant response was, 'Shut up, or we'll throw you to the sharks.' After six months, he was taken to hospital and his nightmares and hysteria suppressed with drugs. He will probably never recover, is perhaps already dead.

The prisoners are between nineteen and seventy-five, previously students, factory workers, lawyers, peasants, teachers, office workers or union men. In a normal society, their ideas would be considered admirable, even elevated. They have never known what freedom is.

'A few letters a year, at most five hundred censored words, may be sent from Robben Island. No prisoner was allowed to keep more than two letters for at the most two months. All other letters had to be burnt. Rare visits filled you with a horrible expectation. You were never forewarned. For days beforehand, we talked about the visit we were hoping for, writing down things we would say, and others who were certain no one would come to see them asked us to send greetings.'

I think about Dennis Brutus, the Coloured poet, who was on Robben Island and wrote a poem about this Saturday waiting for visits, which gradually turned into a paradoxical relief at not having to reckon with the outside world. But first the pain of feeling embalmed. . .

like specimen moths pressed under glass
we were immobile in the sunlit afternoon
waiting;
Visiting time:
until suddenly like a book snapped shut
all possibilities vanished as zero hour passed
and we knew another week would have to pass.

It is the wives and mothers who come, perhaps once every other year. They have to travel through the country and pay large sums to get to the island. A daughter of Albert Lutuli's, the winner of the Peace Prize, has described a visit to her husband, a doctor. She was taken into a little hut with a window. 'I saw him through the glass. I wanted to run up to him and hold him, but there was a wall between us. I hurried over to the glass and was very frightened, for he was very thin, quite different. We began a peculiar conversation. We had been told not to say anything outside family chat. It was unnatural. How are you? He said he was all right. How are the children? They're well. They send their love. That's how we went on and soon the visit was over. Kiss the children from me, my husband said. We cried. Then he was taken away. The other women and I watched them go. They were so thin and weak! One of the women said to me: 'Oh, our men, they shrink here.'

If Mandela, Mbeki and Sisulu – they are in for life – survive another twenty years, they will have seen their wives for fewer than ten days in all that time. No private meetings, no touching, no kissing. And they are not allowed to see their children under eighteen at all.

Men released after a decade or so have contracted tuberculosis from gathering sea-grass for days on end. They have eye-injuries from the glare of the sun and limestone dust. They are taken to a reserve where they regularly have to report to the police. They may not live with their families in town, if the family is still even together. If the family goes with him to the country, they may not return to town. As ex-political prisoners, they are forbidden to seek work anywhere where there are more than six employees. They remain prisoners in their own country.

'What a strange experience, living as if life were a punishment for being black,' I say.

'There are different colours of skin in our company,' Albert Dlomo replies. 'But at the worst moment of despair – which will precede organised rebellion – we will forget that. We won't be able to escape a period of black racism. I only hope it'll be short.'

We sit all night in the little three-roomed house Myrtle has been lent. We manage to talk about a great many things. I ask Albert whether suicide doesn't seem a way out when hopelessness and uncertainty, maltreatment and torture become too much.

'They have to be the ones to kill you,' he replies. 'My death is all I have left. You can't suffer so much and then just give up. They must force you to.'

We talk about small reliefs in the apartheid system.

'It doesn't make any difference to us if we're suddenly allowed to walk straight across the city park in Johannesburg,' says Albert Dlomo.

'But it matters a lot to the whites,' Myrtle maintains. 'That's why a decision of that kind can be politically important. It makes the whites less certain of themselves. Why are the blacks just as good as we are at walking in parks, they ask themselves. Perhaps they're just as good at sitting at table with us, lying in bed with us, sharing our jobs, our wages. Perhaps they ought to have citizenship in the same country. Questions of that kind are disturbing. They get right through to the core of white identity.'

'But the propaganda makes it sound as if apartheid is being abolished,' says Albert. 'Nelson Mandela isn't inside because of parks. Apartheid is a deliberately thought-out system that robs us of all influence over our own lives.'

The society Albert Dlomo is able to talk about rests on a foundation of torture. Trials occur only when government wants publicity among their own people and to show they are doing something for Christian civilisation. Then the judge and lawyers in wigs nod to each other. They have venerable titles and do not accept bribes. Some prisoners have been promised their freedom if they appear as Crown witnesses and give assurances that they are speaking of their own free will, while policemen in civilian clothes observe them from the next bench. The trial goes on. But what it cannot do is administer justice.

That last night in Swaziland is devoted to South Africa, the South Africa which someone likened to the Garden of Eden after the Fall, but before the Banishment. For just as humanity can only through its fall come to feel its joy and its limitations, perhaps South Africa can only experience all its human assets only by going straight through that night which is now enveloping it in darkness.

Apartheid isn't only a psychological tangle of hatred, fear and guilt. The whites have gained power and wealth by robbing the Africans of their birthright, and in various ways, they have motivated this system and its perpetuation so that the Africans will not rebel and retake what is rightly theirs. This is not insanity, but the considered behaviour white civilisation often reserves for people of different cultures, which conveniently often coincides with different pigmentation.

Apartheid has not only racial ties with the rich countries, but also economic and political ties. Despite growing hesitation, these countries see apartheid as an economic asset. For what other nation has been condemned for so long, and with such unity, and open-heartedness, and yet has not only survived but continued to flourish?

Perhaps apartheid is a microcosm of the world. Either you find use for it or you are its victim.

On the bookshelf in the room I am sitting in is a classic of colonialism, John Buchan's *Prester John* (1910), one of the English best-sellers of the century. Several generations have taken quotes out of it, which they themselves do not have to live by – for instance, 'That is the difference between black and white: the gift of responsibility.'

Black and white share a heavy responsibility. It does not divide them, but binds them to each other within the framework of what I call my assignment. I know how much they know and how much I can tell without indefensibly risking the assignment, should they be arrested. I know what we are up against, a vengeful police apparatus, a prestige-ridden bureaucracy, espionage with huge resources, and the assignment is constantly facing me with decisions I must base on almost absurd trust in others.

Outside, the night is clear. A smell of burning from scorching grass hangs in the air. The stars are lined up in bright ribbons, like yellow wood shavings slung across the skies. There does seem to be an order in nature which human beings have been unable to achieve.

I think about most people having behind them moments of no return. In the past lies an event to which they constantly have to return to see if it can be re-done, reinterpreted, forgotten or obliterated. The judge in Camus' *The Fall* remembers the girl who threw herself into the Seine. He could have intervened, but he didn't. Lord Jim in Joseph Conrad's book could also have intervened, but at the crucial moment, he acted against his own inner conviction. There is a man who should not have been dismissed, a friend who should not have been informed against. Whom have we trodden on, to get where we are?

Albert Dlomo named two such moments, one when he undertook to lead the protest on Robben Island, with the result that he had no sign of life from his family for two years, and the other when he accepted an exit visa rather than stay in his own country. The first he does not regret, the other fills him with doubts.

When it comes to Africa, I became an object of other

people's chance choices. In 1958, a scholarship fund examined my application to study the new China for a year at Hong Kong university, or alternatively African literature at the university in Rhodesia. For me they were equal enticements. Unknown people decided. I have often wondered what would have happened if they had decided the other way round.

Five o'clock came round, the air still serene, the day not yet born. It seemed easy to leap away like a Thompson's gazelle, even for someone who had been awake all night. It is tempting to shout out aloud in order to hear the world reply – like a stream, a rolling stone, a volcanic rumble, a new form of address. But it's best to keep quiet. There are other cars and other directions. Swaziland is not a nation that can guard its borders itself.

A flock of guinea-fowl wake behind a hillock and flee in the same direction as Myrtle is driving the car, towards Mozambique.

At nine o'clock, I go down to breakfast at the hotel and as usual exchange a few words with the major about the servants, golf and the weather. I leave Swaziland the same day.

Shortly afterwards, something happens that should not be allowed to happen, although it cannot be directly linked with my assignment.

This concerns Joseph Mdluli from Lamontville, near Durban. He has recruited and smuggled resistance fighters across the border to Swaziland and on to military training in Tanzania. He has long been active within ANC, and was previously a political prisoner and has been held under house arrest for many years. He earned his living selling in the streets and as a pedlar.

In February, 1976, Mdluli was visited by seven Africans who wanted to become guerillas. The same night as they were taken into Swaziland, two security police came to his home in 2952, Mhlongo Road. He was wearing a raincoat and shoes when he was arrested. Twelve hours later, a policeman told his wife he was dead. When she was allowed to identify him in a morgue three days later, she saw his body was deformed by torture.

ANC leaders in Swaziland suspected three of the seven recruits. These reported to the Swaziland police and revealed that they were working for South African security services.

They were discreetly allowed to return to South Africa. The following day, two South Africans who had been given political asylum in Swaziland were persuaded to go to the desolate fence bordering on South Africa. They flashed a torch and said the password in the belief that they were about to receive refugees. But in the darkness were two white policemen, their faces blackened with shoe polish. They jumped over the fence, tied the men up on Swaziland soil and dragged them into South Africa, where they were almost tortured to death to make them name the conspirators. A great many arrests were made, a trial has started and will no doubt last some years. Life sentences will probably be numerous.

The three leading ANC politicians in Swaziland during the winter of 1976 were given protective detention by the country's authorities. They were Albert Dlomo, Jacob Zuma and Thanbo Mbeki, son of Govan Mbeki, who is serving a life sentence on Robben Island. A few days later, for safety's sake, they left Swaziland.

Will Major Swanepoel, Colonel Steenkamp and the other torturers ever be brought to court in a new Nuremberg trial? It should be possible to start a register of people accused of committing atrocities, and their dossiers should be taken out the day it became possible to hold them responsible. For even if the system bears the greatest blame, behind every ruthless action is an individual who carries out or inspires that atrocity. He could at least be named and branded as an international outlaw.

When will Vorster and his government be brought to a world court? Presumably never. Their fellow criminals all over the world are far too numerous to allow such a dangerous precedent.

6. Prohibited Area

We drive through the Botswana night. Badgers and warthogs run across the road. Unusual moonlight, with birds flying silently as if it were quite dark. The night has many recruits. The light on in the back of the car. A thermos of strong tea. The sound of frogs like the roar of a city.

The directions on the piece of paper have been written by Mukayi, in childish handwriting, unformed by experience or practice. The road narrows down to a path which in the rainy season is a quite unusable muddy furrow. Up by the border of a prohibited area – Rhodesia – I get out and lift a simple home-made gate to one side – as if in any Swedish paddock.

Brian is driving, an Englishman, scarcely thirty, surveyor and map-maker, with light metal poles, surveying instruments and maps in the back. He is one of many sent to Africa according to an agreement the British Directorate of Overseas Surveys has made with countries of the Third World. Sketches and reports are sent from all over the world to Tolworth in Surrey.

Brian is a slim, long-nosed man with shaggy sandy-coloured hair. He has come across lions, buffalo and leopards. Worst were the elephants in East Africa and north-west Botswana, where he and his assistants had to construct sixty foot high towers to enable them to see over the treetops and make surveys of the ground, water-courses and hills. They had to escape up the towers from elephants defending their territory. Brian is not bothered by such hardships. What is important to him is to live out in the open air. He doesn't understand that to many people Africa seems far more uneventful than Oxford Street.

In its turn, this has much to do with the fact that after a few years on this continent, he is beginning to be able to demarcate and describe details in the landscape. He has overcome the threat of the nameless. If you think about it, it is only already familiar trees – sycamore, oak, lime, birch – that say anything definite to you. Other trees have to be in some relationship to them. When you notice how few words there are for the forest, the huts, the flowers, the food, you can feel lost in Africa. Then you grow hollyhocks, eat haddock and smoke Capstan. But Brian distinguishes the trees in the lamp light – paramiri, makipoko, dahoma – and can tell you something about them.

Map-maker, he calls himself, rather than Topographical Surveyor, as it says in his passport.

Suddenly a glade appears, trampled earth, goats, hens, mud huts. Sue and Ralph, an American missionary couple, live out of the way in Rhodesia, in what is called tribal trust land, where only missionaries may settle, and then with special permission. It is the worst land in the country, which has been allocated to Africans.

Ralph and Sue are Methodists, but they remind me of Quakers I have met, idealists with their feet firmly on the ground. Like Brian, they are younger than I am, a generation come to Africa to learn something, not just to teach in a patriarchal way the gospels or the best health care. I first met them on a station near Mount Elgon in Kenya a few years earlier.

There are many kinds of missionaries, but over the years I have been impressed by their contributions and way of life. They are often the least bigoted, the most socially involved, and with the most practical attitudes of Christians who have gone to Africa, or perhaps Africans have influenced their view of life. They teach the use of tools, they make bricks and clear pathways, they bandage sores, discuss weddings and funerals, keep accounts and pay wages. They offer strangers coffee and home-made cakes, have a bed ready and occasionally a small store of luxury – a bottle of wine or a glass of whisky.

Sue and Ralph are awake when we arrive and ask us whether we would like a bath. Brian has been here before and warns me with a look that the procedure is troublesome. It turns out that water from an outdoor pump has to be carried in an old tin bath and heated up by a servant, who then bangs on an oil-drum so that his masters or their guests don't let the water grow cold.

A hurricane lamp in the roof provides light good enough to read by, but attracts nocturnal insects. After boiled chilled water and bread, we go to bed. We seem to have crossed some border or other. We are in a part of Rhodesia which is far closer to Botswana and South Africa than it is to the capital of the country. Ian Smith has never been here. North of the area of land inhabited only by blacks and a few missionaries, white farms extend all round the railway line from Bulawayo to Cape Town. There are also state-managed wildernesses there, put to no use at all.

We wake up, and I at once know where I am. Something unites all missions, the simplest of them as well as the best equipped – just like adult education colleges and public baths. Worn oil-cloth, sticky in the heat. Poorly glazed white china, thick as hospital crocks. A prayer mumbled at the start of a meal, no sidelong glances, almost absent-mindedly. The servant watches over the last spoonful of soup, then the plate is whisked away to be washed up during the next course. When the meal is over, the table is cleared and plates set out for the next meal, upside-down so as not to gather dust.

They live in a house made of coarse bricks, white plaster inside, concrete floors and a grass roof. A little way away is an earth-closet, a hollow in the ground and a box with a hole in it. They have radio links with the outside world – should terrorists ('the terrs') appear, explained the authorities, whom Sue and Ralph fear far more.

'So much happens these days,' says Sue. 'We keep hearing rumours. You'd go crazy if you believed half of them.'

We talk, report and instruct as we do the daily round of chores. The little white chapel and its crude wooden benches has a brick altar with a woven altar-cloth, a tin roof and beaten-earth floor. It is used as a meeting-place for the parish council more often than for communion service. Ralph and Sue run a school and try to get the Africans to organise themselves into a co-operative, bartering services for goods. They teach them to mend pumps themselves, eliminate intestinal worms, cultivate and rinse lettuce and beans, and dispose of their own waste far away from food.

Some girls are knitting and whispering together under a tree, and one of them leans back helpless with laughter. A man appears wanting boric acid from the medicine store. Ralph has learnt a lot about medicinal plants which are far more effective than the dubious nutritive preparations some drug firms produce. The teeth of the older children are hollow from the shortage of calcium, those of younger ones still all right for a while. Sue thinks they should have rose-hips and tomatoes. Cassava is good against the worst hunger, the root ground for porridge and soup, the leaves rather like bitter spinach, but it is an artificial satisfaction which largely results in swollen stomachs.

Mothers often don't understand that their children are dying of hunger. They think it is a mysterious disease, and hurriedly place them in a coffin and lower them into the ground while the surviving children look on in bewilderment. Small children don't usually learn to speak until they are two and a half here: too little protein leads to slow brain growth. Children are quiet and good, never cry and have no aggression.

Among the whites in Rhodesia, the Methodists are considered a Bantu sect. Whites aren't Methodists, and their ministers are distrusted. The American bishop has been deported and Abel Muzorewa, one of the resistance leaders, succeeded him. The Methodists spoke up for African rights before most of the others. Catholics, Anglicans and others have followed them when seizures of land and school closures grew conspicuous.

Brian has never had trouble making his way here. The border between Rhodesia and Botswana is erratically guarded. If you arrive from Botswana, it is almost taken for granted you've come from South Africa, and whoever is good enough for South Africa is good enough for Smith. Although Ralph and Sue live remotely, on some occasions they have been an important communication link between north and south, between total oppression and relative freedom.

I feel enlivened by being here, although it is a distant corner of an illicit country. I have friends here, and would very much like to be with them again. Rhodesia has become a kind of African childhood, terrible and inescapable, with occasional marvellous days which lure me back again.

I see before me a brotherhood of different ideologies and faiths, spread across Africa, across the world. Something binds us together, we have our signs of recognition, a wave-length on which we meet. This kind of work often seems meaningless. Documents pile on documents, between the pages the rustle of those who have already starved to death, been betrayed or waited in vain. Yet anemones keep on flowering in Sweden, all things miraculous and untouched continue, and I laugh at an inner vision of my children sleeping hand in hand in a juniper glade, like two gingerbread men stuck together on the oven plate.

A sense of guilt is not a propelling force in me. I prefer to make a mental note of an impression that it should be possible to do something, because it is so easy not to. What happens to others may also happen to me, so I am involved. But I admire people who are deeply and protractedly involved with no foundation of concrete experience.

I am in the same country as my closest African friend, Willie Musarurwa, the man who was my entrée on my very first visit to Africa. In my book on Rhodesia, *Forbidden Territory*, I had to conceal him behind the name Joshua Mutsingi. He is also a journalist. He also has a family, brothers and sisters. What separates us – apart from a latitude, or a shade of colour? Imprisonment is his and freedom mine. He has been imprisoned for a decade, for an indefinite time, though at last I think he is about to be released. Money is mine, too – probably because I could pay for a correspondence course leading to academic qualifications, books, stamp-coupons and paraffin lamps. The state's only gift to him and his friends has been an overall, maize porridge daily, darkness and malarial mosquitoes. Yet in Gonakudzingwa Camp, under the leadership of Joshua Nkomo, they have managed to form a shadow government prepared to act when the time comes.

We have corresponded over the years, which means his letters reach me, but mine are often confiscated and he thought he was forgotten. I have been able to keep in contact by means of invented names and letters posted in other countries. What depresses him is that his wife, a midwife by profession, has hardly ever been allowed to visit him over the years. They have one child, and his wife may be too old to have any more children by him. Otherwise his will to live seems unbroken. With remarkable lack of bitterness, he regards the whites as foolish rather than evil, in other words, possible to deal with once they finally understand that the good life in Africa requires more lasting guarantees than force of arms.

I remember how one Sunday in 1959, Willie and I drove out to Lake McIlwain, the whites' proud artificial bilharzia-free installation. We sat on a rock, concealed for safety's sake, and watched an egret elegantly observing us through the high grass on the shore. We talked about the future, because I knew I would soon be deported, and he knew prison would be his obligatory political schooling. Perhaps we would never meet again, or perhaps we would meet in twenty years time in a free Zimbabwe. The day passed, the trees trembled, and the surface of the great lake shifted from azure-blue to jade-green. The following morning, I received a polite indication from the

Minister of the Interior that judging from my articles in the foreign press I was one of the few people who was not suited to the society of partnership . . .

In the features of a face I have long observed, in a human being I think I have become close to, I can fathom an involvement which spreads out like rings on water to other people, other phenomena. Once again, they are signs of recognition.

Ralph and Sue are the only whites for miles and miles. They think the rôle of white liberals has come to an end. There are some radicals left within the church, otherwise good people who no longer dare appear to be traitors in a tense situation, so say nothing or leave the country. Few whites analyse the situation. They prefer to regard themselves as persecuted by the United Nations, communism or the whole world, and they reply by treating Africans more and more brutally, and by imagining that they themselves live a peaceful, enviable life. The country is in a permanent state of emergency, and censorship more severe than anywhere in the West. On evenings when fighting flares up on the border of Mozambique, the news on television is replaced by a 1950s *Lucy Show*, or another episode of *Upstairs, Downstairs*.

But restaurants are advertised in the newspapers as giving a ten per cent discount to 'members of our uniformed forces'. Three British policemen who have fled the service in Rhodesia tell a reporter from London that they were ordered to shoot Africans with intent to kill in order to save hospital costs. A British school inspector, employed by the Minister of Education in Salisbury, after being threatened with prison and having his passport taken away, slipped across the border into Botswana. His crime – in an internal report he described what he had seen on his inspections. Black teachers in his district were visited in their classrooms by security police, and if they said they knew nothing about the guerillas, they were tied to a tree and brutally beaten. As a result of this, thousands of young people left the schools and were taken across to the guerillas in Mozambique.

Strategic barriers still exist in the north and north-west only. The south-west, where we are, is an apparently peaceful part of the country, where freedom fighters have not stayed for any noticeable length of time. But the day when land-mines are found on the white farms bordering the mission's tribal lands, Ralph and Sue are going to be up against it.

Even here, I am told, farmers have started erecting electric fences round their houses. Searchlights play all round as the family watches television, a Belgian rifle within reach. The farm workers, forty to sixty families on a thousand-acre farm, usually live in a village a mile or so from the farmhouse. The farmers are settlers who have put up tobacco barns, laid down roads, and built houses from termite-stack clay. The wife has occasionally started up a shop in which she sells material and cosmetics to the black women of the district.

It seems to me as if Rhodesia's 260,000 whites should have the right to demand one more advantage – free passage out of the country. Over the years, they have rejected every offer to be included in the creation of a multi-racial society in which their talents and skills would be of great use. They have also renounced all guarantees to life and property which South Africa and their black neighbours jointly wished to offer them. They have said very clearly that they do not wish to live in Rhodesia on the conditions even the most accommodating Africans could accept. So they ought to leave the country.

But everything points to them choosing a war which without intervention from outside could continue for years. They are choosing many dead, all kinds of mental and material destruction, and an irreconcilability between races which will continue on down into the next generation.

At the mission where we are, it seems a long way from politics, fighting and the confusion of the world. Africa feels like an unscrubbed continent here, a reminder of the first days of humanity as it fled across grasslands set on fire by lightning, and when the visible majority consisted of elephants wading in the water up to their stomachs in wide rivers, the early sun shining through their eyelashes.

The land is largely a threadbare carpet, trampled by bony cows, where goats have eaten the sparse foliage and people have worn paths that have obliterated all patterns. One is at rock bottom. Now it is a question of digging below it. There are termites which drill a hundred and twenty feet down to find water. Human beings go looking under the sand on the dry river banks. This is the time when the thorny undergrowth audibly grinds its teeth in the evening breeze and African mothers are tempted to go to the white farms and offer their children free as servants in return for a sack of maize-flour or a few buckets of drinking-water.

Brian looks at the landscape which for him is an internal economic map, every maize-field, hut and cattle path marked on it. He points out red-backed shrikes and wheatears. They look the same as in Europe, so are presumably journeying abroad, as we are.

Ralph wears shorts and sandals, Sue a faded denim skirt and a teeshirt. She is of Norwegian origin and freckled, with strong hard hands. They reckon on a few more years in Rhodesia, and then the USA for further training at some seminary, then Africa again, preferably Uganda if that would obliterate Amin. Meanwhile they are thinking of having children. They appear very secure with each other and their surroundings, life clearly delineated, with no tempting sidetracks, as if God and America had given them an almost innocent confidence.

'If the guerillas appear in the area, they'll probably give us fair warning that it's time we took a holiday,' Ralph says with a laugh.

We look into some huts and see a maths lesson in the mission school, a black girl with five years in primary school behind her doing the teaching. I deliberately avoid taking up political questions with the Africans.

Towards night, we drink strong invigorating tea and eat some strips of sun-dried shoulder of mutton. Then we leave again after finishing our conversation, driving through the pale silvery savanna grass, between rocks stacked on top of each other, primaeval elephant-grey boulders.

Brian tells me that, as I have, he has been to Ralph and Sue's mission at Mount Elgon in Kenya – after their time there. Africa is small and has many points of contact for those who have reason to travel around. Mount Elgon, its slightly curved profile draped in heavy clouds, an extinct volcano which is difficult to climb, although many people have tried. The Africans maintain that a chieftain hid somewhere inside the rock, shaking with prehistoric grief, so that great boulders rolled down on to intruders.

The gravel road glitters with night-eyes, squirrels, wild-cats, a duiker antelope, a porcupine, jackals. Perhaps the rose-finches and the hyenas find some order in this chaos of signals between rivals and relations.

Brian is upset by the poaching of crocodiles all over Africa. Of all the animals, it seems to be the most difficult to identify with and arouses greedy malice. Yet hippos kill more Africans in anger than crocodiles, who have plenty to eat. If you go close to a sleeping crocodile, Brian tells me, you might faint from its repulsive breath, even fall straight into its gaping mouth.

The unchanging landscape is asleep. Our headlights seem to light up the same scene, the same overgrown verges. I remember spending hours in childhood throwing a ball against the school wall, counting to a hundred or two hundred without dropping the ball, a meaningless yet tempting test of endurance. On one occasion, the ball game against a brick wall that Stockholm May evening was interrupted by a visitor. A school friend was suddenly there, eager to join in, at the same time cowed and unlike himself. He said he was going back to school the next day. He had been away a week. His father had died. He had been shaving and had collapsed on the bathroom floor and died on the stretcher. It was my first reminder of the unpredictable and unforgivable behaviour of fathers.

As so often in Africa, I feel the immensity of nature, perhaps one of the reasons why people here so eagerly seek each other's company. The countryside demands a yardstick, the matchbox on the newspaper photograph or the little man on Dutch landscape paintings to help the viewer into the picture, instructing him to find his way in the mountains and the flower-filled fields.

The countryside we are driving through looks cultivated, grazing grounds, meadows and thinned woodlands. But it is wilderness and no one lives within a radius of miles and miles, terrain in which it is easy to disappear. But Africans stick together and seldom go out alone at night nor do they turn off known pathways.

The birds of the night, owls and the jitters, fly soundlessly ahead of the car headlights, like the souls of the departed guarding their territories.

I start telling Brian how I came across an abandoned tin-mine in the interior of Ruanda. I was not prepared for it. An arcadian, unpretentious landscape suddenly became ghostly because people had lived there, then left again – as if after a careless, hasty picnic. Rusty winding machines had stopped and water accumulated far down in the mine-shaft, stumps of rope hanging like lianas from the branches of eucalyptus trees. The barracks had disintegrated, their window frames and doors consumed by ants. An excavator had collapsed like broken meccano. A rubbish heap – a memorial to a civilisation which is a pillaging foray. People had gathered here in wretchedness and expectation, but calculations had gone wrong, transport too distant, the tin insufficient. On the orders of some remote company, they had left again – like myself. Left behind on this detailed topographical map was a special sign indicating human activity that had later ceased.

Then just as unexpectedly as on the way, we arrive at the border, not far from the three-country Rhodesia-South-Africa-Botswana cairn. If there had been a checkpoint, we were ready with our strategy – we were travelling at night because of the cool. Brian was respected in his job and I could show my passport in the certainty that a black-list would not be available at a fence in the wilderness, and it was quite natural that my passport had no entry visa – Rhodesians stamp on loose bits of paper which are easy to lose – 'so that you don't have any trouble with kaffirs when you come from a break-away state', they explain proudly and indulgently.

Africa looks the same in Botswana. We come up on to the wide ridge along the border of South Africa. A small part of my assignment is over, and as the sun rolls up over the horizon like one of those old-fashioned cannon-balls you can see coming at you but you can't stop, the map-maker and I are on our way to sleep and Serowe, previously the main town of Botswana.

7. The African House

On my way to London and north Europe, once again I find myself in transit in the little house by the Indian Ocean where

Eduardo Mondlane died. The gas container under the sink is leaking, as they always do in holiday homes, the broom is standing waiting in the corner and the white plaster has grown grey islands of damp.

Letters from home which have been forwarded several times await me. One contains something like a dried-up insect that has got into the envelope during its journey, but much later, I find it was the first sweet-pea of the summer. I have sent some sweet-scented lemon-eucalyptus leaves, but perhaps there are botanical barriers at the customs. Will the leaves in the envelope rustle and be taken for marijuana?

I carry about thin airmail paper folded so many times the words become illegible, but love gathers in the creases, like the unidentifiable grains at the bottom of a trouser pocket.

It is strange to be alive at this moment, during these years allocated by chance, a time of short-lived empires, fragile nation-building, military coups, local bloodbaths – and a neurotic world peace as an alternative to annihilation. This incredible world where you are carried from continent to continent within a few hours, if you have reason to and sufficient money, where somewhere there is a small green patch where a two year-old will grab me round the knees and say clearly to me; can't we go to bed and have a hug? Where there is a little girl who has been given a puzzle of Africa and has learnt to recognise all the countries. She takes the Mozambique piece with her to play-school, when she knows I am there. And where there's a person I feel I haven't really known long enough or loved enough: I find myself carrying on endless inner conversations with her.

I gobble up a forwarded newspaper and am seized with compassion on behalf of humanity – how hard life is for a Syrian living in a Stockholm suburb, for someone with a handicapped child the neighbours don't want to look at, or another who is unemployed at forty-five or has lost husband and child in a road accident. Sometimes all this – our everyday life during a given twenty-four hours – can disappear into the great cave of resignation. At other times, life seems so unendurable you wish soon to become a handful of ashes. That feeling overcomes me in solitude, seldom when I am working with others. It happens when you stop and try to find an overall view as the cracks open.

Come night, come close things! All else is difficult to understand. Memories of scents flit through Mondlane's house like migrant birds. Words and smiles hurriedly exchanged at post office, self-service store, on buses, both in Africa and at home. Double roots. The waiting letter: expectation's leaflets.

Don't complain, don't make too many demands, I say to myself, remembering Hjalmar Söderberg complaining in letters to his sister, Frida, about everything going wrong. She replied: 'You are nevertheless in the hub of life and I have never even been there.' In the end, it comes down to having the strength to take off so life does not remain unsaid, unlived.

Sometimes I find it difficult to feel myself a coherent person, as if the lives, relationships, landscape and memories of others threaten me and cannot be linked with my own, as if against my own conscious will, I were seeking a lasting order, an order that stayed good, while at the same time I change viewpoint and see new relationships and other landscapes.

When I was young, I saw myself in the future with a variety of faces. With characters from novels as mediums, I practised various rôles, indifferent stroller, brave sea captain, viveur, successful business man, criminal double-nature... where was my centre of gravity? It would appear sooner or later. There was no hurry. I knocked on literary doors and asked them to tell me which I was. I didn't know one was formed early in life. The door you knock on leads into your own apartment.

But I am not quite clear in my mind what it looks like. Perhaps slightly like Mondlane's house, comfortably equipped, but arranged by other people, temporarily furnished, with a beautiful view and, as experience has shown, no guarantee of security.

I blame myself for living so haphazardly. Without plans, in disorder, with no purpose – I find a motive for this by saying what is unforeseen is productive. It has been so in my personal life. I have no sense of my own measure – nor anyone else's. People are their thoughts, dreams and myths. They know they are chemistry, but the knowledge itself is non-chemical. They are not predators, but may resemble one. They belong in several spheres at the same time.

Human behaviour is not measurable, and precisely because history is created by the actions of mankind and not steered by any mechanism or destiny, it is difficult to predict. It is like a rhythm, a mutual game: necessity and freedom, egoism and generosity, bigotry and imaginative experiment.

After the day's work and the fatigue, after all the pamphlets, manifestos and memos which try to document history once and for all and take it a step further, and after all the bitter accusations rival movements hurl at each other, for a moment I am able to feel an incomprehensible warmth breaking through – like a child ploughing its way through a crowd. A name, an association, a glimpse of a solution. I am squeezing a new link out of nothing.

I regard Mondlane's house as a turning point – like the terminal loop of a tramway in the old days. It is lonely here, yet close to people. Half an hour by car, and you are in offices and conference rooms, tobacco smoke hovering above papers signed by a secretary in the name of the head of the Security Service or the Harbour Authority. An hour or so's journey, and you are out among the huts, where bitter maize beer is brewing, vampires are plundering the papaya trees and the old woman, alone and wise, is heating up her thin soup over the firestones after first having fed those younger, those who will carry the vulnerable relay baton on through life.

So many realities ... the glacier on the peak of Kilimanjaro and thyme growing in the shade of a cottage wall. The jaw of the hitherto oldest human being and a new-born Chagga child on the edge of the ditch by the clearing in the coffee co-operative. A dragonfly of primaeval appearance lands on my wristwatch and breathes. I know its spell of life can be contained within the clockface. God is a dragonfly, an African legend says. He reveals himself, is scorched by what he sees during one day on earth, then appears in a new form, dies again from all the evil he sees – one of the numerous African legends about a weak, conquered or banished God.

So many levels ... a measure of joy, a measure of suffering, the one fleeting, the other irrevocable. I see dancers stamping the earth hard with their swift soles while being ecstatically initiated into adulthood. I see lepers tearing at the earth they curse with claw-like hands. But at the same time, there is a fear within the dancers for everything they will now have to face, and within the leper is a happiness that he has learnt to read at the hospital, although he cannot hold a book.

Oh, earth, spurring and whipping you on! What is left behind? Multifarious and sharply memorable experiences, or experience so laborious and burdensome it falls through all the membranes of living, leaving behind emptiness and nothing else, a shake of the head as if nothing essential had occurred except disintegration, the increasingly weary beating of the heart beyond each imperative assignment.

I leave the door open at night. Perhaps he will make it here, the person I am expecting according to my assignment, a black student leader who has fled from South Africa via Botswana. But I am prepared for him not to come, and after one more day, I must leave at dawn.

The person I ought to hear something from is T., a white academic and social worker who fled the same way a week or so ago. I managed to meet T. shortly after his arrival in Botswana. He had brought with him several rolls of film and other testimonies. His family was still in South Africa and were reckoning on emigrating legally. T. himself was to wait for the student leader somewhere in Botswana and take him to Tanzania via Zambia.

T. was in solitary for three months – no charge, no trial. Part of the time he was in a death-cell in Pretoria central prison. Prisoners condemned to death were taken to the gallows at dawn. The night before, from the cells round the open prison yard, came the uninterrupted sound of friends singing hymns, psalms and political songs, a custom tolerated in prison.

After three weeks, having got used to the light and studied every bit of the wall, T. found an inscription. In perpendicular lines as fine as a hair, so that they could only be deciphered by pressing his head to the wall as the light fell in a particular way, were the names of African leaders, messages from condemned men to their successors, revolutionary slogans and Christian prayers. T. told me how his sense of isolation vanished and he felt he had been incorporated into a great circle of friends.

T.'s picture of Johannesburg was of a mentally sick city, where the sense of approaching doom had unconsciously seized the whites. They consume and spend, buy several cars and servants, arrange black-girl shows in their homes, bribe friends to take money out of the country on every journey abroad, ruthlessly breaking the laws. Calculated per capita, white criminality surpasses all statistics from Chicago and Detroit.

T. has lost hope about South Africa. He thinks the destruction will be terrrible, and although he calls himself a Christian, he does not think what the whites have built up is worth saving.

I try to imagine a day when the goldmines are empty and the gold standard gone for ever. Gold is one of the few metals not used for arms or even for useful tools. It is a fantasy product which measures the temperature of world economy and the strength of apartheid. Bridal couples of the world have a gold ring to bind them together for eternity, in prosperity and adversity. At least nine out of ten of those rings come from South Africa. They have been hacked out in hot mine-workings by men forced to leave their wives and children, they themselves never given a glimpse of the strength and joy the rings are supposed to symbolise. It would be worth a less firm faith if it were possible to abolish gold and diamonds, the branded goods of oppression.

Will Africans one day go and stare at the fat bulging dressing-tables in white bedrooms – as the Bolsheviks did in 1919 Russia? Or will they, after sacrifices and pressures brought to bear, find a way to live together? They have been successful up to a point in Kenya and Algeria. But in Zaire, Belgian houses are empty in Kisangani (Stanleyville) and Mbandaka (Coquilhatville), the towns slowly reverting to jungle, the asphalt covered with sand, the cars few, rubbish piling up on white verandas – for Africans have no use for these towns which were run on European conditions. The same is happening in Angola and Mozambique, where the Portuguese have moved out or fled.

The delicate gardens of the Empire will once again sink like mirages into the oblivion of the savanna. Weeds will cling to walls, ferns crack the stone steps. Snapdragons and lobelias will once again bear witness to the elastic capacity of the ancient realm to make itself at home everywhere, to widen the centre until it covers the world.

Yucatan's abandoned pyramids, Zimbabwe's conical bastions, the aqueducts of Rome – historical monuments protected by law – should be compared with the ruins of Dresden and the

East End, with the bombed towns of Eritrea, the dispersed villages of Burundi and plundered villages of Biafra, with Kisangani, Phnom Penh and Hue. Civilisations destroyed, sometimes abandoned, rebuilt in other ways. We see signs of postponed disasters, and completed ones. What will Africa look like in twenty years? Who will then be playing the part of statesmen waving from swift limousines?

'One day,' an African writer said to me, 'the cultural layers beneath will dig out the upper layers. Everything will begin from below.'

Many people are surprised at the adaptability of Africans. Life goes on – without such sharp fractures as in Asia and Latin America. Most seem to be pragmatic rather than fanatical, content with little rather than gloomily destructive. Self-consuming pathetic spirituality is quite lacking in Africa. Animism and ancestor worship are more of a way of remaining in a static existence. Even if superstition can be disturbing in isolated tribes, the magic does not usually run so deeply that it influences all kinds of behaviour. In India, on the other hand, if a wise man maintains he can walk on water, a water tank is arranged and scientists check that the water is real. The holy man steps out on to the surface and sinks. India sighs with disappointment. They wished so very much that someone could walk on water. Such an arrangement would be impossible in Africa. Neither would anyone wish to have a country in which – as V.S. Naipaul says about India – 'at a time of starvation, the pious pour thousands of gallons of milk over the monument of an idol, while air force helicopters drop flowers'.

On the bookshelf in the house, I find Alberto Moravia's African diary from the sixties, full of dubious but stimulating generalisations. Moravia senses a connection between the adaptability of the Africans, i.e. their lack of rebellion, and what he sees as their lack of history. He thinks they have experienced nothing but 'anti-history', i.e. nature, which was too strong because it had to be subdued, and which on the contrary had subdued them outside all courses of history. Perhaps they have suffered more than Bolivia's Indians. They have been exploited, suppressed, sold as slaves, but in contrast to the Indians, they have forgotten everything, remembering at most the tragedies of the past as they remember natural disasters. There is no historically conditioned bitterness in them. They possess a purity of heart which is fundamentally forgetfulness.'

According to Moravia, the African's childish and forgetful nature makes him a victim of neo-capitalism, of the innumerable products of light industry, beautifully packaged, fashionable and superfluous. The African today is selling his birthright for such rubbish, just as he was tempted to exchange gold and ivory for cloth from Lyons and glass beads from Venice.

Would it not be better to make the generalisation that the African's view of life – in contrast to Asian religions – never hindered understanding of industrial culture? On the contrary, the African finds it easy to regard machines and objects as fetishes and magical objects. Neither does puritanism nor the thought of privation stand in the way.

If you have known the proletarian greyness of much of East Africa and Zaire (and even more in Arab countries) and seen the monotony left behind after the vagrancy laws, forced labour and missions wiped out African culture, until nothing much more than their music managed to survive, then you look with tolerance on the cheerful theatre of the West African markets, the people clad in wonderful colours, men in Roman togas, women dressed as if off to an imaginative gala première of a royal opera. Naturally – it is finery and imported. Only the dyed seeds, the necklaces, the faith-healing powders of finely chopped bisamrat hairs, powdered rat-claws and enamel of crushed tusks of wild boar are indigenous.

Europeans come to Africa with goods and exchange them for other goods. It is capitalism's idea that everything can be bought and sold, and nothing has any value except when in relation to other goods. Every object can be exchanged for its opposite, a beautifully illustrated bible for a death-dealing rifle.

Free trade opened up Africa for Europeans, not for themselves. They had to produce far more than they consumed. Suffering was the only surplus. Without any help from Marx, many Africans also reacted quite spontaneously against the white's confident view of the world as a commodity. The blacks usually had no property except tribal land, which was

theirs because of their ancestors' life on that spot. They lived meagrely, for nothing else was possible, and their wealth was neither truly visible nor kept in safes. The idea that the earth and its assets existed for people to lay their hands on through reciprocal competition was quite alien to them.
Many of them still think so, and they are not alone.

I continue my conversation with Moravia. The man I am waiting for has not come. Rain is moving east across the sea and seems to stay where it is least needed. It sounds as if someone is raking a gravel path far away.

Go prudently, travel cautiously, drive carefully . . . African parting words are the same as ours, a mutual consideration, a warning of all dangers ahead. The road runs through different regions and forms of life, and seldom back to the graveyards of our ancestors.

In 1969, Eduardo Mondlane, in the last year of his life, looks forward to the Africa of the 1970s. He has no doubts about liberation from Portugal, achieved five years later. The problem is a continent fragmented into forty countries and unable to unite its policies or, even more important, its economy. What he warned against more than anything is the rise of privileged black groupings, the educated against the uneducated, factory workers against farmers. To prevent wealth and services ending in the hands of the few in a small part of the country requires good national planning which has as its priorities agriculture and whatever people can achieve themselves, wherever they are: village democracy, village co-operatives, village schools.

Here and there in Africa, in countries which call themselves socialist, some of this has been carried out, and as both Mondlane and Amilcar often stated, this is not incompatible with *joie de vivre*, a love of life and its delights, or trust in your own labour and initiative. Or rather, it shouldn't be. For far too long Africa has been to many people the continent of too many expectations, a gathering place for Utopias. Equality and a classless society are a long way off, further in many places in Africa than it has been for centuries with us. If revolution is necessary, it is not as an aim in itself, but because it would be a launching-pad for necessary reforms.

We must keep in sight Bertrand Russell's vision of an unjust world and an Africa of adversity, a world of creative people in which 'life is an adventure full of hope and joy, founded on the impulse to build up rather than the wish to keep what we own or usurp what others own'.

When I go out, the humidity is as heavy as thunder. The huge grey baobab trees have marched up to the coast here, a herd of inquisitive elephants solidified at the sight of the sea. I have eaten the flesh of the baobab tree, a tough white mass tasting of lemon. The leaves can be cooked like spinach. Fishing-nets and clothes are made from the bark. Someone once told me that if I ever got lost and was threatened by thirst, I should climb a baobab tree, and where the big branches leave the trunk there are hollows fill with water.

Baobab trees grow from South Africa to Senegal. They are said to grow to be 2,500 years old. Their roots can be ninety feet long, their creamy flowers ten inches across. But they have no timber. Their thick bark holds them up. In Boma at the mouth of the Congo River is a famous baobab tree on which Stanley scratched his name. Long before him, Portuguese traders hid slaves inside it away from the eyes of British inspectors trying to uphold the ban on slavery: two hundred people could be stacked inside like firewood, and many died in the darkness of the tree.

There is a baobab just behind my African house. It looks as if I could kick it over, but it is almost certainly the other way round. The baobab is slowly approaching the building and it has time behind it as well as ahead of it.

I stand on the shore between sea and inland, a ledge here, and the emptiness out there blows grey, blowing out the whorl of a shell, and at the most I am given a small respite, but that's not much to go on.

Perhaps the lights will soon go out for us Westerners on the stage of the African continent. After our first home, we will deny this other one. I see myself standing here biding my time, in an interval widening and closing, filled as Rilke says 'with a bad taste in the mouth of an unknown future'.

In the evening, migrant birds land on the flat-topped acacias and roost until morning. They perch in soundless clumps and do not fly at night. They are on their way to the temperate zone of the southern hemisphere, if it exists.

I give up hope of my visitor. I know he has got out of South Africa and must be safe somewhere. To wait any longer for him is not essential to my assignment. I have promised to be back home in two days. No more delays for the sake of noble aims. And the assignment remains. Unfortunately it does not abolish itself and its completion does not depend on me.

I write down my address for anyone trying to find me. 'The last person leaving the house must turn out the light.' That notice in official departments, military barracks and warehouses is also here. The little energy you have must be saved.

When I go out on to the slope outside, dawn is just breaking. The disc of the sun lies for a moment on the scales between two waves out at sea, but then rises weightlessly.

Now I am on my way to Swedish October skies, to whortleberries and wormwood, wood blewit and oyster mushrooms, to census forms and newspaper kiosks, to a narrow isthmus of freedom where, perhaps, and despite everything, it is possible both to act and have time to think, where the private self is enclosed by the world without either coming to any harm.

Above my head bee-eaters and blue crows gather in the thin crown of the baobab, the tree stretching its arms out above house and coast. The air feels light, the wind changeable. The rainy season is here, uneasiness and uncertainty reigning among people and plants. Dried-up lakes gasp for water, clay sealing the cracks, Africa twisting its dry body into a better starting point.

I close the shutters of Mondlane's house, lock the door and put the key under the stone. Soon someone will come and find it in its place.